BRAND PSYCHOLOGY

Brand Psychology brings together theory and practice from the fields of psychology, design, and marketing to demystify the brand development process. It explores the behavioral science behind brand building, looking at the psychological principles at play whenever a brand is built and communicated.

Backed by research from various fields of psychology, the book presents practical insights for developing memorable brands through its interdisciplinary character, and emphasis on digital channels. Throughout the book, readers will learn to apply concepts from brand psychology, social learning and persuasion, identity design, and sensory branding to attract and retain their ideal customers. Each chapter presents insights from academic consumer behavior studies, real-life cases from inspiring brands, and unique visual learning tools including infographics, worksheets, and timelines. Ultimately, it serves as a tool to bridge the gap between scientists and entrepreneurs, offering clear, research-backed ideas to drive brand growth and reach human beings in a meaningful way during a time of independent brands and global connectivity. This transformative book shows readers how to:

- Develop memorable brands that resonate with their target audience
- Create powerful brand stories, archetypes, and strategies for growth
- Navigate brand management with mindful communication and active shaping of associations

Containing cutting-edge brand-building tools, this book is a must-read for students and practitioners in brand management, marketing, design management, graphic design, business, advertising, and related spaces that aim to craft an identity that turns heads and hearts.

Laura Busche is a Colombo-German brand strategist helping companies in the public and private sectors bring their message to life with a compelling brand story, memorable visual symbols, and a bold communication strategy. Busche holds a doctoral degree in Psychology, a master's degree in Design Management and is a Bachelor of Science in Business Administration. Her client list has included Dribbble, Creative Market, Webflow, Domestika, Magmic, Grubbrr, Littledata, among many others.

BRAND PSYCHOLOGY

The Art and Science of Building Strong Brands

LAURA BUSCHE, PH.D

Routledge
Taylor & Francis Group

NEW YORK AND LONDON

Designed cover image: © Eugene Mymrin/Getty Images

First published 2024
by Routledge
605 Third Avenue, New York, NY 10158

and by Routledge
4 Park Square, Milton Park, Abingdon, Oxon, OX14 4RN

*Routledge is an imprint of the Taylor & Francis Group, an informa
business*

Library of Congress Cataloging-in-Publication Data
Names: Busche, Laura, author.
Title: Brand psychology : the art and science of building strong
brands /Laura Busche, Ph.D.
Description: New York, NY : Routledge, 2023. | Includes
bibliographical references and index. |
Identifiers: LCCN 2023022170 (print) | LCCN 2023022171 (ebook) |
ISBN 9781032373720 (paperback) | ISBN 9781032373768 (hardback) |
ISBN 9781003336693 (ebook)
Subjects: LCSH: Branding (Marketing)--Psychological aspects. |
Product management--Psychological aspects. | Brand name products.
Classification: LCC HF5415.1255 .B869 2023 (print) |
LCC HF5415.1255 (ebook) | DDC 658.8/27--dc23/eng/20230623
LC record available at https://lccn.loc.gov/2023022170
LC ebook record available at https://lccn.loc.gov/2023022171

ISBN: 978-1-032-37376-8 (hbk)
ISBN: 978-1-032-37372-0 (pbk)
ISBN: 978-1-003-33669-3 (ebk)

DOI: 10.4324/9781003336693

Typeset in Stone Serif and Franklin Gothic
by KnowledgeWorks Global Ltd.

To the brands serving humanity
And the human beings building them

CONTENTS

P 2 INTRODUCTION

P 8 **CHAPTER 1**
WELCOME TO THE WORLD
OF BRANDING

P 38 **CHAPTER 2**
DEFINING "BRAND"

P 60 **CHAPTER 3**
BRAND EQUITY AND
MANAGEMENT

P 76 **SECTION 1**
STORY

P 78 **CHAPTER 4**
BRAND STORY
——

P 96 **CHAPTER 5**
SELF-BRAND IDENTIFICATION
——

P 108 **CHAPTER 6**
RESEARCH, SEGMENTATION, AND PERSONAS
——

P 130 **CHAPTER 7**
ASSOCIATIONS AND POSITIONING
——

P 150 **CHAPTER 8**
NAMING
——

P 160   **CHAPTER 9**
PRICING
———

P 170   **CHAPTER 10**
PERSONALITY AND VOICE
———

P 188   **SECTION 2**
SYMBOLS
———

P 190   **CHAPTER 11**
THE BRANDVERSE
———

P 200   **CHAPTER 12**
VISUAL PERCEPTION
———

P 216   **CHAPTER 13**
LOGO DESIGN
——

P 232   **CHAPTER 14**
TYPOGRAPHY
——

P 246   **CHAPTER 15**
COLOR
——

P 260   **CHAPTER 16**
APPLICATIONS, PACKAGING, AND SYSTEMS
——

P 282   **SECTION 3**
STRATEGY
——

P 286   **CHAPTER 17**
BUILDING STRONG BRAND RELATIONSHIPS
——

P 310   **CHAPTER 18**
UNDERSTANDING CHANNELS
——

P 326   **CHAPTER 19**
DESIGNING MEMORABLE BRAND EXPERIENCES
——

P 336   **CHAPTER 20**
BRAND PORTFOLIO MANAGEMENT: EXTENSIONS, ARCHITECTURE, AND REBRANDING
——

P 356 **CHAPTER 21**
BRAND INTELLIGENCE
——

P 364 **CONCLUSION AND EMERGING DIRECTIONS**

P 376 **INDEX**

INTRODUCTION

DOI: 10.4324/9781003336693-1

You're a strategist, a problem-solver, a maker. You have a brand in mind and want to position it in everyone else's. You reject pseudoscience and understand there's much more than meets the eye in the world of brands. That brought you here.

You're holding this book out of a genuine curiosity to dive deeper: to seek data-driven answers for the non-obvious questions that keep you up:

> *Why are we drawn to certain brands and not others?*
> *Why do some messages stop you in your tracks?*
> *What is this magnetic feel some brands exude and others don't?*

Most importantly,

> *How can I design a brand that feels like this?*

How do I know about these lingering questions?

Because I was there.

I was the curious, ever-dissatisfied business student who devoured consumer behavior courses and was desperate for more. More answers beneath the transactional surface every other business discipline seemed to be obsessed about.

Later in life, I became the business person who studied design management to understand how a brand's symbols are created. I wanted to understand how these graphic, color, typography, and semiotic decisions impacted brand perception. And ultimately, yes, *performance*.

I was then the designer who sought a doctorate in psychology to open doors to a whole new world of clarity. And now I can't wait to show you what's behind that door.

BRAND CLARITY

Supported by decades of behavioral, cognitive, consumer, and design research, I'll share some of the insights that drive memorable brands.

As with all sound, serious science, no answer is definitive. These are principles we've found strong evidence for and can put into practice, to the best of our knowledge.

Different branches of psychology have provided practical answers from a wide range of perspectives: varying understandings of *what drives us* and *how we learn*. This book recounts these findings with a pragmatic perspective: if a brand psychology insight is properly evidenced and carries practical implications, we will review it.

BRANDING IDEAS

The myth that brand building only serves for-profit organizations has to be dismantled. I'll address this misconception first: *branding propels ideas.*

The principles you'll read about in this book will equip you to engage human beings with a construct that appeals to their needs and aspirations—this construct is the brand.

Yes, we'll learn about pricing, but we'll also explore the deep psychological processes at play when you choose a name, symbols to represent you, or deliver a speech.

Whether customers need to pay for something or not is a separate question. Whether it's a product, service or idea is also irrelevant. Brand building is how we bridge the worlds of psychology, design, and marketing to turn a raw concept into a desirable symbol. An idea with attracting and staying power. An idea that, sure, could drive a business forward. But also: *a group of people, a cause, or an entire country.*

A PATH TO MORE INTENTIONAL, MINDFUL BRANDING

I believe the key to better organizations is operating with a high degree of intention: conscious definition and use of symbols to express important messages.

When brands don't cross the realm of the utilitarian, we're left with decadent marketing messages that speak to no one, say nothing, and sell nothing.

Because at the very core of a brand's ability to persuade is its *connection* with a buyer's aspirations. His needs, her desires, and the drivers that influence their behaviors.

Throughout this book, you'll learn to harness the immense power of brand psychology to attract and retain your ideal customer. In doing so, you will apply concepts from type, color, language, and marketing theory. Ideas that have been put to the test again and again.

If you have a message to share, a brand to design, and an audience to build, these are science's best answers to the questions that'll get you there. And I'm determined to pass those on.

Quite literally, dear reader, here's **every trick in the branding book.** Enjoy.

BUT FIRST, A MANIFESTO

Over the last 12 years, my clients have inspired me more than they know. It's the faith, the resilient we'll-try-again-tomorrow strength with which they knock on impossible doors; their signature stubbornness that eventually gets those exact doors to open.

From the first potters who burnt their initials onto their art, to the young entrepreneurs dreaming up fashion labels, the vocation to build symbols is unmistakable. You can *feel* the intentional desire to leave a mark. The unapologetic drive to create something lasting, meaningful, transcendent. There's no doubt in my mind: *brand building is a battle to recover the soul of business.*

And I couldn't possibly walk you through this journey of symbolic meaning without sharing what the next 21 chapters *truly* mean.

I work with brands that understand they're building for human beings, *with* human beings. That is why you're holding *Brand Psychology* and not "brand strategy"—because there is simply no enduring growth without a genuine understanding of human behavior.

This book is reaching you at a radically innovative point in history: an era of independent brands. A time when information, resources, and yes, **brands**, spread frictionless across the globe.

To that end, this book is here to bridge the gap between scientists and entrepreneurs, offering the tools and knowledge that can turn brands around with clear, research-backed ideas. I wrote this book to pull insights out from the shelves of academia to make them visible to brand visionaries eager to fulfill their potential. *Human beings like you.*

With incredibly low barriers to entry, the right disposition, and the insights we'll review in this book, I believe there is no stopping you.

CHAPTER 1

WELCOME TO THE WORLD OF BRANDING

DOI: 10.4324/9781003336693-2

BRANDING AND PSYCHOLOGY

Regardless of how little or much you've studied the subject, you have been personally exposed to branding all your life. Companies, large and small, have long used the principles of brand building, positioning, and design to influence your perception of their offer.

Whether that offer is an idea, a product, a service, or a combination of those, branding has defined how you've experienced it. But what is a brand, exactly? Which psychological forces are at play when we interact with a brand? How can we design a strategy to influence the way that brand is perceived and purchased over time?

Throughout this chapter, we will review some of the basic definitions related to branding and explore its connection with consumer behavior. The concepts you're about to read will lay the ground for the in-depth discussions about brand storytelling, visual symbols, and strategy presented in the rest of this book. As you read along, think about your favorite apparel brand. It can be helpful to consider how all of these ideas apply to your relationship with that brand.

AN INTRODUCTION TO THE WORLD OF CONSUMER BEHAVIOR

Our ideas about how consumers interact with brands in the marketplace have changed significantly in the last three centuries. To understand what brands are and what they're capable of, we must first recognize the space in which the concept emerged and continues to develop. No exploration of branding is complete without context, and that context is the field of consumer behavior.

Consumer behavior is the study of how individuals and companies fulfill their wants and needs by searching for, deciding on, acquiring, using, and disposing of a product. While there are various definitions of consumer behavior in academic literature, most coincide in that the idea of "consumption" isn't limited to a mere purchase act: the process begins earlier, when consumers are first recognizing their needs and figuring out what options can best serve them.

The seemingly small difference between *buyer* and *consumer* is worth noting, as it has real implications for brand managers. While buyer simply hints at someone who has an active role in the purchase transaction, the term consumer is more extensive: this individual or entity takes part in the use of the purchased product, actively experiencing the value it offers.

Having clarified that, let's explore how consumer behavior has been understood differently over time. As explained before, there are three major disciplines that have contributed to shaping consumer behavior: psychology, design, and business. Over time, these three domains have promoted a certain understanding of human behavior, hence consumer behavior. The different understandings have been driven by larger, predominant paradigms in the scientific community of each time period.

The timeline below generalizes when each paradigm rose to popularity and places them in roughly chronological order, but by no means does it indicate the end of one phase or the start of another[1]. All of these dominant perspectives continued to be studied for decades after their initial period of popularity, and some are even in expansion today. In the next few pages, we'll take a closer look at these paradigms.

FIGURE 1.1: Consumer behavior approaches

THE ECONOMIC MAN

Around the 1800s, the dominant paradigm in economics was the idea of a rationally-driven consumer. The so-called "Economic Man" or *Homo Economicus* became the most popular explanation for why we make certain decisions in the market. According to this approach, humans decide in pursuit of their self-interest, making rational choices with the end goal of maximizing their **utility**.

The concept was shaped by multiple economists over the course of the nineteenth and twentieth centuries, but it was perhaps Adam Smith who spearheaded the effort when he wrote in *The Wealth of Nations*:

> It is not from the benevolence of the butcher, the brewer, or the baker that we expect our dinner, but from their regard to their own interest[2].

Decades later, economist William Stanley Jevons described consumers as "utility maximizers"[3]. Alfred Marshall expanded on this concept, proposing specific calculations to quantify just how much utility we get from a purchased item[4]. This mathematical reduction of consumer behavior has some obvious challenges: is every single one of our purchases exclusively driven by a rational decision-making process? Don't emotions, social experiences, and context play a role?

These were the questions that motivated the next wave of consumer theorists. Fortunately, in 1879 a crucial milestone would open the door to a better understanding of those human questions: the birth of psychology as a scientific field. German scientist Wilhelm Wundt, the first researcher to label himself as a psychologist, founded the first experimental psychology lab in Leipzig[5]. In doing so, he would pave the way for debates, discoveries, and theories that added a whole new depth to our understanding of consumer behavior.

BEHAVIORISM

Around the 1890s, a Russian physiologist called Ivan Pavlov was carrying out tests related to dog digestion when he noticed that the animals wouldn't only salivate when they had food in front of them. Pavlov's dogs would also drool in mere *anticipation* of the food whenever they heard his assistant's footsteps. Interested in how that event could have connected to the idea of food, Pavlov carried out a new series of tests to understand how behavior could be influenced by a strategically applied set of cues.

In Pavlov's experiments, dogs would be given food every time a sound-making device called a *metronome* rang. With time, dogs would associate the sound with the idea of getting fed. You can already start to picture what happened: food or not, every time they heard the metronome, dogs would salivate in anticipation of a reward they had grown used to; more accurately, *conditioned* to[6].

Pavlov's tests gave birth to **classical conditioning**, and a lasting paradigm in psychology called **behaviorism**. Behind behaviorism is the idea that conduct can be modified with the intentional use of certain cues. Those cues, in turn, are associated with an idea or event. It is through these associations, marketers began to believe, that one could influence how con-sumers viewed and remembered certain products. Stimulating these associations will become a central topic further along when we discuss brand-building.

Even though the connection between stimuli and response was promising, a few years later psychologist B.F. Skinner would contribute a key element that was missing from that initial scheme: **reinforcement**. Pavlov had focused on involuntary responses (i.e., salivation) associated with cer-tain cues (i.e., sounds) that went from being totally neu-tral to inducing or *conditioned* stimulus. Instead, Skinner focused on what happened after a response. He proposed the notion of **operant conditioning**, where positive or negative reinforcement can actively encourage or discour-age behavior[7].

The rationale was simple but compelling: human beings would be eager to repeat behaviors that they were rewarded for and quit behaviors for which they got punished. Examples abound, but the sole mention of reward and punishment reminds many of their experiences growing up. Maybe you remember getting treats in celebration of your accomplish-ments and being grounded whenever your behavior was inappropriate. Marketers leverage this theory every time they roll out a discount to boost sales. Conversely, governments levy taxes to discourage unhealthy consumption, as is the case with cigarettes. In both cases, positive and negative rein-forcement are used as behavior modification instruments.

For all its virtues, behaviorism still didn't fully explain the complex process that is consumption. Neither could the idea of a rational consumer championed by nineteenth-century economists. Reason, stimuli, and reinforcement alone simply cannot explain many purchase behaviors.

THE PSYCHODYNAMIC PERSPECTIVE

At around the same time Pavlov was studying his dogs, a young Austrian neuropathologist called Sigmund Freud was breaking ground with a new approach to human behavior that would be later labeled as **psychodynamic**. Freud, and the many who followed his steps, introduced a new element to our understanding of decision-making processes: the unconscious mind. While those before him had refused to go down the dark, deep hole ("black box") that was the human mind, Freud's psychoanalytic practice put a spotlight on it. Instinct, inner conflict, anxiety, personality, dreams, pleasure, and other previously discarded areas of the inner self were all suddenly on the table[8].

Another important voice in this period was that of Swiss psychiatrist Carl Jung. He is responsible for a wide range of concepts that we use in consumer behavior, and even regular conversations, to this day: introversion, extroversion, archetypes, complexes, the self, and many others[9]. Jung's contributions, specifically around personality types and the self, went on to inspire the first generations of consumer behaviorists.

By the 1920s the split in the academic world was evident: on one hand, you had a group of scientists advocating for observable, measurable behavior as the single source of truth. On the other, you had a growing group that was fixed on unveiling the complexities of the mind, most of which cannot be quantified or measured objectively. Behaviorists were convinced that they had found a way to finally make human conduct measurable and thus more like a natural science.

John Watson, often recognized as the founder of behaviorism, described the mind as an utterly mysterious and indecipherable entity that wasn't directly observable[10]. Debates continue to this day, but it's important to recognize that both perspectives have contributed greatly to our understanding of consumer behavior. Together, they paint a more complete picture of what's really involved in this multifaceted process that is consumption.

THE COGNITIVE PERSPECTIVE

But was the human mind really that inaccessible? The second half of the twentieth century would bring a whole new understanding of how we decide and learn: the **cognitive** perspective. A group of scientists that, this time around, included early computing theorists started to compare the human mind with a computer. Humans, hence consumers, started to be recognized as problem-solvers, information processors, memory builders, and active learners. With George Miller's "The Magical Number Seven Plus or Minus Two" in 1956, cognitive psychology was officially born[11].

Like behaviorists, cognitive psychologists believed that any study of behavior should be rigorous, controlled, and measured. Unlike behaviorism, however, cognitive psychology refused to ignore mental events, seeing them as powerful behavior triggers that could be studied scientifically using experiments. Human thinking *could* be demystified, and in 1957 computer scientists Newell and Simon published a program that showcased a theory of human problem-solving. It was aptly called "General Problem Solver", and continues to influence our understanding of how consumers go about processing the information they are exposed to and use it to solve their pressing problems and desires[12]. The complexities of the mind didn't discourage cognitive scientists: it just made their investigations that much more interesting.

THE HUMANISTIC PERSPECTIVE

Regardless of human beings' ability to process information and solve problems, one intriguing question remained: how do we prioritize which of those problems to solve first? What does our train of thought look like as we figure out which needs are most important to us?

These and other questions related to the role of will and power gave rise to the **humanistic** perspective. Abraham Maslow, one of its most influential figures, proposed the idea of **self-actualization** and a series of needs that took over other needs in a relatively ordered fashion triggered by our motivations. Maslow's hierarchy of needs was a major contribution to the world of consumer behavior, and continues to be referenced widely today. According to Maslow, we go about satisfying our needs in subsequent levels, as follows: physiological, safety, belonging and love, esteem, and self-actualization needs[13].

Self-actualization became a recurring theme in consumer behavior. American social psychologists Hazel Markus and Paula Nurius developed the concept of **possible selves** to describe those ideal states that we aspire to and that guide our decision-making[14]. For example, your behavior may be driven by trying to achieve a certain "professional possible self": the ideal state within the career path you've selected. Over time, this *possible self* influences many kinds of decisions in your life, from the school you attend to the books you read on a regular basis—perhaps even the one you're holding now.

At around the same time, but on the other side of the world, French philosopher Paul Ricoeur introduced the idea of the **narrative identity** of the self, describing how we require stories (narratives) to make sense of our time, essence, and place[15].

We come to know and identify ourselves through these narratives, a notion that has deep implications for brands and how they are simultaneously perceived as stories and allow us to complement our own life stories.

Narrative identity theory is easy to experience, and we're constantly enacting it in our lives. Just remember the last time someone asked you to introduce yourself. You immediately thought of some beginning, middle, and end story structure. Perhaps you pulled in characters, locations, dates, and even certain events that defined the plot of this narrative that is your life. In doing so, you used storytelling as a device to explain your identity to others and yourself.

THE SOCIOCULTURAL PERSPECTIVE

The colorful picture of human behavior was starting to become less of a mystery. We had explored the role of utility, external stimuli, memory, motivation, self-actualization, and self-identity construction, but what influence, if any, did our social context have in all of this? According to those that led the **sociocultural** perspective, plenty.

In one of the most famous experiments in psychology, Albert Bandura found that when children were exposed to aggressive models of behavior (i.e. an adult being violent to a doll), they were more likely to act in physically aggressive ways themselves. Children's own behavior was influenced by observing adults kicking, hitting, and punching an inflatable doll known as Bobo, a round-bottomed toy that brings itself back up whenever it is pushed[16]. Based on these and other findings, Bandura developed what is now known as the **social learning theory**. Put simply, he proposed that human beings can acquire or learn new behaviors by observing and imitating others[17]. This theory will become incredibly important when we discuss brand strategy and the role of ambassadors and influencers further along in this book.

Another key contribution from the sociocultural perspective was that of **symbolic interactionism,** which sees the self as a social object. Symbolic interactionism suggests that we tend to define ourselves based on our perception of others' responses toward us. Whatever definition we land on becomes our self-concept, which in turn guides our behavior. Insofar as products can play a role in expressing our identity to others, they can become powerful social stimuli within this theory.

Simply put, we act based on the kind of human being we *think* we are, and that thought is heavily influenced by our interpretation of others' responses toward us. Sociologist George Herbert Mead[18] and his student Herbert Blumer are some of the main figures linked to this perspective, with the latter actually coining the term "symbolic interactionism"[19].

In part, the idea of a social self was inspired by one of psychology's founding fathers: William James. Back in 1890, James had described four different parts of the self: the social self, the spiritual self, pure ego, and an interesting notion called the **material self.** According to him, we are also defined by the material objects we come to possess[20]. They become an inextricable part of who we are and how we explain ourselves to the world around us. In other words, they become *symbols*.

Symbolic interactionism paved the way for a new understanding of products and brands: they could help us communicate *meaning* in this ongoing attempt to build our identity.

Professor Sidney Levy pioneered this approach when he spoke of "Symbols for Sale" in the Harvard Business Review in 1959[21]. **Symbolic consumption** became a research area in consumer behavior, and for good reason: we were finally recognizing products' value beyond their functional features or a mathematical formula for utility. Products carry symbolic significance and branding can add that valuable layer of meaning in ways consumers can understand, remember, and respond to.

Researcher Russell Belk also used James' work as a starting point for his concept of a consumption-enabled extension of the self in his seminal article "Possessions and the Extended Self". To Belk, the **extended self** was that augmented identity composed of our core self plus the layers of meaning that certain products could add[22]. Our desired self-concept plays a role in the brand choices we make, and this idea will be explored in depth throughout this book.

The shift from a merely rational, to-the-point buyer to a dynamic, emotional, often unpredictable human being that consumes fueled the evolution of branding as a core business process[23]. We no longer see the consumption process as mere utility maximization, with simple price and quality variables. We now understand the holistic nature of a consumer's relationship with our offer: they experience motivation, stimuli, impulse, needs, problem resolution, satisfaction—independently or all at once.

What was once reduced to a go or no-go decision process is now understood as much more complex, even colorful to some extent. The new variables at play have opened the door for branding to take center stage: in a market where exchanges get more and more sophisticated, building a unique identity offers a leg up.

WHAT IS A BRAND?

Over time, the different paradigms we reviewed in the previous section have shaped our understanding of a brand's impact. Seen through the lens of behavioral psychology, a brand enacts the role of a cue or **stimulus.** In being exposed to a brand, whether for the first time or not, we activate different kinds of associations. From the cognitive perspective, brands exert influence in information processing through the meanings that are captured in the consumer's **memory** and he or she retrieves in the various phases of the process—from need recognition to post-consumption.

From a more humanistic understanding, a brand presents itself as a vehicle for **self-actualization**: its success depends on its ability to take you from an actual state to a desired state, or *possible self* in Markus and Nurius' terms. Lastly, the sociocultural approach stresses the importance of context in human behavior, with clear implications when building and sustaining brands. In this view, individuals learn through social and cultural interactions, which go on to shape their perception of the brands presented to them. These same social interactions become the scene for **symbolic consumption**: consumers acquire products that convey specific meanings that they'd like to associate with their identity. The branding process imbues products with those layers of meaning, therefore making them valuable instruments in individuals' assertion of their ideal selves.

THE HISTORICAL EVOLUTION OF BRANDING

In its most literal sense, the term "branding" references the act of marking an object by burning some kind of symbol onto it.

Until modern marketers adopted the word, *branding* merely indicated a form of burning a symbol to communicate ownership. Ancient Greeks, Romans, and Egyptians all "branded" animals to express that sense of belonging in a property stamp of sorts.

With time, the concept of branding to mark something's origin slowly made its way into the realm of commercial goods. As early as 3000 BCE, tradesmen were marking their items with special symbols to announce who had produced them, in an early attempt to convey reliability and quality.

Around 2000 BCE, merchants from the Harappan civilization used picture characters to mark their items in what is sometimes known as the earliest example of branding. Archaeologist David Wengrow places the beginning of a pseudo-branding practice even earlier, at around 4000 BCE in Early Mesopotamia, when cylinder seals and vase caps were marked to convey specific product information. Later on, kin groups in Shang China created family crests that they would imprint on the products they were known for, e.g. "pottery", "cooking pot", or "vessels". At around 500 BCE, Phoenicians were using red paint and purple dye to identify their commercial ceramics and garments, respectively. By 300 BCE, Greek potters were signing their work to promote themselves. Some of these inscriptions went as far as to include verbiage that resembles modern brand slogans, such as "Exekias painted and made me".

All of these seal forms are just examples of what we now know to be a widespread practice in ancient civilizations. Moore and Reid labeled these early seals as **proto-brands**, to distinguish them from the more elaborate and intentional brand identity strategies in place today[24]. Even before alphabets and words came into play, pictorial symbols were applied to items to indicate one or more of these three types of information:

- **Possession:** Marks reflected a ruler's authority, as well as individuals' ownership over land, animals, and property.
- **Authorship:** Creators took pride in their work and labeled it in a way that promoted their craftsmanship.
- **Origin:** Used as trademarks, special seals could indicate a product's provenance, which in turn hinted at its quality and value.

WHERE DOES THE WORD COME FROM?

As for the word "brand" itself, etymologists trace its origin back to the Old English term for "burning", which in turn comes from Old High German, the earliest form of the modern German language. The word "brand" was first spotted in the *Beowulf* story around 1000 AD. This epic poem was written in Old English, or Anglo-Saxon, and the events in it took place around the late fifth century AD.

HOW BRANDING ENTERED THE BUSINESS VOCABULARY

Our contemporary understanding of a *brand*, at least in a business context, emerged long after the word entered the dictionary. Professor Barbara Stern argues that the term had actually been in use for 15 centuries before it entered marketing in the form of the expression **brand name** in 1922[25].

Now, if you recall our overview of the main paradigms in consumer behavior history, Psychology became a formal, influential discipline in the first part of the twentieth century. After Wundt opened his lab, the incipient field of marketing cross-bred with some of psychology's new principles to give birth to a deeper, more integrative vision of what brands could do.

The 1930s marked a key era in the evolution of modern branding. Consumer behavior analysis got richer, the marketer's toolkit expanded, and consumers were getting more and more sophisticated about their purchases. Previously, mass products like soap were sold in a generic, commoditized fashion that left little room for differentiation. However, as media outlets developed, the emergence of channels like magazines, TV, and radio drove companies to find new ways to stand out. Adding brand names to products helped manufacturers differentiate their offer and send much-needed quality signals.

The two World Wars were notoriously gray periods for brands. Consumer spending and confidence hit all-time lows and the exciting, new advertising channels that had emerged in the first part of the century were dominated by war efforts and political propaganda. However, after the Second World War, the market would see an unprecedented surge—something economists often call the "Golden Age of Capitalism". The economic expansion, rising employment levels, and renewed consumer confidence propelled existing brands and encouraged new brands to join the market. As they did, consumer researchers found new behaviors to analyze and the field developed like never before.

In 1955, Gardner and Levy proposed what would be another cornerstone concept in branding history: the **brand image**. In their words, a brand image was a "governing product and brand personality that is unified and coherently meaningful"[26]. This new understanding of a brand and its wider significance was followed by another publication titled "Symbols for Sale" by the same authors. In that second paper, Gardner and Levy mention one of the most influential principles in branding history: "People buy things not only for what they can do, but also for what they mean".

As the idea of "brand" escaped the confines of a literal mark to encompass the complexity of symbolic meaning, the 1950s brought about a boom of advertising agencies that could leverage this new potential. New York's Madison Avenue became the epicenter of advertising innovation, housing David Ogilvy's renowned agency. Ogilvy was heavily influenced by these initial ideas of a brand's symbolic significance and connection to the self, and evidenced it when he created the agency's 12-point "Creative Credo". Heavily inspired by Gardner and Levy's 1955 "The Product and the Brand", one of the 12 points read: "Every advertisement is part of the long-term investment in the personality of the brand".[27]

A period of growth ensued in the branding world through the rest of the twentieth century. In 1991 David Aaker wrote the book *Managing Brand Equity*, in which he described a framework to measure the true value of a brand to a business[28]. Up until this point brand research had focused on defining the concept and understanding some of the brand's key functions. However, as more companies started investing in brand building, it became evident that these efforts had to be tracked and measured somehow. Defined as a measure of a brand's strength and health, **brand equity** provided an answer to that performance tracking challenge. That's why Aaker's introduction of a succinct brand equity model was so instrumental: it helped monitor and understand the impact of brand initiatives in a market that desperately needed that kind of validation. Later on in this book, we will review Aaker's brand equity framework and the set of measures he proposed to evaluate each dimension's strength.

Consumer researchers continued to pull from psychology concepts and in 1997 Jennifer Aaker, extending her father's legacy, published a model of brand personality that linked humane personality traits with brands in different categories. She went on to define **brand personality** as "the set of human characteristics associated with a brand" and uncovered five basic dimensions to group those characteristics: sincerity, excitement, competence, sophistication, and ruggedness[29].

With time, brand management became a formal functional area within businesses, and in 1997 Professor Kevin Keller authored *Strategic Brand Management*, a book that provided specific strategy guidelines for this emerging field[30]. A few years later, Keller would join forces with Phillip Kotler to co-author the 12th edition of another key textbook in the larger marketing field: *Marketing Management*[31]. The title provides an actionable definition for **branding** itself, describing it as the act of "endowing products and services with the power of a brand".

BRAND HISTORY TIMELINE

Let's now visualize some key milestones in brand management history. As we just saw, brand management has a rich and fascinating history that began long before the modern era. Early examples include the branding of cattle in ancient Rome and the use of trademarks in medieval Europe. As commerce expanded and communication technologies improved, brand management became more sophisticated.

Today, brand management is a vital aspect of any successful business, and it involves a wide range of activities, from market research and advertising to social media and public relations.

TABLE 1.1: Brand history timeline proto-brands

-4000	Ancient Egyptian merchants develop distinctive marks to distinguish their products, possibly the earliest form of branding.
-2700	Egyptians brand oxen with hieroglyphics. Ancient Greeks and Romans mark their livestock.
-2000	The Indus Valley or Harappan civilization (located in India) uses seals to mark commercial wares and indicate their origin.
-1500	Kin groups (zu) in Shang China use crests to identify their families and the responsibilities assigned to them within the local economy.
-1000	Phoenicians from the city of Tyre use purple-dyed garments and red-slip ceramics to identify their origin and quality.
-700	Greek potters identify their products adding their signature, distinctive decorations, and mottos.
1200	England requires breadmakers, goldsmiths, and silversmiths to put their marks on goods to ensure honesty.
1400	Makers of luxury goods in Europe begin using crests, coats of arms, and other symbols to denote quality and exclusivity.
1448	The printing press is invented by Johann Gutenberg in 1448, an invention that altered the history of communications[33].

This timeline will provide you with an overview of some of the most important events and trends in the history of brand management, and it will help you understand how this field has evolved over time.

Proto-brands

As defined by Moore and Reid[32], early branding efforts result in *proto-brands* where specific symbols are used to mark product ownership and origin.

1700-1800s

The Industrial Revolution enables mass production and the rise of consumer culture. Technological advances in photography and film fuel a new realm of multimedia messaging possibilities for brands.

TABLE 1.2: Brand history timeline 1700-1800s

1816	William Caslon IV designs the first sans serif typeface, Caslon Egyptian[34].
1837	Charles Lewis Tiffany establishes Tiffany & Co., which becomes a global icon of luxury and quality[35].
1837	Louis Daguerre creates the first photograph, revolutionizing the world of advertising[36].
1873	Colgate starts selling aromatic toothpaste in jars[37].
1876	*Bass Brewery* registers its Red Triangle trademark, regarded as the first registered trademark in Britain[38].
1881	US congress passes its first trademark act. It would be amended numerous times, but paved the way for trademark protection in the country[39].
1886	Dr. John Pemberton sells the first glass of Coca-Cola at Jacobs' Pharmacy in downtown Atlanta. Coca-Cola is invented and becomes one of the most recognizable brands in the world[40].
1888	Kodak introduces the first camera with roll film[41], allowing consumers to take and print their own pictures.
1895	The Lumière brothers invent the first motion picture projector, creating an entirely new avenue for advertising[42].
1899	The introduction and patent of the Uneeda Biscuits package, one of the first containers for packaged consumer goods, plays an important role in the development of the paperboard box industry[43].

1900-1930s

Branding vocabulary is slowly but steadily becoming more prevalent in the business world. The rise of consumer culture enables the emergence of iconic brands like Ford, Chanel, and Lego.

1940-1950s

The post-Second World War economic boom creates a new era of mass consumption and advertising. TVs become popular in the home, providing a new way for companies to send sales messages to the mass market.

1960-1970s

Consumer psychology becomes a recognized academic field, with scholars like Ernest Dichter and Herbert Krugman leading

TABLE 1.3: Brand history timeline 1900-1930s

1903	Ford Motor Company is founded[44].
1903	Walter Dill Scott publishes *The Theory of Advertising*, a groundbreaking work that introduces the concept of audience segmentation[45].
1910	Coco, as she had come to be called, opens a hat boutique at 21 rue Cambon under the name Chanel Modes[46]. Global fashion brand Chanel is born.
1919	The Bauhaus School is founded in Germany, which would influence modernist design and typography for years to come[47].
1922	The expression "brand name" enters the marketing vocabulary when it appears in the article "Brand names on menus?" in *Hotel World*[48].
1923	Claude Hopkins publishes *Scientific Advertising*,[49] which becomes a bible for modern advertising techniques.
1929	Edward Bernays introduces the concept of "public relations" and published his seminal work *Propaganda*, shaping the way companies communicate with consumers and the media[50].
1931	Procter & Gamble's Neil McElroy sends his famous "Brand Man" memo[51] outlining one of the first formal brand management programs.
1932	Lego is founded. "LEGO" is an abbreviation of the two Danish words "leg godt", meaning "play well"[52].
1937	The National Association of Marketing Teachers and the American Marketing Society merge to form the American Marketing Association, helping to define the profession of marketing[53].

TABLE 1.4: Brand history timeline 1940-1950s

1941	The first TV commercial airs: an advertisement for a Bulova watch during a baseball game on a New York station[54].
1955	McDonald's Corporation is founded and revolutionizes the fast food industry.
1955	Gardner and Levy publish their seminal piece "The Product and the Brand"[55] on *Harvard Business Review*, defining the term "brand image" as a "long-term investment in the reputation of the brand".
1956	Graphic designer Paul Rand creates the iconic logo for IBM, revolutionizing the way brands are visually represented[56].
1957	Helvetica, a typeface designed by Max Miedinger, is released and would become one of the most widely used typefaces in the world[57].

the way. Research on consumer decision-making shifts from a focus on rational factors to a consideration of emotional and cognitive factors.

1980-1990s

Branding becomes a key focus of consumer psychology research, with researchers exploring how consumers develop relationships with brands.

TABLE 1.5: Brand history timeline 1960-1970s

1963	David Ogilvy publishes *Confessions of an Advertising Man*, a seminal work on advertising that remains influential to this day. He pioneers the concept of positioning, emphasizing the importance of differentiating a brand in the minds of consumers[58].
1963	Pantone is launched as a graphic standards system for professional designers, specializing in color charts for the cosmetic, fashion, and medical industries[59].
1963	The idea of vector graphics and a vector file format emerges. "Sketchpad: A Man-Machine Graphical Communication System" is presented by Ivan Sutherland, who uses vector graphics to run his program[60].
1971	Intel introduces the first microprocessor, allowing for the development of the personal computer.
1971	Nike, Inc. is founded and becomes a leader in sports apparel and footwear. The Nike "swoosh" logo is created, marking a shift towards minimalist and iconic branding[61].
1971	Ray Tomlinson sends the first email[62], which eventually leads to email marketing.
1976	Apple launches the first personal computer, revolutionizing the way people interact with technology[63].

TABLE 1.6: Brand history timeline 1980-1990s

1982	Sony launches the first compact disc and player, leading to a revolution in music distribution and branding[64].
1987	Adobe Illustrator launches, changing the course of brand design forever. Using Illustrator, designers could apply PostScript's Bézier curves to hand-crafted shapes[65].
1988	Russell Belk publishes "Possessions and the Extended Self"[66], suggesting that products could convey and provide meaning.
1988	Nike introduces its "Just Do It"[67] campaign, which becomes one of the most recognizable and effective advertising slogans in history.
1990	Adobe releases Photoshop 1. The software and its associated PSD format have evolved dramatically over time, transforming the design industry[68].
1991	The World Wide Web is invented[69], leading to a new era of digital marketing, advertising, and e-commerce.
1991	David Aaker publishes "Managing Brand Equity"[70], his seminal work defining the idea of brand equity and a framework for its measurement.
1991	The emergence of brand storytelling with the publication of *The Hero's Journey*[71] by Joseph Campbell.
1993	Keller develops the customer-based brand equity model[72], which emphasizes the importance of building strong relationships with customers to create valuable brands.
1993	Fournier publishes "Consumers and Their Brands: Developing Relationship Theory in Consumer Research"[73], which expands the understanding of brand–consumer relationships beyond simple transactions.
1994	The FedEx logo is redesigned by Lindon Leader[74], featuring a hidden arrow between the "E" and the "X" that has become one of the most famous examples of a hidden message in a logo.
1994	De Chernatony and McDonald publish *Creating Powerful Brands*, which outlines a practical framework for brand building[75].

(Continued)

TABLE 1.6: (Continued)

1995	The launch of Amazon.com[76] introduces the concept of e-commerce and changing the way we shop.
1997	Jennifer Aaker defines brand personality and introduces its five basic dimensions: sincerity, excitement, competence, sophistication, and ruggedness[77].
1997	Keller publishes *Strategic Brand Management*[78], a book that provides specific strategy guidelines for this emerging field.
1999	The World Wide Web Consortium adopts a standard file format for vector graphics—the SVG or scalable vector graphic. The first version of SVG was approved as a W3C Recommendation in September 2001[79].

TABLE 1.7: Brand history timeline 2000s

2003	Schmitt publishes *Customer Experience Management: A Revolutionary Approach to Connecting with Your Customers*[80], emphasizing the importance of creating memorable experiences for customers.
2003	Facebook is launched, creating an entirely new platform for marketing and branding[81].
2005	YouTube is founded, providing a platform for consumers to create and share videos[82].
2006	Twitter is launched, giving brands a new platform for engaging with customers and promoting their products[83].

2000s

Researchers begin to study the impact of technology on consumer behavior, including the effects of e-commerce and the rise of social media. The growth of the internet leads to new branding and marketing opportunities.

2010–2020s

Behavioral economics gains prominence as a way to understand consumer decision-making, with researchers like Richard Thaler winning a Nobel Prize for their work.

TABLE 1.8: Brand history timeline 2010–2020s

2010	Instagram is launched, creating new opportunities for brands to showcase their products and engage with consumers[84].
2011	Berthon et al. introduce the concept of "brand mystique"[85], which refers to the symbolic, mythic, and ritualistic aspects of brands that create deep connections with consumers.
2012	The rise of influencer marketing with the creation of Instagram and the emergence of social media influencers.
2013	Canva launches as an online design and publishing tool with a mission to empower everyone in the world to design anything—including brand materials[86].
2014	Alibaba Group launches the largest IPO in history[87], solidifying China's position as a major player in the global e-commerce industry.
2014	Facebook buys Oculus VR[88], powering the adoption of virtual reality among the consumer market and an entirely new platform for advertising and branding.
2016	The European Union adopts the General Data Protection Regulation (GDPR), changing the way companies collect and use consumer data[89]. GDPR becomes enforceable two years later.
2020	The COVID-19 pandemic accelerates the shift toward digital branding, as e-commerce and online communication become even more central to consumers' lives.
2023	Consumer design and content creation AI apps take off, radically changing how brand assets are created.

NOTES

1. Bray, J. P. (2008). *Consumer Behaviour Theory: Approaches and Models.* Keizer, P. (2015). *Psychology for Economists.* https://doi.org/10.1093/acprof:oso/9780199686490.003.0010

2. Smith, A. (1776). *An Inquiry Into the Nature and Causes of the Wealth of Nations.* W. Strahan; and T. Cadell, in the Strand.

3. Jevons, W. S. (1879). *The Theory of Political Economy.* Macmillan and Company.

4. Marshall, A. (1960). *Principles of Economics.* Palgrave Macmillan. https://link.springer.com/book/9780333056462

5. Harper, R. S. (1950). The first psychological laboratory. *Isis, 41*(2), 158–161.

6. Pavlov, P. I. (1927), (2010). Conditioned reflexes: An investigation of the physiological activity of the cerebral cortex. *Annals of Neurosciences, 17*(3), 136–141. https://doi.org/10.5214/ans.0972-7531.1017309

7. Skinner, B. F. (1938). *The Behavior of Organisms: An Experimental Analysis* (p. 457). Appleton-Century.

8. Freud, S. (1997). *The Interpretation of Dreams.* Wordsworth Editions.

9. Jung, C. G. (1969). *Collected Works of C.G. Jung, Volume 9 (Part 1): Archetypes and the Collective Unconscious.* Princeton University Press. https://www.jstor.org/stable/j.ctt5hhrnk

10. Watson, J. B. (1924). *Behaviorism.* W.W. Norton.

11. Miller, G. A. (1956). The magical number seven, plus or minus two: Some limits on our capacity for processing information. *Psychological Review, 63,* 81–97. https://doi.org/10.1037/h0043158

12. Newell, A., Shaw, J., & Simon, H. (1959). *Report on a General Problem-solving Program.* Proceedings of the International Conference on Information Processing. Paris: UNESCO House.

13. Maslow, A. H. (1943). A theory of human motivation. *Psychological Review, 50*(4), 370.

14. Markus, H., & Nurius, P. (1986). Possible selves. *American Psychologist, 41*(9), 954–969. https://doi.org/10.1037/0003-066X.41.9.954

15. Ricoeur, P. (1990). *Time and Narrative, Volume 1* (K. McLaughlin & D. Pellauer, Trans.). University of Chicago Press. https://press.uchicago.edu/ucp/books/book/chicago/T/bo5962044.html

16. Bandura, A., Ross, D., & Ross, S. A. (1961). Transmission of aggression through imitation of aggressive models. *The Journal of Abnormal and Social Psychology, 63,* 575–582. https://doi.org/10.1037/h0045925

17. Bandura, A. (1977). *Social Learning Theory.* Prentice Hall.

18. Mead, G. H. (2015). *Mind, Self, and Society: The Definitive Edition* (Morris, C. W., Huebner, D. R., & Joas, H. (Eds.). University of Chicago Press. https://press.uchicago.edu/ucp/books/book/chicago/M/bo20099389.html

19. Blumer, H. (1969). *Symbolic Interactionism; Perspective and Method.* Prentice-Hall.

20. James, W. (1890). *The Principles of Psychology, Vol I.* (pp. xii, 697). Henry Holt and Co. https://doi.org/10.1037/10538-000

21. Levy, S. J. (1959). Symbols for sale. *Harvard Business Review, 37*(4), 117–124.

22. Belk, R. W. (1988). Possessions and the extended self. *Journal of Consumer Research, 15*(2), 139–168. http://dx.doi.org/10.1086/209154

23. Bastos, W., & Levy, S. J. (2012). A history of the concept of branding: Practice and theory. *Journal of Historical Research in Marketing, 4*(3), 347–368. https://doi.org/10.1108/17557501211252934

24. Moore, K., & Reid, S. (2008). The birth of brand: 4000 years of branding. *Business History, 50*(4), 419–432. https://doi.org/10.1080/00076790802106299

25. Stern, B. B. (2006). What does brand mean? Historical-analysis method and construct definition. *Journal of the Academy of Marketing Science, 34*(2), 216–223.

26. Gardner, B. B., & Levy, S. J. (1955). The product and the brand. *Harvard Business Review, 33*(2), 33–39.

27. Ogilvy, D. (1955). The Image of the Brand–A new approach to creative operations. Speech delivered at the American Marketing Association conference.

28. Aaker, D. A. (1991). *Managing Brand Equity: Capitalizing on the Value of a Brand Name.* Free Press; Maxwell Macmillan Canada.

29. Aaker, J. L. (1997). Dimensions of brand personality. *Journal of Marketing Research, 34*(3), 347–356. https://doi.org/10.2307/3151897

30. Keller, K. L. (1997). *Strategic Brand Management: Building, Measuring, and Managing Brand Equity.* Prentice Hall.

31. Kotler, P., & Keller, K. L. (2006). *Marketing Management.* Pearson Prentice Hall.

32. Moore, K., & Reid, S. (2008). The birth of brand: 4000 years of branding. *Business History, 50*(4), 419–432. https://doi.org/10.1080/00076790802106299

33. MIT. *Johann Gutenberg | Lemelson.* Massachusetts Institute of Technology. Retrieved from https://lemelson.mit.edu/resources/johann-gutenberg

34. Monotype. (2019, February 25). *Why brands love to use sans serifs (and how you can choose one, too).* Monotype. https://www.monotype.com/resources/articles/why-brands-love-to-use-sans-serifs-and-how-you-can-choose-one-too

35. Tiffany & Co. *The World of Tiffany.* Retrieved from https://www.tiffany.com/world-of-tiffany/

36. Google Arts & Culture. *Daguerreotypes: The First Photograph.* Google Arts & Culture. Retrieved from https://artsandculture.google.com/story/daguerreotypes-the-first-photograph/5AXR7pXeExqLJA

37. Colgate-Palmolive. *Our History | Colgate-Palmolive.* Retrieved from https://www.colgatepalmolive.com/en-us/who-we-are/history

38. Campaign Live. *History of advertising: No 128: Bass Brewery's red triangle.* Retrieved from https://www.campaignlive.co.uk/article/history-advertising-no-128-bass-brewerys-red-triangle/1342646

39. American Bar Association. *Federal Trademark Law: From Its Beginnings.* Retrieved from https://www.americanbar.org/groups/intellectual_property_law/publications/landslide/2018-19/march-april/federal-trademark-law/

40. The Coca Cola Company. *Coca-Cola History*. Retrieved from https://www.coca-colacompany.com/company/history
41. Fineman, A. M. *Kodak and the Rise of Amateur Photography*. The Metropolitan Museum of Art's Heilbrunn Timeline of Art History. Retrieved from https://www.metmuseum.org/toah/hd/kodk/hd_kodk.htm
42. National Geographic. (2019, February 22). *How the Lumière brothers invented the movies*. History. https://www.nationalgeographic.com/history/history-magazine/article/creation-of-the-motion-picture-lumiere-brothers
43. Twede, D. (1997). Uneeda Biscuit: The first consumer package? *Journal of Macromarketing, 17*(2), 82–88. https://doi.org/10.1177/027614679701700208
44. Ford Motor Company. *Our History*. Retrieved from https://corporate.ford.com/about/history.html
45. Scott, W. D. (1903). *The Theory of Advertising: A Simple Exposition of the Principles of Psychology in their Relation to Successful Advertising*. Small, Maynard & Company.
46. Chanel. *Chanel History: 1910s*. Chanel. Retrieved from https://www.chanel.com/us/about-chanel/the-history/1910/
47. Winton, A. A. G. *The Bauhaus, 1919–1933*. The Metropolitan Museum of Art's Heilbrunn Timeline of Art History. Retrieved from https://www.metmuseum.org/toah/hd/bauh/hd_bauh.htm
48. Stern, B. B. (2006). What does brand mean? Historical-Analysis method and construct definition. *Journal of the Academy of Marketing Science, 34*(2), 216–223.
49. Hopkins, C. (1923). *Scientific Advertising*. Infobase Holdings, Incorporated.
50. Bernays, E. (1928). *Propaganda*. http://archive.org/details/Bernays Propaganda
51. McElroy, N. H. (1931). *1931 Memo: Brand Management at Procter & Gamble*. 1931 Memo from Neil H. McElroy. https://commons.wikimedia.org/wiki/File:Neil_Mcelroy%27s_1931_Brand_Man_Memo.pdf
52. Lego. *The LEGO Group History—About Us*. Retrieved from https://www.lego.com/en-us/aboutus/lego-group/the-lego-group-history
53. Agnew, H. E. (1941). The history of the American Marketing Association. *Journal of Marketing (Pre-1986), 5*(000004), 374.
54. Matthei, H. (1997). Inventing the commercial: The imperium of modern television advertising was born in desperate improvisation. *American Heritage, 48*(3), 62–73.

55. Gardner, B. B., & Levy, S. J. (1955). The product and the brand. *Harvard Business Review, 33*(2), 33–39.

56. IBM. (2003, January 23). *IBM Archives: IBM continuity (1956–1972).* (2003, January 23). https://www.ibm.com/ibm/history/exhibits/logo/logo_7.html

57. Hustwit, G., Siegel, S., Geissbuhler, L., Swiss Dots (Firm), V. (Firm), & Plexifilm (Firm). (2007). *Helvetica.* https://ecommons.cornell.edu/handle/1813/36252

58. Ogilvy, D. (1963). *Confessions of an Advertising Man.*

59. Budds, D. (2015, September 18). *How Pantone Became the Definitive Language of Color.* Fast Company. https://www.fastcompany.com/3050240/how-pantone-became-the-definitive-language-of-color

60. Sito, T. (2013). *Moving Innovation: A History of Computer Animation.* MIT Press.

61. Newcomb, T. *The History of the Swoosh on Nike's Sneakers.* Complex. Retrieved from https://www.complex.com/sneakers/nike-swoosh-sneaker-logo-history

62. Swatman, R. (2015, August 19). *1971: First Ever Email.* Guinness World Records. https://www.guinnessworldrecords.com/news/60at60/2015/8/1971-first-ever-email-392973

63. Smithsonian Institution. *Apple I Microcomputer.* National Museum of American History. Retrieved from https://americanhistory.si.edu/collections/search/object/nmah_1692121

64. Kelly, H. (2012, September 28). *Rock on! The compact disc turns 30.* CNN Business. https://www.cnn.com/2012/09/28/tech/innovation/compact-disc-turns-30/index.html

65. Adobe. (2014, May 14). *The Story Behind Adobe Illustrator (Part 1 of 3).* Adobe Creative Cloud. https://www.youtube.com/watch?v=1gaCKT_Ncdk

66. Belk, R. W. (1988). Possessions and the extended self. *Journal of Consumer Research, 15*(2), 139–168. http://dx.doi.org/10.1086/209154

67. Restrepo, M. L. (2022, October 6). Just Do It: How the iconic Nike tagline built a career for the late Dan Wieden. *NPR.* https://www.npr.org/2022/10/06/1127032721/nike-just-do-it-slogan-success-dan-wieden-kennedy-dies

68. Adobe. *Learn About PSD Files.* Adobe. Retrieved from https://www.adobe.com/creativecloud/file-types/image/raster/psd-file.html

69. CERN. *A Short History of the Web.* Retrieved from https://home.cern/science/computing/birth-web/short-history-web

70. Aaker, D. A. (1991). *Managing brand equity: Capitalizing on the value of a brand name.* Free Press ; Maxwell Macmillan Canada.

71. Campbell, J. (1991). *The Hero's Journey: The World of Joseph Campbell: Joseph Campbell on His Life and Work*. HarperSanFrancisco.

72. Keller, K. L. (1993). Conceptualizing, measuring, and managing customer-based brand equity. *Journal of Marketing, 57*(1), 1.

73. Fournier, S. (1998). Consumers and Their Brands: Developing Relationship Theory in Consumer Research. *Journal of Consumer Research, 24*(4), 343–353. https://doi.org/10.1086/209515

74. ArtCenter College of Design. *Lindon Leader: Advertising Alumni Story*. Retrieved from http://www.artcenter.edu/about/alumni/alumni-stories/lindon-leader.html

75. de Chernatony L. and McDonald M. (1994). *Creating Powerful Brands*. Oxford: Butterworth Heinemann.

76. Stone, B. (2013). *The Everything Store: Jeff Bezos and the Age of Amazon*. Random House.

77. Aaker, J. L. (1997). Dimensions of brand personality. *Journal of Marketing Research, 34*(3), 347–356. https://doi.org/10.2307/3151897

78. Keller, K. L. (1997). *Strategic Brand Management: Building, Measuring, and Managing Brand Equity*. Prentice Hall.

79. Library of Congress. (2022, May 10). *Scalable Vector Graphics (SVG) File Format Family* [Web page]. https://www.loc.gov/preservation/digital/formats/fdd/fdd000515.shtml

80. Schmitt, B. H. (2003). *Customer Experience Management: A Revolutionary Approach to Connecting with Your Customers*. John Wiley & Sons, Incorporated.

81. Encyclopedia Britannica. *Facebook | Overview, History, & Facts*. Britannica. https://www.britannica.com/topic/Facebook

82. Encyclopedia Britannica. *YouTube | History, Founders, & Facts*. Britannica. https://www.britannica.com/topic/YouTube

83. Vanian, J. (2022, October 29). *Twitter is now owned by Elon Musk—Here's a brief history from the app's founding in 2006 to the present*. CNBC. https://www.cnbc.com/2022/10/29/a-brief-history-of-twitter-from-its-founding-in-2006-to-musk-takeover.html

84. Web Design Museum. *Instagram—2010*. Retrieved from https://www.webdesignmuseum.org/web-design-history/instagram-2010

85. Berthon, P., Pitt, L. F., Chakrabarti, R., Berthon, J.-P., & Simon, M. (2011). Brand worlds: From articulation to integration. *Journal of Advertising Research, 51*(1 50th Ann), 182.

86. Canva. *About Canva*. Retrieved from https://www.canva.com/about/

87. Sun, L. *If You'd Invested $5,000 in Alibaba in 2014, This Is How Much You Would Have Today.* NASDAQ. Retrieved from https://www. nasdaq.com/articles/if-youd-invested-%245000-in-alibaba-in-2014-this-is-how-much-you-would-have-today

88. Meta. (2014, March 25). Facebook to Acquire Oculus. https:// about.fb.com/news/2014/03/facebook-to-acquire-oculus/

89. EUR Lex. *Regulation (EU) 2016/679 of the European Parliament and of the Council of 27 April 2016.* Retrieved from https://eur-lex. europa.eu/eli/reg/2016/679/oj

CHAPTER 2

DEFINING "BRAND"

DOI: 10.4324/9781003336693-3

As we've discussed, "brand" hasn't always been part of the management vocabulary. From its early definitions as an origin marker, to a differentiator, to a meaning carrier, the concept of a "brand" has evolved from a strictly utilitarian label to a meaning-making signifier.

Today, we know the power of a brand lies in its ability to create meaning beyond its functional purposes. A strong brand can evoke emotions, connect with customers on a deeper level, and create a sense of identity and belonging. As businesses continue to compete in crowded markets, the importance of building a meaningful brand has never been greater.

TABLE 2.1: Popular definitions of a brand

A brand name is more than the label employed to differentiate among the manufacturers of a product. It is a complex symbol that represents a variety of ideas and attributes[1].	**Gardner and Levy**
A name, term, sign, symbol, or design or a combination of them intended to identify the goods and services of one seller or group of sellers and to differentiate them from those of competitors[2].	**AMA**
A brand is not the name of a product. It is the vision that drives the creation of products and services under that name. That vision, the key belief of the brands and its core values is called identity[3].	**Kapferer**
A "value system" which transforms the usage experience through the subjective meanings the brand represents for consumers. [...] The interface between the firm's activities and consumers' interpretations[4].	**De Chernatony and Dall'Olmo Riley**
An identifiable product, service, person, or place, augmented in such a way that a buyer or user perceives relevant and unique added values which match their needs more closely. Furthermore, its success results from being able to sustain these added values in the face of competition[5].	**De Chernatony and McDonald**
[...] an evolving mental collection of actual (offer related) and emotional (human-like) characteristics and associations which convey benefits of an offer identified through a symbol, or a collection of symbols, and differentiates this offer from the rest of the marketplace[6].	**Velotsou and Delgado-Ballester**
A brand is the unique story that consumers recall when they think of you. This story associates your product with their personal stories, a particular personality, what you promise to solve, and your position relative to your competitors. Your brand is represented by your visual symbols and feeds from multiple conversations where you must participate strategically[7].	**Busche**

(Continued)

TABLE 2.1: (Continued)

A brand is a repository of meanings fueled by a combination of marketers' intentions, consumers' interpretations, and numerous sociocultural networks' associations[8].	Parmentier
(Brand) image means personality. Products, like people, have personalities, and they can make or break them in the marketplace. The personality of a product is an amalgam of many things—its name, its packaging, its price, the style of its advertising, and, above all, the nature of the product itself. Every advertisement should be thought of as a contribution to the brand image[9].	Ogilvy
A brand is a "trust mark". It's shorthand. It's a sorting device[10].	Peters
Brand is the promise, the big idea, and the expectations that reside in each customer's mind about a product, service, or a company. People fall in love with brands, trust them, develop strong loyalties to them, buy them, and believe in their superiority. The brand is shorthand. It stands for something[11].	Wheeler
Brands represent consumers' perceptions and feelings about a product and its performance—everything that the product or the service means to consumers. In the final analysis, brands exist in the heads of consumers[12].	Kotler & Armstrong
A singular idea or concept that you own inside the mind of the prospect[13].	Ries
Brands serve as markers for the offerings of a firm. (They) are built on the product itself, the accompanying marketing activity, and the use (or nonuse) by customers as well as others. Brands, thus, reflect the complete experience that customers have with products. Brands manifest their impact at three primary levels: customer market, product market, and financial market[14].	Keller & Lehmann
A set of assets and liabilities linked to a brand, its name and symbol, that adds to or subtracts from the value provided by a product or service to a firm and/or to that firm's customers[15].	Aaker
A brand is a mechanism for achieving competitive advantage for firms, through differentiation (purpose). The attributes that differentiate a brand provide the customer with satisfaction and benefits for which they are willing to pay (mechanism)[16].	Wood
Brands are re-defined as complex multidimensional constructs with varying degrees of meaning, independence, co-creation and scope. Brands are semiotic marketing systems that generate value for direct and indirect participants, society, and the broader environment, through the exchange of co-created meaning[17].	Conejo
A brand is the set of expectations, memories, stories, and relationships that, taken together, account for a consumer's decision to choose one product or service over another[18].	Seth Godin
Brand means the total identity of a product or service, which a current or prospective consumer relates to and connects with intellectually, psychologically, and/or emotionally. "Brand" is a complex, multi-layered promise of what will be delivered to and experienced by the consumer[19].	INTA
Think of the brand as the culture of the product. Brands are cultures that circulate in society as conventional stories[20].	Holt
A brand is the sum of all expressions by which an entity (person, organization, company, business unit, city, nation, etc.) intends to be recognized[21].	Interbrand

Here's a summary of some of the most influential conceptualizations of a brand's building blocks we've heard over the last few decades.

BRAND EQUITY (AAKER)

David Aaker's Brand Equity model emphasizes the multidimensional nature of brand value by focusing on five key components: Brand Loyalty, Brand Awareness, Perceived Quality, Brand Associations, and Other Proprietary Assets[22].

Brand Loyalty represents customers' commitment to your brand, while **Brand Awareness** refers to how easily they can recognize it. **Perceived Quality** elucidates, regardless of objective feature sets, what is ultimately being perceived by customers. **Brand Associations** reveal the brand-related attributes, benefits, and attitudes stored in customers' memories. Lastly, **Other Proprietary Assets** include legal and competitive perks that make your brand stand out.

This holistic and deeply influential brand equity model highlights the importance of nurturing not just brand recognition, but also the emotional and functional aspects of a brand that

AAKER'S
Brand Equity Ten

Loyalty Measures	Awareness Measures	Perceived Quality / Leadership Measures	Associations / Differentiation Measures	Market Behavior Measures
LOYALTY / SATISFACTION	BRAND AWARENESS	LEADERSHIP	BRAND PERSONALITY	MARKET SHARE
PRICE PREMIUM		PERCEIVED QUALITY	ORGANIZATIONAL ASSOCIATIONS	PRICE AND DISTRIBUTION INDICES
			PERCEIVED VALUE	

FIGURE 2.1: Brand Equity Ten (Aaker)

create consumer attachment. As a brand manager, Aaker's Brand Equity model is invaluable for understanding and maximizing the long-term value of your brand.

Along with the original five dimensions, Aaker recommended a set of related measures to assess our brand equity's strength[23]. He denominated these indicators as the **Brand Equity Ten:**

1. **Brand Loyalty**
   - **Price Premium:** The extra amount consumers are willing to pay for your brand over others.
   - **Satisfaction/Loyalty:** The degree to which consumers are content with your brand and keep coming back.
2. **Brand Awareness**
   - **Brand Recognition:** The extent to which consumers can identify your brand when prompted.
   - **Brand Recall:** How well consumers can spontaneously remember your brand.
3. **Perceived Quality**
   - **Perceived Quality Level:** The overall consumer perception of your brand's quality.
   - **Quality Value:** The consumer's evaluation of your brand's quality relative to its price.
4. **Brand Associations**
   - **Perceived Value:** The consumer's assessment of the benefits and costs of your brand.
   - **Brand Personality:** The human-like traits and characteristics associated with your brand.
   - **Organizational Associations:** The perceived traits of the organization behind the brand, such as innovation or reliability.
5. **Other Proprietary Assets**
   - Patents, Trademarks, and Channel Relationships: The legal rights and market advantages that protect and promote your brand.

BRAND HEXAGON

Mats Urde's Brand Hexagon presents building blocks that relate harmoniously in brand-oriented organizations: Positioning, Trademark, Product, Corporate Identity, Corporate Name, Brand Vision, and Target Group.[24]

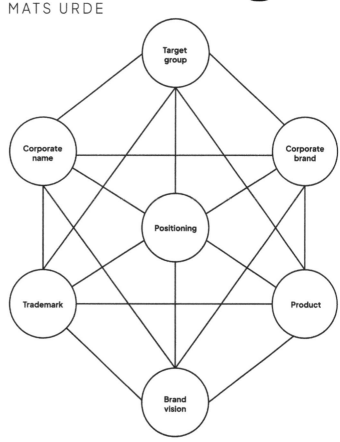

FIGURE 2.2: Brand Hexagon (Urde)

The model elucidates how an organization can communicate a cohesive message emanating from the Brand Vision to reach its Target Group. The Brand Vision can be seen as its essential strategy, a principle that guides all executions. This vision informs the brand's message, which is composed of the Corporate Name, Identity, Trademark, Product, and Position. Together, these elements serve as points of contact that shape the Target Group's impression of the company.

Brand Orientation is an integrative approach that resolves the disconnect between product and marketing in many companies today. Simply put, the Brand Vision provides a set of long-term objectives and a unifying narrative that an organization can rally around, understanding that multiple touchpoints must interact cohesively to bring this vision to life.

BRAND IDENTITY PRISM

The Brand Identity Prism, developed by Jean-Noël Kapferer, captures the essence of a brand's identity through six facets: **Physique** (tangible features), **Personality** (character traits projected by the brand), **Culture** (values and beliefs underpinning the brand), **Relationship** (bonds created between a brand and its consumers), **Reflection** (the consumer's ideal self-image projected by the brand), and **Self-image** (how consumers see themselves when using the brand)[25].

This model's uniqueness lies in its deeper exploration of a brand's essence and its attempt to tie it back to consumer's own self-management activities, making it an excellent tool for brand managers defining a brand's identity. Addressing each facet helps to create a cohesive and compelling brand narrative that resonates with consumers. Unlike other models focusing on a brand's financial or customer equity, Kapferer's

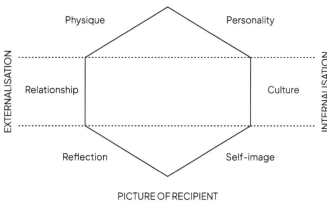

Brand Identity Prism

KAPFERER

PICTURE OF SENDER

Physique — Personality

EXTERNALISATION — INTERNALISATION

Relationship — Culture

Reflection — Self-image

PICTURE OF RECIPIENT

FIGURE 2.3: Brand Identity Prism (Kapferer)

Identity Prism is a comprehensive deep dive into your brand's unique character and associated meanings.

BRAND ESSENCE PYRAMID

Leslie De Chernatony's Brand Essence Pyramid is a strategic tool that helps brand managers distill a brand's core values and attributes into a simplified hierarchy[26].

As a brand manager, one of your main goals is to seek alignment: you want to make sure the whole team is on the same page when it comes to your brand. Enter the Brand Pyramid. This tool helps you define your brand's core promise and communicate it effectively to everyone in your organization. It's like a blueprint for the brand's identity, focusing on the elements that matter most to consumers.

The base layer is all about finding untapped opportunities in the market and leveraging your company's strengths to create a unique set of attributes. Think of this as the "What" of your brand—the special technology or process that sets it apart.

But consumers care more about the "Why" than the "What". They're interested in the benefits your brand offers. With time, these benefits lead to emotional rewards. To resonate with consumers, these emotional rewards need to connect to a value they appreciate.

But here's the thing—consumers have limited time and resources, making it difficult to absorb this identity you're carefully trying to build. That's where the top of the pyramid comes in: the brand's personality. By associating your brand with a celebrity or public figure who embodies its values, consumers can quickly make connections between your brand and its promise. Let's see how each of the pyramid's layers plays a role when defining an eco-friendly fashion brand:

1. **Attributes:** A clothing brand that uses eco-friendly materials and ethical manufacturing processes.
2. **Benefits:** Customers can wear stylish clothes while knowing they're making a positive impact on the environment and supporting fair labor practices.
3. **Emotional rewards:** Wearing the brand's clothing brings a sense of pride and satisfaction in contributing to a greener future.
4. **Values:** The brand aligns with consumers' values of sustainability, ethical practices, and environmental consciousness.
5. **Brand personality:** A well-known environmental activist or an influencer with a passion for sustainable living could represent the brand, reinforcing the brand's promise to create stylish, eco-friendly clothing that makes a difference.

Brand Essence Pyramid

DE CHERNATONY

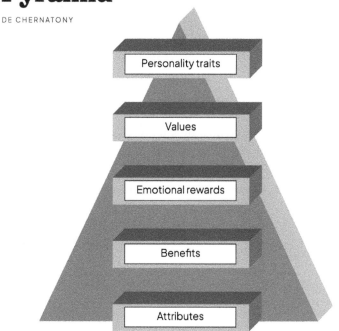

Personality traits

Values

Emotional rewards

Benefits

Attributes

FIGURE 2.4: Brand Essence Pyramid (De Chernatony)

The Brand Pyramid is grounded in means–end theory, which suggests that a brand's attributes (the means) have consequences for consumers, reinforcing their values (the ends) (Gutman, 1982)[27]. We'll review means–end theory in greater detail in Chapter 7 when we discuss brand associations.

Like Kapferer's, this model is particularly useful for brand managers looking to create or refine their brand's positioning, as it emphasizes the importance of leveraging the brand's differentiating values. By mastering the pyramid, managers can develop a powerful and authentic brand message that connects with consumers on a deeper level.

TOWARDS A HOLISTIC DEFINITION OF BRAND

It is only by integrating these various perspectives that we are able to arrive at a holistic, robust definition of a brand.

At its core, a brand is the **story** that consumers recall when they think about you. This story associates your product with their personal stories, a particular personality, what you promise to solve, and your position relative to your competitors. Your brand is represented by a set of visual **symbols** and is shared with a defined audience through a specific communication **strategy.** Three brand components become immediately evident: a story, symbols, and a strategy.

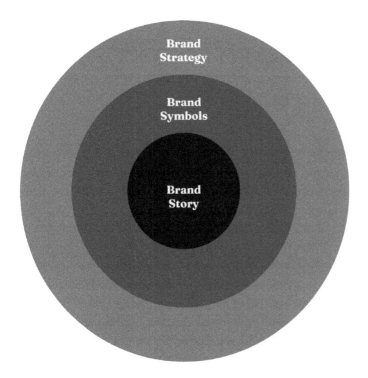

FIGURE 2.5: Brand System (Busche)

A brand serves as a repository of meaning: it summarizes a larger value story and becomes a shortcut to recall that story's connection to our own needs and wants. In a way, the definition I'm proposing above leans on the original, literal meaning of the word brand. However, instead of referring to a physical mark, this brand leaves a lasting mental impression that consumers recall when they are exposed to elements of its story, symbols, or strategy. Like the literal definition, the final meaning of a brand depends on the surface it is imprinted on. In consumers, this surface corresponds to their unique individual traits and environmental context.

Throughout this book, we will explore the concepts of story, symbols, and strategy in depth, including insights from business, design, and psychology. We will also expand on this three-part structure of brands to shape the Brand System, a helpful framework to unify, capture, and manage the brand concept over time.

BRAND SYSTEMS: A FRAMEWORK TO CAPTURE THE BRAND CONCEPT

One of our main issues in the brand management space is unifying seemingly disparate, ever-evolving concepts into useful frameworks that are clear, consistent, and practical.

I've faced this challenge over the years and have consolidated insights from business, psychology, and design literature into a single framework: Brand Systems.

At their core, **Brand Systems** are shared libraries that define a brand's story, symbols, and strategy. Within teams, Brand Systems help avoid fragmentation, confusion, and exclusion. Consumer-facing, they become a script to deliver the most compelling brand experience possible — at every touchpoint, every single time.

A robust brand system goes from the concrete to the symbolic, expanding a brand concept far beyond the utilitarian realm. If we've learned anything in the last 50 years, and throughout this book, it's that human beings purchase products and services for reasons beyond their objective features.

Understanding this, Brand Systems capture the various layers of value that are perceived and appreciated by customers in their journey with a brand.

Let's take a look.

Brand System components

At its core, a Brand System stems from a basic value **promise.** We will cover how to shape this promise in depth later on in this section. In the meantime, this core value proposition is the most essential benefit or set of benefits brought about by this brand.

Next up is the **story** layer. This is where a brand's narrative unfolds: we learn how it creates value, for whom, in what ways, what this brand sounds like and feels like, how it positions itself in relation to competitors, and what it aims to do.

This Story is then represented through a wide array of **symbols.** The third layer in our brand system is a set of symbolic elements we associate with the brand. Enter the realm of the senses, imagination, emotions, aesthetics, beliefs, and experiences—a more immersive definition of this brand where customers feel brought into a distinct universe. A space where this brand's essence is on display and can be fully experienced.

Lastly, **strategy** is an instrumental part of any Brand System.

Strong brands are the dreams they enable, the needs they resolve, and the aspirations they realize. Brands are what they do, not what they say they're going to do. That's why strategy—the *how*— is so tightly connected to a brand's identity.

Throughout this book, we will review a brand's story, symbols, and strategy in detail. The following section will focus on that first layer of our brand's system: shaping a compelling story.

HOW BRANDS ADD SYMBOLIC SIGNIFICANCE TO A PRODUCT

Brands act as meaning carriers: they both contain associations and assist in their recall. Over time, well-positioned brands become shorthand for specific functional or deeper values. In this context, a brand manager's role is twofold:

1. **To unveil existing meanings associated with the brand.** A brand manager must conduct ongoing research to uncover and unpack the kinds of associations triggered by the brand, understanding the vital role they play in the information processing and decision-making processes that we saw before.
2. **To reinforce intended meanings** by designing a brand story, symbols and strategy. Certain marketing actions can strengthen the level of perceived association between a brand and its target concepts/meanings.

STRATEGY: COMMUNICATING THE BRAND STORY

But how can we go about fulfilling that second part of the role? Brand building is, at its heart, an education effort. As mentioned before, the brand story that ends up residing in a customer's memory is not only shaped by his or her individual variables; the way we present brand stimuli can also make a difference.

Through **consumer learning**, a brand can actively foster education processes to create and reinforce desired associations. It can also make a case for the product it offers: why it's worth acquiring, what kinds of needs it solves, and, perhaps most importantly, how it constitutes a clear benefit for the consumer's own needs.

Going back to the three-part brand structure introduced earlier in this chapter, a brand's **strategy** is ultimately responsible for conveying its value **story** and visual **symbols** effectively. Regardless of how this story ends up reading in consumers' minds, brands can improve their chances of building successful relationships if they are mindful of the benefits they can potentially create—the value they can truly add. After defining these benefits, brands can communicate them through consumer learning. When we discuss brand strategy more extensively in Section 3, we will review tactics to design, foster, and maintain these learning processes.

TOWARDS A BENEFIT-CENTRIC BRAND STRATEGY

Often known as "wins", consumers' triumphal moments should be the primary obsession of any team branding a product. Designing and generating these moments turn brands into genuine vehicles for self-realization. Given their power to move consumers into action, benefits are the associations that should be at the core of every consumer learning effort.

What kinds of benefits can a brand possibly generate for consumers? Researchers have studied many of these positive effects closely over the years. Let's take a look at some of the most important ones:

HOW BRANDS CAN BENEFIT CONSUMERS

- A certain brand can provide a sense of **group identification**, helping individuals express their commitment to collective identities. The values attached to a given brand can extend symbolically to its users, connecting them through its use.
- Brands can become **choice heuristics** or shortcuts to simplify and make the decision-making process more efficient[28]. All else constant, human beings aim at creating rules of thumb to make sense of the reality that surrounds them. These shortcuts are the reason we create stereotypes. While applying stereotypes to other human beings can lead to misjudgment and injustice, assigning certain meanings to brands *a priori* contributes to rapid purchase decisions. Van Osselaer and Janiszewski found that customers have innate learning processes that allow them to use brand names to predict consumption benefits[29].
- Brand stories can become part of individuals' **personal narratives**, helping them convey meanings that tie back to their personalities, attitudes, and lifestyles. The symbolic interactionism theory we reviewed in Chapter 1 describes how human beings exchange meanings in their daily interactions. Inspired by that theory, Robert

Wicklund and Peter Gollwitzer introduced the notion of "symbolic self-completion", proposing that human beings are driven by the desire to come across as "complete" in a given domain area, using various resources at their disposal to "self-symbolize"[30]. In this context, brands can assist us in the purpose of intentionally designing our identity and communicating it to our social circle.

- **Aspirational** brands can offer a path or shortcut to the realization of a desired self. In our review of consumer behavior history, we discussed the possible selves concept as a source of motivation for individuals to engage in certain behaviors. In industries where brands are closely tied to personal image, such as fashion and beauty, the consumption of certain brands can signal desired values like prestige, a certain social position, and a level of taste.

It's important to mention that you won't find the same level of symbolic consumption in the decision to purchase every single brand. Some industries are dominated by commoditized products where variables like price and accessibility are enough signals to stimulate consumption. However, even those industries are now trying to move towards a value-based differentiation by building brands that capture and convey the product's benefits. The branding landscape is shifting as you read this.

SUSTAINING BRAND RELATIONSHIPS OVER TIME

Successful brands build strong relationships with consumers. They aim to engage with them continuously, delivering consistent value over time. In order to succeed brands must:

- **Define** what that value looks like for the audience it serves. What do they want, need, or aspire to? What does the ideal scenario look like for them? What is their desired self?

- **Design** a brand experience that offers that value. How does this audience want to be served? What are the components that need to be in place to bring their ideal scenario to life?
- **Deliver** that value consistently over the customer's life cycle. Does this audience need to consume this value again? Do they need a complementary experience?

WHY BRAND? BENEFITS FOR COMPANIES

There are multiple benefits for companies that build a long-term brand strategy, especially in today's saturated market. Globalization, the internet, and free trade agreements have leveled the playing field and made competing on functional attributes increasingly harder. Price advantages are feeble: a simple tariff change or new free trade agreement could decimate anyone's cost-based competitive advantage in seconds. Capturing and conveying superior value is the way to survive. Consumers want more, and brand differentiation is the name of this new game. Here are some of the specific benefits companies can obtain by investing in brand building:

- **Premium pricing.** Premium pricing is the differential amount of money a consumer is willing to pay for a good or service above what others charge for similar offers in the market. While not desirable for every product or company, premium pricing makes sense for brands trying to convey a level of luxury and/or reach a specific market segment with higher purchasing power. Regardless of the specific goals behind this business decision, one truth remains: a sustainable price premium strategy relies heavily on successful brand building. It is the values and associations consistently linked to the brand that allow it to command a price that is well above production costs for a product or service that other brands offer for less.

- **Top-of-mind awareness.** When a brand is actively trying to build relationships with its target audience, it makes itself more salient (top of mind) in the **consideration set** that consumers entertain when they make certain purchase decisions. When facing the purchase process, our mind tends to filter through an **awareness set** (brands that we know exist), to an **evoked set** (brands we know could satisfy our need or want), to a **consideration set** that we shortlist for our final decision. Top-of-mind awareness makes brands easier to remember, recall, and settle for at the end of the day.
- **Brand extension potential.** A high-equity brand can serve as a solid foundation for one or multiple **brand extensions.** As consumers, we tend to extend the loyalty and trust we've built up towards a certain brand to its new products or services. Strengthening a brand enables it to provide that kind of leverage to such extensions, as we will analyze in Chapter 20.

Steve Hoeffler and Kevin Keller analyzed brand strength literature and distilled a comprehensive overview of the key benefits a strong brand can bring about. The figure below illustrates some of the benefits we've outlined here and more. There are overarching benefits like increased brand strength, incentivized consumer behaviors, and a differentiated customer response to certain marketing activities. In general, building a strong brand increases awareness of its offerings, the proneness to acquire them, and reception towards new initiatives[31].

Brand Strength

A SUMMARY

| BRAND STRENGTH | → | CONSUMER BEHAVIOUR | → | DIFFERENTIAL MARKETING EFFORTS |

Brand familiarity

- Awareness

Brand knowledge

- Strong, favourable and unique brand associations
- High-quality brand

Brand performance

- Market share leader
- Dominant brand

Attention and learning

- Consideration
- Selective attention

Interpretation and evaluation

- Direct
- Indirect

Choice

- Heuristic

Post-purchase

- Extension evaluation
- Loyalty

Product

- More favourable attribute and benefit perceptions
- Overall preference

Extensions

- More favourable consumer response
- More efficient marketing programme

Price

- Greater price premiums
- More favourable response to price increases and decreases

Communications

- Pay greater attention
- React more positively
- Retain more information

FIGURE 2.6: Brand strength

NOTES

1. Gardner, B. B., & Levy, S. J. (1955). The product and the brand. *Harvard Business Review, 33*(2), 33–39.
2. American Marketing Association. Branding Archives. *American Marketing Association.* Retrieved from https://www.ama.org/topics/branding/
3. Kapferer, J.-N. (2008). *The New Strategic Brand Management: Creating and Sustaining Brand Equity Long Term.* Kogan Page Publishers.
4. De Chernatony, L., & Dall'Olmo Riley, F. (1998). Defining a "brand": Beyond the literature with experts' interpretations. *Journal of Marketing Management, 14*(5), 417–443. https://doi.org/10.1362/026725798784867798
5. De Chernatony L. and McDonald M. (1994) *Creating Powerful Brands.* Oxford: Butterworth Heinemann.
6. Veloutsou, C., & Delgado-Ballester, E. (2018). New challenges in brand management. *Spanish Journal of Marketing - ESIC, 22*(3), 254–271. https://doi.org/10.1108/SJME-12-2018-036
7. Busche, L. (2014). *Lean Branding: Creating Dynamic Brands to Generate Conversion* (1st edition). O'Reilly Media.
8. Parmentier, M. (2011). When David met Victoria: Forging a strong family brand. *Family Business Review, 23*, 217–232. https://doi.org/10.1177/0894486511408415
9. Ogilvy, D. (1985). *Ogilvy on Advertising.* New York: Vintage Books.
10. Peters, T. *The Brand Called You.* Fast Company. Retrieved from https://www.fastcompany.com/28905/brand-called-you
11. Wheeler, A. (2006). *Designing Brand Identity: A Complete Guide to Creating, Building and Maintaining Strong Brands.* Hoboken, N.J.: John Wiley.
12. Kotler, P., & Armstrong, G. M. (2010). *Principles of Marketing.* Prentice Hall.
13. Ries, A., & Ries, L. (2002). *The 22 Immutable Laws of Branding.* HarperCollins.
14. Keller, K. L., & Lehmann, D. R. (2006). Brands and branding: Research findings and future priorities. *Marketing Science, 25*(6), 740–759.
15. Aaker, D. A. (1991). *Managing Brand Equity: Capitalizing on the Value of a Brand Name.* Free Press; Maxwell Macmillan Canada.

16. Wood, L. (2000). Brands and brand equity: Definition and management. *Management Decision, 38*(9), 662–669. https://doi.org/10.1108/00251740010379100

17. Conejo, F., & Wooliscroft, B. (2015). Brands defined as semiotic marketing systems. *Journal of Macromarketing, 35*(3), 287–301. https://doi.org/10.1177/0276146714531147

18. Godin, S. (2009, December 13). *define: Brand*. Seth's Blog. https://seths.blog/2009/12/define-brand

19. INTA. *Brand Value Special Task Force Report: Executive Summary.* Retrieved from https://www.inta.org/wp-content/uploads/public-files/perspectives/industry-research/Brand-Value-Special-Task-Force-Report-Executive-Summary-1.pdf

20. Holt, D. (2003). *Brands and Branding*. MBA Note.
    Holt, D. B. (2004). *How Brands Become Icons: The Principles of Cultural Branding*. Harvard Business Review Press.

21. Interbrand. (2018, April 18). *What is a Brand?* https://interbrand.com/london/thinking/what-is-a-brand/, https://interbrand.com/london/thinking/what-is-a-brand/

22. Aaker, D. A. (1991). *Managing Brand Equity: Capitalizing on the Value of a Brand Name*. Free Press; Maxwell Macmillan Canada.

23. Aaker, D. A. (1996). Measuring brand equity across products and markets. *California Management Review, 38*(3).

24. Urde, M. (1994). Brand orientation–A strategy for survival. *Journal of Consumer Marketing, 11*(3), 18–32.

25. Kapferer, J.-N. (2008). *The New Strategic Brand Management: Creating and Sustaining Brand Equity Long Term*. Kogan Page Publishers.

26. De Chernatony, L. (2010). *From Brand Vision to Brand Evaluation: The Strategic Process of Growing and Strengthening Brands*. Routledge.

27. Gutman, Gutman, J. (1982). A Means-End Chain Model Based on Consumer Categorization Processes. *Journal of Marketing, 46*(2), 60–72. https://doi.org/10.2307/3203341

28. Hoeffler, S., & Keller, K. L. (2003). The marketing advantages of strong brands. *Journal of Brand Management, 10*, 421–445.

29. Van Osselaer, S. M., & Janiszewski, C. (2001). Two ways of learning brand associations. *Journal of Consumer Research, 28*(2), 202–223.

30. Wicklund, R. A., & Gollwitzer, P. M. (1981). Symbolic self-completion, attempted influence, and self-deprecation. *Basic and Applied Social Psychology, 2*, 89–114. https://doi.org/10.1207/s15324834basp0202_2

31. Hoeffler, S., & Keller, K. L. (2003). The marketing advantages of strong brands. *Journal of Brand Management, 10*, 421–445.

CHAPTER 3

BRAND EQUITY AND MANAGEMENT

DOI: 10.4324/9781003336693-4

Brand marketing is often treated as a "soft" discipline. A set of investments without an objective, measurable return. This common misconception sabotages worthy ventures every day, turning brand positioning, innovation, and other activities into second-class business functions. In deprioritizing and defunding these initiatives, brands are undercutting their growth potential.

BRAND EQUITY OFFERS A PATH FORWARD

Brand equity is a structured measurement of a brand's impact. How that impact is defined results in a number of brand equity metrics one can track and optimize. Objective indicators demonstrate a company's ability to engage, convert, and retain human beings' intentions long term.

Essentially, brand equity is an answer to the question of how much a brand is worth. Over the last decades, we've seen two major approaches to size this impact:

- Customer-based brand equity
- Firm-based brand equity

Customer-based brand equity is about defining the brand's value as it manifests in solving a customer's need or want.

On the other hand, firm-based brand equity focuses on a brand's business value—the net worth it adds as an asset.

Ultimately, both of these perspectives are complementary in that financial value can be a reflection of strong customer brand equity. While large consultancies like Interbrand offer signature brand valuation systems, every brand manager should be aware of accessible scales that allow you to monitor brand impact on an internal, managerial level.

Luckily, brand management theorists and practitioners have proposed multiple scales we can lean on to measure brand equity. Up next, we will review the *Multidimensional Customer-Based Brand Equity Scale*—a tool that allows brands to self-assess and strengthen equity. Then, we will also look at the *Online Retail Service Brand Equity Scale*, specifically designed to analyze the strength of digital retail brands.

Drawing from Aaker's conceptualization of brand equity, Yoo and Donthu built a consumer-based brand equity scale (MBE) based on three dimensions: brand loyalty, perceived quality, brand awareness/associations. As you'll likely remember, these constructs were part of Aaker's understanding of a brand's equity: consumer loyalty, quality perceptions, and heightened awareness are all positive effects a strong brand can add to a product. In fact, Yoo and Donthu see brand equity as "consumers' different response between a focal brand and an unbranded product when both have the same level of marketing stimuli and product attributes".[1] All else equal, a strong

TABLE 3.1: Multi-dimensional Brand Equity Scale (Yoo & Donthu, 2001)

Scale name	Multidimensional Consumer-Based Brand Equity (MBE) Scale
Authors	Yoo & Donthu (2001)
Type of scale	5-point Likert
Anchors	From "Strongly disagree" (1) to "Strongly agree" (5)
Dimensions	*Brand loyalty, perceived quality, brand awareness/associations*
Items	**Brand loyalty** • I consider myself to be loyal to (brand X) • (Brand X) would be my first choice • I will not buy other brands if (brand X) is available at the store **Perceived quality** • The likely quality of (brand X) is extremely high • The likelihood that (brand X) would be functional is very high **Brand awareness/associations** • I can recognize (brand X) among other competing brands • I am aware of (brand X) • Some characteristics of (brand X) come to my mind quickly • I can quickly recall the symbol or logo of (brand X) • I have difficulty in imagining (brand X) in my mind (R)* ** Item should be reverse coded*

brand equity should improve customers' response to a given product and this instrument gives us a way to measure it.

Online retail brands face unique challenges when it comes to building strong brands. Much of the customer/brand experience is intangible, taking place through a series of digital interactions that can feel disjointed. Christodoulides et al. observed that user experience and customer support played a crucial role in positioning these types of brands. Therefore, they built a scale that evaluates customers' level of emotional connection, the quality of their online experience, the extent to which the brand's service has felt responsive, the sense of trust it instils, and its ability to fulfill orders accurately as described[2].

TABLE 3.2: ORS Brand Equity Scale (Christodoulides et al., 2006)

Scale name	Online Retail/Service (ORS) Brand Equity Scale
Authors	Christodoulides et al. (2006)
Type of scale	7-point Likert
Anchors	From "Strongly disagree" (1) to "Strongly agree" (7)
Scoring	The ORS brand equity index equals 0.21 (the mean of emotional connection) + 0.18 (the mean of online experience) + 0.18 (the mean of responsive service nature) + 0.20 (the mean of trust) + 0.23 (the mean of fulfillment).
Dimensions	*Emotional Connection, Online Experience, Responsive Service Nature, Trust, Fulfillment*
Items	**Emotional connection** • I feel related to the type of people who are [X]'s customers • I feel like [X] actually cares about me • I feel as though [X] really understands me **Online experience** • [X]'s website provides easy-to-follow search paths • I never feel lost when navigating through [X]'s website • I was able to obtain the information I wanted without any delay **Responsive service nature** • [X] is willing and ready to respond to customer needs • [X]'s website gives visitors the opportunity to 'talk back' to [X] **Trust** • I trust [X] to keep my personal information safe • I feel safe in my transactions with [X] **Fulfillment** • I got what I ordered from [X]'s website • The product was delivered by the time promised by [X]

BRAND MANAGEMENT

If brand equity answers what a brand's real value is, brand management answers **how** that value is created over time.

Brand management is the ongoing process of defining a brand's position, identity, and message. Brand managers analyze the network of associations conveyed by the brand and actively intervene to reshape or reinforce them. To do so, they seek a holistic view of the brand's presence, diving deep into customer perceptions to calibrate what is being communicated.

Brand managers understand that every business function plays a role in enacting the brand. They aim for a cohesive experience where customers are left with a value story they feel compelled to return to. No touchpoint is too small, no channel is too foreign. If the brand is at play, so are they.

Over time, brand management paradigms have shifted from mere image management to customer-centric storytelling, to our contemporary view: one where brands are seen as networks of meaning one imbues in products, services, and ideas.

Let's now turn our attention to some of the most popular brand management models of the last century and a new proposal to manage brands moving forward. Lastly, we will review the human-centered brand management framework proposed as an integrative approach to branding rooted in human motivations and the communication process.

BRAND ASSET MANAGEMENT (DAVIS)

The Brand Asset Management model, developed by Scott M. Davis in 2002, is a comprehensive framework that emphasizes the strategic management of brand equity to maximize long-term value.

The model consists of 11 steps in four primary phases: Brand Vision, BrandPicture, Brand Asset Management Strategy, and Brand Asset Management Culture[3].

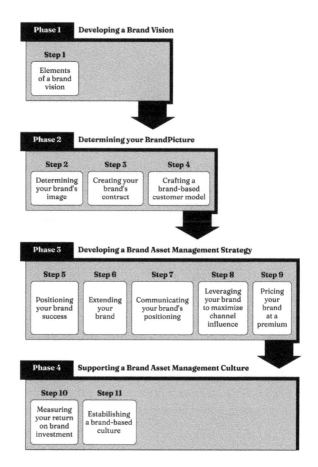

FIGURE 3.1: Brand Asset Management (Davis)

In Phase 1, brand managers define a **Brand Vision** that is linked to the organization's broader vision and fills a financial growth gap. This vision will be shared by senior management and guides all brand-building efforts.

Phase 2 is about determining a clear **BrandPicture.** This phase involves taking a deep dive into how your customers view your brand and what it stands for. With these perceptions in mind, the next step is crafting a brand-based customer model that answers:

- How customers choose one brand over another
- How your brand stacks up against others
- What opportunities exist for brand growth

Finally, you'll design a strategy to deliver on the promise your brand makes to customers, which Davis denominates "brand contract".

Phase 3 is about creating a **Brand Asset Management Strategy** that explains the how. You position your brand, extend into new areas, and decide when to charge a premium price. This strategy allows you to keep your brand fresh and innovative over time, so it can continue to stand out in a crowded marketplace.

Finally, Phase 4 involves designing a **Brand Asset Management Culture** that gets the entire organization aligned and motivated around the brand. Davis recommends establishing a brand-based culture that affects the roles of every functional area, from top management to internal communications to reward and measurement systems. He proposes measuring your return on brand investment (ROBI) to track progress and adjust strategies as needed.

BRAND CONCEPT MANAGEMENT (PARK ET AL.)

The Brand Concept Management (BCM) model, proposed by C. Whan Park, Bernard J. Jaworski, and Deborah J. MacInnis, focuses on the psychological aspects of branding by suggesting that a strong brand must establish a clear and compelling brand concept[4].

This model consists of three types of brand concepts: functional, symbolic, and experiential. **Functional** concepts are centered around the product's utilitarian features, **symbolic** concepts emphasize the social or personal meaning behind the brand, and **experiential** concepts focus on the sensory or emotional appeal of the brand.

The uniqueness of the BCM model lies in its emphasis on the consumer's psychological connection with the brand. It

Brand Concept Management

C. WHAN PARK, BERNARD J. JAWORSKI AND DEBORAH J. MACLNNIS

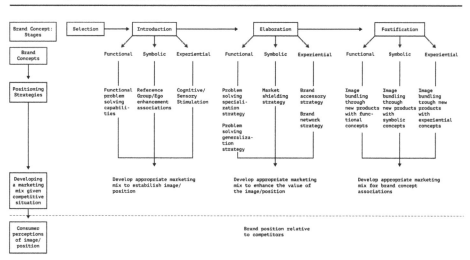

FIGURE 3.2: Brand Concept Management (Park et al.)

serves as a valuable tool for brand managers when developing marketing strategies that resonate with their target audience and foster brand loyalty.

LOGMAN MODEL (LOGMAN)

The LOGMAN model, proposed by Marc Logman in 2004, focuses on the need for alignment and balance between a brand's learning, process, customer, and financial perspectives[5]. It is strongly based on the classic Balanced Scorecard instrument widely used in management since the 90s[6].

Put simply, brands should balance these four perspectives when evaluating their performance over time. They must optimize the **processes** with which they serve their key customer segments, review the brand and customers' **financial** value to the organization, monitor **customers' perceptions** of key brand drivers, and maintain an ongoing **learning** practice that fuels innovation.

This framework sees brand management as both a proactive and reactive discipline. Proactive brand managers influence the drivers affecting customer perception: including those stemming from the company's actions (internal) as well as those coming from external sources. Also reactive at times, brand managers must integrate a learning perspective to learn from financial outcomes and better address customer segments in the future.

For brand managers, the LOGMAN model is particularly useful when aiming to achieve consistency in brand messaging and experience over time, ensuring that all aspects of the brand align with the overall organizational strategy.

The Logical Brand Management Model

MARC LOGMAN

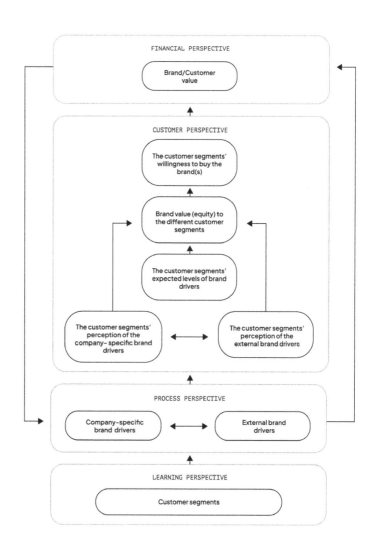

FIGURE 3.3: Logical brand management model (Logman)

BRAND DESIGN MANAGEMENT (MONTAÑA, GUZMÁN, AND MOLL)

The Brand Design Management model, introduced by Jordi Montaña, Francisco Guzmán, and Isa Moll emphasizes the role of design in creating and sustaining a powerful brand identity.

For a brand to be strong, recognized, and remembered, every brand message must be aligned to project a consistent meaning. Design plays a central role in achieving this. Given that different managers at various levels typically handle brand design decisions, it is crucial to have a coordinated brand design management strategy in place.

This is where the Brand Design Management model comes in. Design can act as a manager for consistency and coherence, but it must be understood throughout the organization first. This model outlines a collaborative process for building and maintaining a strong brand identity[7]. It involves four main activities:

1. **Concept generation:** Gathering internal and external information and stimuli to create a potential offering.
2. **Design strategy:** Outlining the necessary activities to refine the potential offering.
3. **Resource procurement:** Assembling all required internal and external resources to execute the design process.
4. **Strategy implementation:** Executing the strategy, with the design orientation of the firm guiding all activities.

This model's unique value comes from its detailed focus on the design aspects of branding, making it a valuable resource

Brand Design Management Model

JORDI MONTAÑA , FRANCISCO GUZMÁN & ISA MOLL

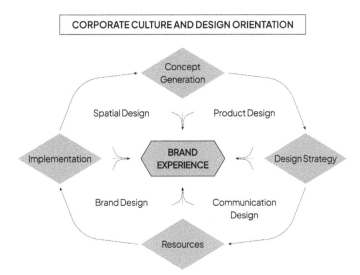

CORPORATE CULTURE AND DESIGN ORIENTATION

FIGURE 3.4: Brand Design Management (Montaña, Guzmán, and Moll)

for brand managers seeking to create a strong and memorable brand identity through design.

HUMAN-CENTERED BRAND MANAGEMENT

Over the last 10 years, I've worked with brands of all sizes to design an empathetic, sustainable strategy that propels them forward. Along the way, I've built a brand management framework rooted in principles of human psychology, design thinking, communication, and management.

At their core, **effective brand managers are communicators.** They understand that what *isn't* said is also part of the message. They recognize that a brand is, ultimately, a co-constructed story where receivers and senders build off each other's inputs. They operate knowing brand development is a feedback loop accelerated by brand activities and fine-tuned through diligent research.

This model entertains each human being's pains, wants, and needs, identifying these factors as behavior drivers. The systematic literature review involved in developing this book as well as industry insights have led to this synthetic framework based on interactional and transactional models of interpersonal communication such as Barnlund's and Schramm's.

The diagram below illustrates some of the processes involved in Human-Centered Brand Management as well as the activities and initiatives brand managers can perform proactively (underlined).

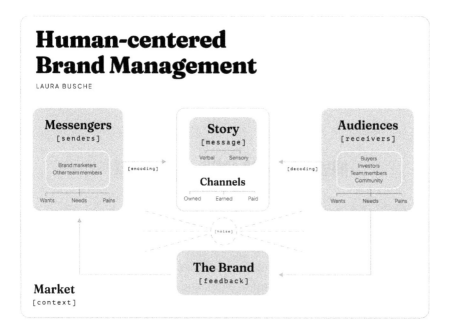

FIGURE 3.5: Human-Centered Brand Management (Busche)

Here are some of the core ideas behind this model:

- Brands are **co-constructed** and ultimately the outcome of customer/firm interactions that can be influenced but not wholly controlled. In Chernatony & O'Reilly's words, "the firm's activities (input) and consumers' perceptions (output) emerge as the two main boundaries of the brand construct, [...] the values and expectations imbued in the brand object (product or service) are set and enacted by the firm's staff and interpreted and redefined by the consumers"[8].

- Cultural **context** plays an active role in brand perception, preference, and relationships.

- **Noise** impacts the process at every stage. It includes media and competitive exposure that will vary according to the context.

- Brands can leverage mediums to communicate their key messages, exercising varying levels of **channel ownership.** This input is an important influence in the brand construct, but is not the only one. Explore some of the channels listed in Chapter 18 to understand the range of options at your disposal.

- Everyone is on the **"brand team"**: team members outside of the functional brand communication team are simultaneously senders and receivers in this process. To unveil team members' perspectives on the brand, you can leverage the EBE scale we will cover in Chapter 17 or a similar tool.

- Strong brand stories are defined both **verbally and sensorially**, offering customers an immersive experience (more on this when we cover the Brandverse in Chapter 11).

- Auditing prevalent brand associations is key to managing them. Brand managers must put an ongoing **research process** in place that works for their organization long term. One-time measurements won't suffice:

to establish benchmarks and analyze the brand's trajectory, continuous measurement is key. Leverage one or more of the brand equity scales we reviewed in this chapter and apply it consistently.

Arising from these principles, there are three essential initiatives brand managers must lead on an ongoing basis: **brand research**, **alignment**, and **communication**.

1. **Brand research:** This activity track entails active audience, context, and impact measurement to inform brand executions.
   a. **Audience:** Empathize with your receiver (target audience) to the point where you're constantly listening. Identify their core needs, pains, and wants and address them as often as possible.
   b. **Context:** Analyze the brandspace to forecast trends and get ahead of meaningful context shifts. Maintain an active brand radar to identify changing needs and wants. We will cover more details on how this is done in Chapter 21.
   c. **Impact:** Track the outcome of your efforts. Ongoing brand image and equity audits can help detect outstanding associations and reinforce them. Reshape your story as often as needed. Identify channels where customers leave unprompted feedback.
2. **Brand alignment:** Can every team member confidently advocate for this brand? Contribute to its ideal experience at key touchpoints? Brand managers document essential story, symbol, and strategy principles to shape a Brand System stakeholders can align around. Internal branding, brand appropriation, and brand system maintenance all fall under this realm.
3. **Brand communication:** Again, effective brand managers are clear communicators— they know how to convey a message that is both verbal and sensory. Designing

a strategic positioning statement, promise, and brand story are all part of this category.

Brand managers influence customers' perceived brand by crafting messages that reinforce desired associations. They leverage owned, earned, and paid channels to accomplish this goal.

To cater to a range of customer engagement levels, brand managers craft a messaging mix that blends cognitive, affective, and behavioral cues (see Chapter 18).

NOTES

1. Yoo, B., & Donthu, N. (2001). Developing and validating a multidimensional consumer-based brand equity scale. *Journal of Business Research, 52*(1), 14.
2. Christodoulides, G., Furrer, O., & Shiu, E. (2006). Conceptualising and Measuring the Equity of Online Brands. *Journal of Marketing Management, 22*, 799–825.
3. Davis, S. M. (2002). *Brand Asset Management: Driving Profitable Growth Through Your Brands.* John Wiley & Sons.
4. Park, C., Jaworski, B., & Macinnis, D. (1986). Strategic brand concept-image management. *Journal of Marketing, 50*, 135. https://doi.org/10.2307/1251291
5. Logman, M. (2004). The LOGMAN model: A logical brand management model. *The Journal of Product and Brand Management, 13*(2/3), 94–104. https://doi.org/10.1108/10610420410529726
6. Kaplan, R. S., & Norton, D. P. (1992). The balanced scorecard: Measures that drive performance. *Harvard Business Review, 70*.
7. Montaña, J., Guzmán, F., & Moll, I. (2007). Branding and design management: A brand design management model. *Journal of Marketing Management, 23*(9–10), 829–840. https://doi.org/10.1362/026725707X250340
8. Chernatony, L., & Dall'Olmo Riley, F. (1998). Modeling the components of brand. *European Journal of Marketing, 32*. https://doi.org/10.1108/03090569810243721

SECTION 1

STORY

DOI: 10.4324/9781003336693-5

INTRODUCTION

Take a moment to think about your favorite brand. Bring its name to mind and take note of the first few ideas you are able to recall. Brands are more than just a name or a logo; they are deeply meaningful concepts, constructed and developed over time.

Brands crystallize meaning.

In essence, they are concepts we build and define over time, messaging desired associations alongside them as we construct a whole network of meaning.

Brands that have closer relationships with us will become more powerful entities, taking on a life of their own as they are associated with more and more touch points, linked to more and more memories, and informed by a greater variety of experiences.

Loyal customers will be privy to the inner workings of brands, engaging with different people from different parts of the business to form their opinion. These customers will even be able to tell when something is out of step with the brand concept they have come to know. They'll be able to spot events, messages, or decisions that don't match up with the brand concept that has been crafted so carefully over time.

CHAPTER 4

BRAND STORY

DOI: 10.4324/9781003336693-6

Stories are how we weave our perceptions and experiences into a meaningful narrative. They help us make sense of our past, present, and future, our own selves and others.

Stories are the most universal form of language, transcending national and ethnic boundaries in the most natural of ways.

Parables, fables, myths, legends: this is how we nurture our imaginations and immerse ourselves in the answers to our most complex questions.

At the heart of every strong brand is an authentic, resonant story. Don't think about this story as something you read. Instead, consider the brand's story an immersive, personally meaningful narrative that comes to life in every interaction you have with it.

This story is the key to unlocking a connection between the brand and its customers, allowing both to be heard and understood in a meaningful way. This is not a story you're *told*, it's a story you experience.

As such, powerful brand stories contain narrative elements that pull us in:

- A captivating **plot,** related to how our needs are solved by this brand
- A vivid, relatable **setting**
- **Characters**, where your target customer is a protagonist

Naturally, customers also play a creative role in shaping this story: they interpret what is being presented in light of previous experiences, knowledge, and their unique worldview. For instance, a customer being presented with a new product may interpret it through the lens of their personal values, seeing it as a vehicle for self-expression or a way to show off their success.

However, brand strategists can design a brand universe that is put forward at every customer touchpoint. This larger enthralling story is the subject of this chapter. By crafting a compelling narrative that can be shared throughout the customer journey, brand strategists can leverage the power of storytelling to build a deeper connection with their customers.

We will borrow insights from psychology, design, marketing, and even cinema literature to construct a captivating brand story that stands the test of time. By studying the successful techniques used by those disciplines, we will be able to create a narrative that resonates with our target audience and is memorable enough to keep them engaged.

DEFINING A BRAND'S VALUE STORY

For the amount of talk about "value" in the business space today, there is little or no exploration of what that value actually looks like for consumers. What it means, deeply and directly, within the context of their decision-making process.

Fortunately, consumer psychology sheds light on this concept— which falls nothing short of the heart of a brand's mission. When we talk about a brand being a value story, we're referring to its ability to satisfy consumers' wants in the manner that they need or wish these to be fulfilled/realized. The **brand story** is a narrative stored by consumers in their attempt to understand the role this brand plays in their lives.

Saying that the narrative is captured by consumers themselves elucidates the two processes that define every brand story. On one hand, you have the brand's outward messaging: the official narrative promoted by whoever is behind the product or service. On the other hand, you have consumers' perception and inner interpretation of that story, contingent on their mediated and lived experiences. In this chapter, we'll take a closer look at both of these processes, starting with the consumer's perception of the brand story.

HOW CONSUMERS SHAPE AND RECALL THE BRAND STORY

In order to understand how the brand story is received by consumers, it's important to analyze how we go about interpreting the stimuli around us and making decisions in reaction to them. The brand's outbound story, symbols, and strategy interact with the consumer's own memory, traits, and environment to result in a final understanding of the brand. Throughout this section, we will take a closer look at how that memory is built, which individual differences affect our reactions, and how our environment influences our decisions.

In cognitive psychology, **information processing** is the set of events through which we recognize, interpret, and store the stimuli presented to us. Now, you may remember from our review of consumer behavior history that, at one point in time, cognitive scientists started comparing the human mind to a computer. Information processing is one of that perspective's most important contributions to the consumer behavior field.

Essentially, when branding stimuli are presented to us we go through five initial steps: exposure, attention, comprehension, acceptance, and retention[1]. These steps are prerequisites to be able to store any given message in our memory. **Exposure** happens when the stimulus is close enough to our senses for us to take note of its existence. As you've probably experienced, sometimes we are too distracted to even recognize the stimuli around us, no matter how "obvious".

In an ideal world, every message brands have spent so much time crafting would get noticed, but that is not how **selective exposure** works. The more saturated our environment gets, the more we avoid certain types of stimuli in order to reduce overwhelm. Ad blockers, skimming, and zapping are not unusual activities for twenty-first-century consumers. Sometimes, however, we are so interested in a subject matter that we actually seek out information in what is known as **voluntary exposure**.

Attention is the natural next step. We have been effectively exposed to the brand stimuli and everything we experience in relation to it is being processed by the brain. But what does this raw information we are sensing actually mean? Well, it depends on who you ask. So here comes one of the most distinctively human processes to the rescue: **comprehension**.

As the popular saying goes, beauty is in the eye of the beholder—and so is the brand. Comprehension is our attempt to make sense of the information we've been exposed to and have attended to. To comprehend is, at once, to understand and interpret. You will often hear that something is "up for interpretation" when it is left open to individuals' subjective points of view about the matter. Comprehension is the step prior to memory storage where we get remarkably creative with what we're about to save. It is also one of the hardest truths for brand managers to assimilate: *the brand will ultimately mean whatever consumers interpret it to mean.* Finally, the last two steps involve **accepting** the message as one has understood it and **retaining** it for later recall from memory.

Throughout this entire information processing sequence there are individual traits that come into play, but there is also something to be said for the **brand stimuli** themselves. Is the brand story engaging enough to capture consumers' attention? Are the brand symbols large, vibrant, or distinctive enough to stand out in the midst of so much visual saturation?

Is the brand strategy leveraging the right channels to engage the intended audience? We will resolve all of these questions in the Strategy section later on in this book.

While important, the information stored in our memory is just one of the many influences at play in the consumption process. We will revisit the role of stimuli further along but, for the time being, let's explore some of the individual traits and environmental factors that influence a consumer's decision-making process.

The Overall Model of Consumer Behavior proposed by Hawkins, Mothersbaugh, and Best[2] offers a comprehensive framework to visualize the most important forces at play:

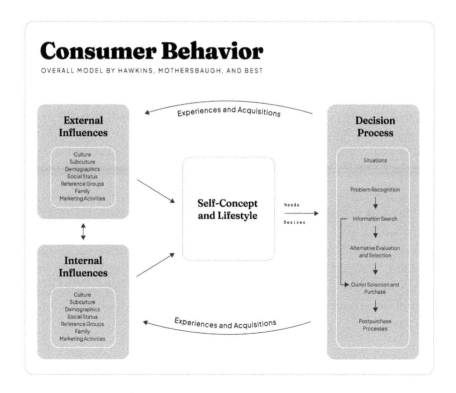

FIGURE 4.1: Overall Model of Consumer Behavior

When we find ourselves in the middle of a consumption decision-making process, we pull from the information previously stored in our memory as a resource.

According to the model above, in a scenario where we are involved with the purchase decision, we will progress from basic **problem recognition** to an active **information search** for solutions, to an **evaluation of existing alternatives**, and then on to **purchase**, **consumption**, and **post-consumption** behaviors. Brand managers must strive to make their brands as salient as possible during that search phase, and even before that, as they actively associate desired meanings to reside in consumers' memories.

THE ROLE OF INDIVIDUAL PERCEPTION

As is evident in the model above, individual perception has an impact in multiple stages of the consumption process: when consumers decide how to interpret the information conveyed to them, when they recognize existing needs, when they consider alternative options, and even as they consume the actual product.

In the world of consumer psychology, perception is a powerful construct with implications in every step of the purchase decision. Think about the last time you experienced a need, visited a retail store (on or offline), and were exposed to a product that could potentially satisfy said need. Your perception of this product, initial or sustained over time, was likely shaped by:

- Your culture
- Your personal history
- Your age

- Your motivations
- Your attitude
- Your level of involvement
- Your lifestyle

This list is by no means exhaustive. The unique traits that make us who we are intervene when we're exposed to brand stimuli, for the first or thousandth time. When you've used a brand before, it's easy to see how it would trigger existing associations. You've had good or bad experiences with it, know more about its story, are familiar with its symbols, and have been exposed to its strategy. However, there are also meanings that come to mind when a brand is entirely new to you.

Think about the last time you used a brand for the first time, in any category. I want you to go back to that initial discovery moment, your very first impression. Even though there may have not been anything to recall from your past personal experience with it, something immediately came to mind upon interacting with its symbols or message. Perception is not something we can switch on and off, but a personal lens in our ongoing attempt to understand reality. Here are some examples of thoughts you may have had:

- Someone else's story about how they experienced this brand. "So this is the brand X told me about". Going back to the social learning theory in our overview of consumer behavior history, consumers will often recall recommendations given to them by influential figures in their social life.
- Ideas related to the brand's visual identity elements, such as the color palette, imagery, logo, icons, shapes, or typography. "I like how rustic this looks" or "this feels dark and boring". At the lack of any previous exposure to the brand's visuals, your attention may have been drawn to the individual symbols and your personal

connection to them. In the Brand Symbols section of this book, we will discuss how visual elements like typography and color play a role in shaping and triggering these associations.

- Ideas related to the brand's voice and tone. Consumers have a natural reaction to the messaging they are exposed to. Consider the last time you read some brand's messaging and thought "that was funny" or "that was too much". Stemming out of a brand's personality, the style with which it communicates can make you feel closer or alienated, depending on how it resonates with your personal preferences.

- A competitor or substitute product that helped you understand what this brand did, by analogy. At some point during your interaction with the brand, you may have thought "Oh, this brand is like X, but instead it Y", where X is a familiar entity and Y is this novel brand's differentiator. We try to rationalize new ideas using what we already know as a basis of comparison, effectively learning by analogy. This phenomenon is called **analogical learning** in psychology and was largely popularized by Northeastern University Professor Dedre Gentner in the late 80s and early 90s[3].

- Ideas related to the brand's messaging. Perhaps you saw elements of the brand's promise, recalled your own needs, and debated whether, at first glance, this brand would be able to satisfy them: "I wonder if they can do X", where X is a function related to your needs and wants. Your own constraints may have also come to mind: "What does the pricing look like? Can I realistically afford this?"

At the end of the day, the brand your audience recalls is a combination of their individual perception and your brand stimuli in varying proportions. The brand story could be defined exactly by what is communicated to them, strictly what they've experienced, or, most probably, by some kind of mix of those. In other words, an individual's salient brand story emerges from a combination of **reception and perception**.

As consumers, we don't just process information as it is. We process information as *we are*. We interpret reality depending on where and who we've been, the values we uphold, our personality type, the unique context in which we will use a product, and a virtually endless list of personal variables that make my life lens completely different than yours.

FOUR ELEMENTS OF COMPELLING BRAND STORIES

What is it about a brand's story that enthralls the audience and imprints a memorable narrative? Chiu et al. took a rigorous approach to answer this question. They reviewed the literature extensively and found four elements that contribute to a good brand story[4]:

- **Authenticity:** points to how relatable, hence credible, the narrative is
- **Conciseness:** the story's succinctness and clarity for customers
- **Reversal:** there's a pivotal inflection point that serves as a climax
- **Humor:** lighthearted, engaging entertainment

After identifying these factors, they went ahead and tested their impact on different kinds of brands. As a result, the authors found that authenticity is more important for products that are meant to be experienced, rather than products that are searched for. Succinctness, or concise messaging, has a significant impact on brand attitude, but only for products that are actively searched.

For experience products, it is more critical to focus on reversal, which boosts brand attitude through the brand's unique, arousing narrative. Lastly, humor is a more effective tool for improving brand attitude in the case of products that are searched, rather than experienced.

WHAT MAKES A STRONG BRAND STORY?

Beyond the structural aspects we just reviewed, a compelling brand narrative must also be *communicated* strategically. It isn't enough to have a solid story to tell: brand managers must also excel at amplifying it. Consider these four pillars when planning your brand story's rollout:

- **Authentic:** a genuine, credible brand story starts with internal branding and is shared with customers in every touchpoint. Team members are engaged, active characters in conveying this story.
- **Immersive:** A memorable brand plays with our senses, offering tangible opportunities to experience its offerings and store them in memory for later recall.
- **Omnichannel:** the story is communicated cohesively across owned, earned, and paid channels in a way that solidifies the narrative in its target customers' minds.
- **Customer-centric:** built and rebuilt based on customers' evolving needs. Brands establish deep, sustainable relationships and feedback channels with customers that enable this ever-relevant, ever-satisfying feature set while maintaining benefit-centric messaging that hits home every time.

NOT SO FAST, BRAND STORIES ARE CO-CONSTRUCTED

In this chapter's introduction, I mentioned that customers play a creative role in shaping brands. Chernatony & Dall'Olmo Riley proposed that a company's brand-building activities work as an input in the process, while consumers' perceptions emerge as the output[5].

These two boundaries define the construct of what a brand ultimately represents. It's an ongoing, ever-evolving interface between what we're told a brand does and what our experiences and worldviews lead us to perceive.

BUILDING YOUR BRAND'S STORYBOARD

For the last 10 years, I've worked with entrepreneurs to shape memorable, resonant brand stories that connect with their target audiences. Along the way, I developed a brand storyboard that has helped us distill the narratives embedded in each company's value proposition, making customers the main characters and defining some brand-strategic scenes. Some of the teams I've used this tool with include:

- A city
- Early-stage tech startups
- Fintech
- Lawyer firm
- Global design companies
- A game development agency

Brand Storyboard

Once upon a time...	He/she always...	But had a problem...	He/she tried to solve it...
But he/she wished that...	Until one day...	Unlike his/her solution, this...	His/her wish came true: to...

FIGURE 4.2: Brand storyboard

By completing each of these scenes, you will be answering some of the key questions behind powerful brand storytelling. Let's go over some considerations as you fill out the storyboard:

Once upon a time

In this scene, you will describe the audience you're currently targeting. *Who is the main character in your brand story?* We will dive deeper into this concept when we discuss personas and segmentation research in Chapter 6.

He/she always

Define some of the main tasks that your customer is regularly involved with. What does she do every day? What are her main responsibilities in life and work, as related to the product or service that you offer? This scene is all about capturing context: what does your target customer's lifestyle look like? What's on their to-do list? What are their everyday experiences like?

But always had a problem

State the main issue that your customer faces when trying to complete his/her tasks. What is the unsatisfied need or aspiration in this story?

He/she tried to solve it

If the previous problem is real, your customer is probably already solving it. What are some alternate solutions to the issue at hand? How is your customer managing to partially satisfy this aspiration?

But he/she wished that

Outline the flaws in the solutions your customer is currently using. Despite purchasing these other products or services, your customer is still unsatisfied. What are existing solutions lacking?

Until one day

Describe how your customer will most probably learn about your brand. What happened on the day he/she first heard about you?

Unlike his/her solution, this

List some of the aspects related to your product experience that set you apart from competitors. How does your offer differ from your customer's current solution?

His/her wish came true, to

Clearly define the aspiration that your brand fulfills. What is your customer's "wish come true"?

BRAND PROMISE

As a brand, you are relevant to the extent that you're providing a shortcut to self-realization. "What's in it for me?" is one of the most underrated rules of thumb every brand marketer should operate by.

- Are we sharing a message about who we are or about **what they need**?
- About what we can do or about what **we can do for them**?
- About how much we've grown or about **how much we'll help them grow**?
- Are these vanity features **or clear benefits**?

A great way to stay customer-centered is to construct a **brand promise**. Your promise is a succinct recap of the core value you're adding to customers' lives.

As with any promise, there are expectations of consistency, coherence, and fulfillment:

- **Consistency:** Is this brand acting in ways that are conducive to this promise?
- **Coherence:** Does it make sense for this particular brand to offer this promise? Based on what I know and perceive, can it realistically deliver on it?
- **Fulfillment:** How well is this promise being honored?

Effective brand management is about finding increasingly clever ways to fulfill this promise.

Let's look at an example:

"Creative finds to organize your daily life"

Breaking down this promise shows us some coherent paths for delivery:

- To emphasize the brand's **"creative"** character, innovate with brand messaging and activities. Test out various content formats, channels, and tactics that showcase the creativity you're trying to associate with the brand.
- To strengthen the quality of your **"finds"**, invest time and resources in extraordinary curation that leads to increasingly unique and distinctive product selections.
- To associate with the **"organize"** verb more closely, you can develop a dedicated content pillar that focuses on productivity and organization techniques. Reflect internal organization at all times and lead by example.
- To demonstrate your brand's usefulness for **"daily life"**, craft campaigns that highlight everyday scenarios and the product's impact. Avoid imagery and content that makes the brand's use cases feel exceptional and rare.

There are hundreds of copywriting and advertising books. You are holding *Brand Psychology*. It is my duty to tell you that coming up with a clever brand promise isn't nearly as important as delivering on it. When thoroughly distilled, a single promise statement can drive a brand's entire strategy. Communications, partnerships, product updates, pricing, and most strategic decisions can be guided by the commitment a brand makes to serve its audience in a specific way.

All brand activities can hinge on keeping one's word to customers: it's that simple and that complex.

NOTES

1. Blackwell, R. D., Miniard, P. W., & Engel, J. F. (2006). *Consumer Behavior*. Thomson South-Western.
2. Hawkins, D., Mothersbaugh, D., & Best, R. (2009). *Consumer Behavior: Building Marketing Strategy*.
3. Gentner, D. (1987). *Mechanisms of Analogical Learning*. Illinois University Department of Computer Science.
4. Chiu, H.-C., Hsieh, Y.-C., & Kuo, Y.-C. (2012). How to align your brand stories with your products. *Journal of Retailing, 88*(2), 262–275. https://doi.org/10.1016/j.jretai.2012.02.001
5. De Chernatony, L., & Dall'Olmo Riley, F. (1998). Defining a "brand": Beyond the literature with experts' interpretations. *Journal of Marketing Management, 14*(5), 417–443. https://doi.org/10.1362/026725798784867798

CHAPTER 5

SELF-BRAND IDENTIFICATION

DOI: 10.4324/9781003336693-7

In our ongoing challenge of defining and expressing our identity, we leverage symbols and integrate them into our **material self**. We run on both *value* and *values*, growing fond of brands based on their utility but also on the deeper ideas they encapsulate.

As William James asserted[1], these elements *complement* our spiritual selves and become tokens for self-expression. Insofar as they reflect our choices, preferences, and beliefs, these material elements represent us in our relationships with others.

As we relate more closely with the brands that speak to us, they become devices to strengthen various self-management activities:

- Self-affirmation
- Self-enhancement
- Self-expression

Products don't determine who we are, but they can become shortcuts to advance and express it.

We look in the mirror and define how it is that we'd like to project ourselves in the world, and certain material objects complement that reflection—that *desired self.*

Social psychologists Markus and Nurius defined the concept of **actual** and **possible selves** to capture this sense of aspiration. We consistently find ourselves at a point A in life, looking at an aspirational point B from afar. The gap between who we are and who we long to be is where this "possible self" resides[2].

This is where brands come in: with customer-centric products and services, they are able to bridge that gap in a faster, simpler, or more efficient way. Brands, then, become enablers of our possible selves. Not sole enablers, but one of the factors driving our ongoing self-realization.

SYMBOLIC CONSUMPTION

Consumer behavior has been studied extensively since the early 1900s. However, it was in the 1970s that research became more in-depth, as the growth of trade and manufacturing increased consumption in numerous countries. Social sciences have tackled the concept of consumption from various angles, including psychology, anthropology, sociology, and with the help of unconventional economists. This multidisciplinary approach has significantly enhanced scientific research, which now incorporates terms associated with emotions, pleasure-seeking, and symbolism.

Gone is the exclusively utilitarian conception of consumption decisions, where individuals rationally evaluate the features that goods and services offer them. As mentioned in Chapter 1, one of the most important researchers in the area of consumer psychology is Russell Belk, who challenged the prevailing paradigm regarding consumption with the following words[3]:

> We find desire to be an overwhelmingly positive emotion, despite our occasional feelings of immorality and ambivalent feelings about our desires [...] That these feelings depend upon the social imagination to construct objects that are sufficiently powerful symbols to become objects of obsessive desires, should neither be disillusioning nor a cause for rationalizing our existence. Perhaps the greatest miracle is that we collectively and individually find imaginative ways to enchant our world through desire.

In his longstanding research interest in the phenomenon of consumption, Belk redefined the perspective on what it meant for an individual to acquire a product or service. Belk emphasizes that the consumption of products plays at least two important roles in the development of the extended self, previously defined as a self-concept expanded through the possession of certain products[4]:

1. Possessions allow us to alter or manipulate our possibilities for presenting the self in a way that obtains feedback from others who might not be as open to interacting with the non-extended self.

2. Possessions that are part of our extended self create a personal museum or archive that allows us to reflect on our history and how we have changed. This applies to individuals, families, communities, nations, and other levels of self-grouping.

While Belk acknowledges that materialism can have negative consequences for the individual when there is extreme dependence, he considers it vital to recognize the positive contribution that possessions make to the development of the identity that forms our extended self.

In addition to Belk, other authors have extensively explored the relationship between consumption and self-development. For Solomon, the symbolism of acquired products becomes important when establishing interpersonal relationships, where they play the role of social stimulants[5].

In other words, the products we possess send a message about who we are and what we are capable of, particularly in environments where the roles we must play have not yet been internalized because they are new to us. Solomon highlights five conclusions regarding symbolic consumption:

1. The symbolism represented in many products is the main reason for their purchase and use.

2. Individuals are evaluated and placed in social networks largely due to the products surrounding them.
3. The construct of reflexive evaluation implies that product symbolism, instrumental in assigning meaning to others, is also used by ourselves to assign social identity.
4. The outcome of this self-identification process guides our behavior through the "script" it evokes for us.
5. Symbolic consumption can have an a priori effect on role definition and interaction, especially in scenarios where we lack internalized behavioral responses.

Kleine, for her part, empirically demonstrated that we are attracted to products that are consistent with, and allow us to represent, the multiple social identities that constitute our sense of self; the more important an identity is to us, the more attractive its associated products will be[6]. In addition to their connection with our personal identity, aesthetically appealing products have the capacity to help us affirm the self[7]. In two studies with 159 students, Townsend & Sood found that choosing a well-designed product positively affected self-assurance and contributed to self-affirmation.

Understanding the implicit meanings in acquiring a brand's offerings is the starting point for grasping the potential of branding for the preservation and strengthening of personal identity. Yes, a new shirt can protect us from the cold, allow us to comply with a dress code, or replace an aged one. However, that same shirt, by virtue of its design, can become a significant reminder of our origin, history, and identity: that shirt can be a symbol.

BRANDS AS SOCIAL AND SELF-SYMBOLISM

Elliott and Wattanasuwan describe this ongoing construction of an identity as the "project of the self"[8]. As we saw in our discussion about symbolic consumption, human beings ascribe deeper-rooted values to goods and services, adding layers of meaning we come to know as the brand.

As we define our identity, we are simultaneously constructing inward meaning (self-symbolism) and outward expression (social symbolism) in a dialectical relationship (Elliot and Wattanasuwan, 1998). Throughout the remainder of this chapter, we will dive deeper into two self-symbolism functions of brands, **self-affirmation** and **self-enhancement**, and one social symbolism function: **self-expression:**

- **Self-affirmation:** *this is who I am*
- **Self-enhancement:** *this is who I long to be*
- **Self-expression:** *this is how I'd like to be perceived*

Self-affirmation

Brands become increasingly meaningful as they become more closely connected to our self[9].

In a way, self-affirmation processes are a way to explain ourselves *to* ourselves[10]. Through self-affirmation, we justify the motives behind our actions and preferences to maintain a sense of personal integrity. These ongoing rationalizations help us perceive ourselves as sufficient, coherent, and competent in different scenarios:

This is what I'm about.
This is what I'm not.
This is what, being who I am, I should do.

Brands can play an active role in these internal arguments. When we select a specific product or service, we observe its associated values and match those against the principles we

101

TABLE 5.1: Self-Brand Connection Scale

Scale name	Self-Brand Connection Scale
Authors	Escalas (2004)
Type of scale	7-point scale
Anchors	From "Not at all" (−3) to Neutral (0) to "Extremely well" (3)
Items	• Brand X reflects who I am
	• I can identify with Brand X
	• I feel a personal connection to Brand X
	• I (can) use Brand X to communicate who I am to other people
	• I think Brand X (could) help(s) me become the type of person I want to be
	• I consider Brand X to be "me" (it reflects who I consider myself to be or the way that I want to present myself to others)
	• Brand X suits me well

live or would like to live by. The brands we use, then, become **symbolic** devices to remind ourselves of what matters to us. Totems of personal meaning.

Professor Jennifer Escalas developed the Self-Brand Connection Scale[11] to unveil whether a certain brand affirms our identity and how.

Self-enhancement

The link between the activation of a possible self and the decision to buy has been studied by various consumer researchers. Russell Belk, in particular, revisited William James's idea of the material self to define what he calls the extended self: a self-concept realized through the symbolic consumption of objects (brands or products) that represent desired identities[12]. He posited that our possessions contribute to extending and actualizing these self-concepts (selves) symbolically.

Far from being conditioned like machines, humans make decisions to reduce the tension (distance) between the actual and desired self[13]; a process in which possessions play a fundamental role as symbolic (cognitive) bridges between who we have been (past self), who we are (current self), and who we can become (possible self).

As individuals, we enhance and advance our self-concept through the goods that allow us to represent who we are in social settings[14]. This process is simultaneously personal and interpersonal: the reason these brands represent desirable ideas (to us) is we've learned their symbolic meaning from public sources. This leads us to the third self-management function in this chapter: self-expression.

Self-expression

When we recognize the symbolic nature of the brands we choose to acquire, the possibility of expressing ourselves through them becomes evident. This function is irrespective of price points or categories: even freely available brands can grant the sought-after associations we wish to be identified with.

We are not passive consumers, but active agents who use brands and products to create, negotiate, and communicate our self-concepts in relation to others.

We are, after all, innately social selves. According to George Herbert Mead's seminal theory of the self, we are a product of the social processes we undergo. His theory is primarily based on two key concepts: the "I" and the "Me". The "I" represents the spontaneous, impulsive, and creative aspects of an individual, whereas the "Me" reflects the socialized and learned behaviors that conform to societal expectations.

If the "I" speaks, the "me" hears. If the "I" strikes, the "me" feels the blow. Mead[15]

Symbolic brand purchases can be understood as a way for individuals to express and reinforce their "Me". By choosing brands that align with their desired social image, individuals project a particular version of themselves that conforms to the expectations of the "generalized other". This projection of the self in social settings is crucial for establishing and maintaining social identities, fostering group affiliations, and garnering approval from others.

There are at least three meaningful ways in which brands can enhance our self-expression:

- **Helping us enact our desired social identities:** We are attracted to products that are consistent with, and that enable the enactment of, the various social identities which make up our sense of self; the more important an identity to us, the more attractive its associated products[16].
- **Signaling group affiliation:** We place value on certain material things insofar as they express our commitment to group identity and reinforce belonging[17].
- **Guiding our social performance:** We might rely on the social meanings inherent in products as a motivation or guide to perform certain social roles, especially when they are new to us[18]. The idea is that our connection to a certain good evokes a specific script we follow to fulfill this novel role.

The power of brands as tools for self-expression is deeply rooted in our social nature and the desire to construct and communicate our identities. Whether it's through the acquisition of products aligned with our desired social selves, signaling our commitment to a particular group, or guiding us in the performance of new roles, brands play an essential part in shaping our individual and collective narratives.

As we actively engage with brands, we are also engaging in a continuous process of self-creation, negotiation, and communication. It's a vivid reminder that our choices hold symbolic weight, painting a picture of who we are and who we aspire to be in the eyes of the "generalized other". As we navigate the rich landscape of brand offerings, we ought to remember that every selection we make is a brushstroke on the canvas of our self-expression.

NOTES

1. James, W. (1890). *The principles of psychology, Vol I.* (pp. xii, 697). Henry Holt and Co. https://doi.org/10.1037/10538-000
2. Markus, H., & Nurius, P. (1986). Possible selves. *American Psychologist, 41*(9), 954–969. https://doi.org/10.1037/0003-066X.41.9.954
3. Belk, R., Ger, G., & Askegaard, S. (2000). The missing streetcar named desire. *The Why of Consumption*, 98–119. Routledge.
4. Belk, R. W. (1988). Possessions and the extended self. *Journal of Consumer Research, 15*(2), 139–168. http://dx.doi.org/10.1086/209154
5. Solomon, M. R. (1983). The role of products as social stimuli: A symbolic interactionism perspective. *Journal of Consumer Research, 10*(3), 319–329.
6. Kleine, R. E., Kleine, S. S., & Kernan, J. B. (1993). Mundane consumption and the self: A social-identity perspective. *Journal of Consumer Psychology, 2*(3), 209–235.
7. Townsend, C., & Sood, S. (2012). Self-affirmation through the choice of highly aesthetic products. *Journal of Consumer Research, 39*(2), 415–428. https://doi.org/10.1086/663775
8. Elliott, R., & Wattanasuwan, K. (1998). Consumption and the symbolic project of the self. *ACR European Advances, E-03.* https://www.acrwebsite.org/volumes/11147/volumes/e03/E-03/full
9. Escalas, J. E., & Bettman, J. R. (2005). Self-construal, reference groups, and brand meaning. *Journal of Consumer Research, 32*(3), 378–389. https://doi.org/10.1086/497549
10. Steele, C. M. (1988). The psychology of self-affirmation: Sustaining the integrity of the self. In L. Berkowitz (Ed.), *Advances in Experimental Social Psychology* (Vol. 21, pp. 261–302). Academic Press. https://doi.org/10.1016/S0065-2601(08)60229-4

11. Escalas, J. E. (2004). Narrative processing: Building consumer con-nections to brands. *Journal of Consumer Psychology, 14*(1/2), 168–180.
12. Belk, R. W. (1988). Possessions and the extended self. *Journal of Consumer Research, 15*(2), 139–168. https://doi.org/10.2307/2489522
13. Markus, H., & Nurius, P. (1986). Possible selves. *American Psychologist, 41*(9), 954–969. https://doi.org/10.1037/0003-066X.41.9.954
14 Grubb, E. L., & Grathwohl, H. L. (1967). Consumer self-concept, symbolism and market behavior: A theoretical approach. *Journal of Marketing, 31*(4), 22–27. https://doi.org/10.2307/1249461
15. Mead, G. H. (1913). The social self. *The Journal of Philosophy, Psychology and Scientific Methods, 10*(14), 374–380. https://doi.org/10.2307/2012910
16. Kleine, R. E., Kleine, S. S., & Kernan, J. B. (1993). Mundane con-sumption and the self: A social-identity perspective. *Journal of Consumer Psychology, 2*(3), 209–235.
17. Ledgerwood, A., Liviatan, I., & Carnevale, P. J. (2007). Group-identity completion and the symbolic value of property. *Psychological Science, 18*(10), 873–878.
18. Solomon, M. R. (1983). The role of products as social stimuli: A symbolic interactionism perspective. *Journal of Consumer Research, 10*(3), 319–329.

CHAPTER 6

RESEARCH, SEGMENTATION, AND PERSONAS

DOI: 10.4324/9781003336693-8

A brand story's main character is the customer. Not the peculiar CEO, or the unicorn story, or the splashy graphics. This is a story about people, problem-solving, self-realizing human beings, looking for answers, and the brands that provide them.

Effective targeting takes empathizing with human beings. People, personas, who have found a solution or desire, met by the brand you're building.

Brand marketing isn't treachery. It's not a zero-sum game. If you're doing this right, a group of human beings will feel gratitude when your name comes to mind.

The fact that your product is "needed" is not an excuse to be lazy in your relationship with customers, if anything, it's a shortcut to a speedy divorce. Great brands are built on communication, trust, and re-engagement. They care about customers and respect them enough to listen. They insist. They ask.

Throughout this chapter, we will learn how to ask.

We will explore ways to fine-tune our awareness of who it is we are bringing to and branding with. We will build **persona profiles** to help create clarity around these human beings' needs and hopes.

SEGMENTATION RESEARCH

Research is customer empathy. If you love your customers, you listen to them. Period.

Invest time and effort in connecting with their evolving needs and desires, leaving space for the unimagined. Go into this exercise with curiosity and openness: this will help mute your natural biases and raise the volume of novel insights.

For its first 50 years as a field, quantitatively-led experimental research techniques drove consumer research. As we saw in Chapter 1, psychologists were largely trying to adapt predominant research paradigms to this emerging interest in consumer behavior.

The 1980s marked a departure from this stance, opening a new path for qualitative and mixed research to flourish. This pragmatic take on consumer studies prioritized the question being asked and designed research methods that properly satisfied the nature of the inquiry.

Segmentation, targeting, and positioning

We're diving deeper into segmentation research because it is the first of several steps needed to reach a target audience effectively. Phillip Kotler first defined the STP (segmentation, targeting, positioning) formula as the essence of strategic marketing around 1969, inspired by the ideas of market segmentation and positioning that were popular at the time[1].

Segmentation involves identifying similar needs, preferences, and lifestyles among consumers in a particular market. Through research, the commonalities between consumer groups are revealed, allowing for thorough segmentation. As part of the **targeting** phase, we pick one or more segments that we will market to. Lastly, **positioning** is about tailoring a specific offer (marketing mix) that effectively fulfills that segment's needs, using methods and channels that are relevant to them. As you can tell, research holds the key to

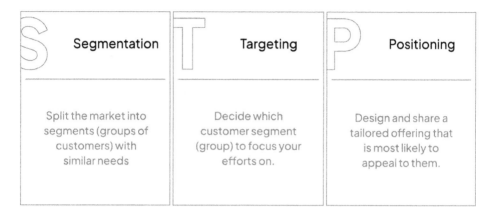

FIGURE 6.1: STP Framework

a sound marketing strategy, opening the door to solid consumer insights.

PRIMARY AND SECONDARY RESEARCH

When it comes to understanding segments in brand management, there are two main approaches: primary and secondary segmentation research. Primary research is all about gathering new data directly from consumers, while secondary research involves analyzing data that has already been collected.

Primary segmentation research focuses on collecting new, first-hand information from the target market to help brands understand their audience's needs, preferences, and behavior. This type of research is typically conducted through surveys, interviews, focus groups, observations, and experiments.

Ultimately, primary research is all about getting up close and personal with the target market to gain a deeper understanding of their behavior and preferences. By doing so, brands can develop more effective marketing strategies and create products that better meet the needs of their customers.

What does primary research look like for a brand trying to define market segments? Here are some ideas:

- **Attitude-based segmentation:** A furniture company might conduct a survey to assess consumers' attitudes toward ethically sourced materials, helping them target a market for their socially responsible product line.
- **Benefit-based segmentation:** An electric vehicle manufacturer could use focus groups to explore the desired features and benefits among different consumer groups, allowing them to create products that cater to specific needs.
- **Behavioral segmentation:** A streaming platform may analyze viewership data and customer feedback to understand the content consumption habits of their users, enabling them to tailor their content strategies accordingly.
- **Psychographic segmentation:** A luxury watch brand could conduct in-depth interviews to explore the lifestyle, values, and aspirations of potential buyers, informing the development of targeted marketing campaigns.
- **Geographic segmentation:** A grocery delivery service may analyze the geographic distribution of their customers, helping them optimize delivery routes and identify underserved areas for expansion.

Secondary research, on the other hand, utilizes existing data to inform brand management decisions. This type of research typically involves analyzing data from sources such as government publications, market research reports, and academic articles. Here are some sample sources for secondary research aimed at segmenting the market:

- Market reports
- (Public) company reports
- Trade publications
- Case studies
- Competitor analysis
- Media analysis
- Social media listening
- Patent analysis
- Trend analysis
- Historical research
- Academic journals

Compared to primary research, secondary research can be more cost-effective and time-efficient since the data already exists. However, it may not always provide the specific insights a brand needs to address its unique goals.

Secondary segmentation research might look like the following examples:

- **Demographic segmentation:** A sportswear company may analyze census data to identify the age, gender, and income distribution of potential customers, allowing them to target their marketing efforts accordingly.
- **Market trend analysis:** A snack company could study market trends to identify emerging preferences in consumer taste, informing the development of new product offerings.
- **Competitor analysis:** A hotel chain might analyze competitor marketing strategies and customer reviews to identify areas of differentiation and improvement in their own brand positioning.

- **Industry analysis:** A renewable energy firm may examine articles and reports to explore the impact of regulatory changes on their industry, enabling them to adapt their business strategies accordingly.
- **Cross-cultural analysis:** A multinational restaurant chain could analyze global consumption patterns to identify cultural differences in consumer preferences, informing the localization of their menu offerings.

GENERATIONAL COHORTS

While it isn't accurate, or fair, to make blanket behavioral assumptions about an entire generation, consumers born and raised in specific eras may share traits worth noting. On one hand, generational cohorts are broadly exposed to the same technological developments—at least as it relates to advances that reach the masses.

On the other hand, different age groups cross high-level life stages within the same historical context. Generation Z, for instance, faced schooling and college disruptions as a result of the Covid-19 pandemic. Millennials, or Generation Y, lived that same life stage in the midst of a different threat: the war on terrorism unleashed by the events of September 11, 2001.

As you look at the generational commonalities below, however, think critically about how different events may have unfolded for human beings in the geographic, cultural, social, or income group of interest to your brand. There may be additional commonalities to keep in mind or broad generational experiences that don't apply. Birth ranges for each cohort may also vary depending on the source you look at, but broad historical events should be largely consistent. Take these guidelines as an additional source of secondary research to complement with your brand's own (primary) findings.

Marketing Generations

A SUMMARY

1925 - 1945

Silent Generation

This generation is known for its loyalty and work ethic, having lived through the Great Depression and World War II. They experienced the rise of the automobile, television, and nuclear power.

1946 - 1964

Baby Boomers

This generation is defined by its optimism and enthusiasm for new technologies. They experienced the Civil Rights Movement and witnessed steep technological revolution, from space exploration to the rise of the computer.

1965 - 1980

Generation X

This generation is known for its independent, self-reliant attitude and entrepreneurial spirit. They experienced the end of the Cold War, the rise of the internet, and the dawn of globalization.

1981 - 1996

Generation Y or Millennials

This generation is notable for its fluency in digital media and technology. They are the first generation to grow up with the internet, and saw the rise of mobile devices and social media.

1997 - 2012

Generation Z

This generation is characterized by its creativity, boldness, and innovation. They are the first truly global generation, and experienced the rise of the gig economy and rapid advancements in technology.

FIGURE 6.2: Marketing generational cohorts

The Silent Generation (born ~1925–1945) experienced the Great Depression and the Second World War, which led to a strong emphasis on financial security and hard work[2]. They tend to be loyal to brands and are less likely to adopt new technologies[3].

Baby Boomers (born 1946–1964) grew up during the post-war economic boom and the Civil Rights Movement, which fostered a sense of optimism and social change[4]. Baby Boomers value personal growth and individualism and are characterized by a strong work ethic[5]. They are more open to adopting new technologies than the Silent Generation but may still be hesitant.

Generation X (born 1965–1980) experienced economic uncertainty, the rise of dual-income families, and the emergence of personal computing[6]. They are often described as self-reliant, skeptical, and pragmatic, and tend to prioritize work–life balance[7]. They are comfortable with technology and prefer authenticity in marketing messages[8].

Generation Y or Millennials (born 1981–1996) came of age during the digital revolution and experienced significant social and economic change, including the rise of globalization and the 2008 financial crisis[9]. They are characterized by high levels of education, diversity, and technological proficiency, and they place a premium on experiences and personal values[10]. Millennials are highly influenced by social media and word-of-mouth recommendations[11].

Generation Z (born 1997–2012) is the first truly digital-native generation, having been exposed to the internet, smartphones, and social media from an early age[12]. They are known for their entrepreneurial spirit, pragmatism, and global-mindedness[13]. Generation Z is highly responsive to personalized, authentic, and socially conscious marketing efforts[14].

Each generation has unique characteristics based on histori-cal events and technological advances that have shaped their lives[15]. When combined with primary research data points, this awareness of generational cohorts can provide meaning-ful context for effective segmentation.

PRIMARY RESEARCH: QUANTITATIVE AND QUALITATIVE TECHNIQUES

Brand research is the process of gathering information about customers, competitors, and the market to inform strategy and decision-making. There are two main types of brand research: **qualitative** and **quantitative** research.

Qualitative research focuses on understanding people's atti-tudes, beliefs, and opinions about a brand. It is exploratory in nature and aims to provide insights into why people behave in a certain way. Qualitative research methods include focus groups, interviews, and observation.

TABLE 6.1: Quantitative and qualitative brand research methods

Quantitative Research Techniques	Qualitative Research Techniques
Surveys	Interviews
Experiments	Focus groups
Observational studies	Ethnography and nethnography
Content analysis	Case study
Conjoint analysis	Narrative analysis
Market basket studies	Projective techniques
Sales tracking	Photo elicitation
Scanner data analysis	Video diaries
Social media analytics	Semiotic analysis
Eye tracking	Laddering interviews
A/B testing	Collage creation
Cluster analysis	Cognitive mapping
Price sensitivity analysis	Shadowing
Panel data analysis	Repertory grid technique

Focus groups involve bringing together a small group of people to discuss a brand. The discussion is led by a moderator who asks open-ended questions and encourages participants to share their thoughts and opinions. **Interviews** are one-on-one conversations between a researcher and a participant. The researcher asks questions to gain insights into the participant's attitudes and beliefs. **Observation** involves watching people use a product or service and taking notes on their behavior.

Empathy maps can be helpful tools to capture observations about our target audience's goals, actions, feelings, and fears.

Empathy Map

GOALS

Who is this person we're trying to serve?

What is he/she trying to accomplish?

WHAT THEY HEAR

What are friends, colleagues, and family members telling them?

WHAT THEY FEEL

Pain points

What are their fears, frustrations, and anxieties?

Wins

What are their dreams, hopes, and desires?

WHAT THEY SEE

What are they observing in the marketplace, social circle, and society?

WHAT THEY SAY

What can you find them saying?

WHAT THEY DO

Which behaviors or habits are part of their everyday life?

FIGURE 6.3: Empathy map

Developed by design consultancy XPLANE[16], this instrument synthesizes the insights we collect and invites us to think holistically about this persona's deeper intentions and needs—beyond the utilitarian.

Qualitative research provides rich insights into people's attitudes, beliefs, and opinions, and can help brand managers identify key themes and trends. However, because the sample sizes are small, its results may not be representative of the entire market. Additionally, the results are often subjective and open to interpretation.

Quantitative research, on the other hand, focuses on gathering numerical data to measure and analyze customer behavior. It is often used to test hypotheses and make predictions. Quantitative research methods include surveys, experiments, and statistical analysis.

Surveys or questionnaires involve asking a large number of people a set of standardized questions to gather data. **Experiments,** in turn, are about manipulating one or more variables to see how customer behavior is affected. **Statistical analysis** involves using mathematical models to analyze and interpret data.

Quantitative research provides objective data that can be analyzed and compared over time. It is often used to measure the effectiveness of brand campaigns and make data-driven decisions. However, because it is based on numerical data, it may not provide the same level of depth and nuance as qualitative research.

Both methods have their strengths and weaknesses, and the choice of which to use will depend on the research questions and goals.

QUESTIONNAIRE DESIGN

Because of their prevalence in marketing research, let's take a closer look at questionnaires and the principles involved in their design.

The first and most crucial step in effective brand research through questionnaires is asking the right questions. No matter how sophisticated research and statistical analysis tools get, there is no replacement for a strategically designed question with the right scale for the job.

At a high level, questionnaires can include nominal, ordinal, interval, or ratio scales, depending on the type of data they intend to collect[17]. It's important to define the type of analysis you'd like to perform on your data at the questionnaire design stage so the answers can effectively provide the input you'll need. Let's dive a bit deeper into each type of measurement scale and how they can be applied in brand marketing research.

First, let's start with **nominal scales**. These scales measure variables that cannot be ranked in any particular order. For example, gender, nationality, or product categories are nominal variables. A common question we might ask using nominal scales is: "What is your preferred brand of soda?" Since there is no inherent order to the response options, this is a nominal scale question.

Next, we have **ordinal scales**, which measure variables that have an inherent order but the distance between the values is not necessarily uniform. For instance, customer satisfaction surveys often use ordinal scales where respondents are asked to rate their satisfaction on a scale of 1–5. A question might be, "On a scale of 1 to 5, how satisfied are you with our customer service?" Since the response options have an order, but the distance between each value is not necessarily equal, this is an ordinal scale question.

Moving on, we have **interval scales.** These scales measure variables where the distance between the values is uniform, but there is no true zero point. Temperature is an example of an interval scale, where the distance between 20 and 30 degrees Celsius is the same as the distance between 30 and 40 degrees Celsius. An example question using an interval scale might be: "On a scale of 1 to 10, how likely are you to recommend our brand to a friend?" Since the distance between each value is the same, but there is no true zero point, this is an interval scale question.

Lastly, we have **ratio scales.** These scales measure variables where the distance between values is uniform and there is a true zero point. Examples of ratio scales include height, weight, and revenue. An example question using a ratio scale might be: "How many times have you purchased from our brand in the past month?" Since there is a true zero point (i.e., zero purchases), and the distance between each value is uniform, this is a ratio scale question.

By understanding the differences between each type of measurement scale, we can tailor our research questions to capture the most accurate and meaningful data for our brand marketing efforts. When it comes to marketing research, specifically, here are some commonly applied scales and corresponding examples for each:

Throughout this book, we will review practical brand measurement scales that demystify seemingly abstract brand attributes/phenomena by breaking them down into dimensions that can be scored with relevant items.

TABLE 6.2: Common questionnaire scales

Scale	Description	Example
Likert Scale	Respondents are asked to indicate their level of agreement or disagreement with a statement on a 5 or 7-point scale. Also used to assess behavioral intention	On a scale of 1–7, how likely are you to recommend our product to a friend?
Semantic Differential Scale	Measures the respondent's perception of an object, event, or concept on a bipolar scale with two anchors	How would you rate our product on a scale of "unreliable" to "reliable"?
Thurstone Scale	Respondents are presented with a list of judge-weighted statements and asked to indicate whether they agree or disagree	I am inspired to finish my tasks using this product Agree Disagree
Guttman Scale	Measures the strength of the respondent's agreement with a series of statements arranged in hierarchical order, increasing in specificity.	Please check whether you agree with the following statements: "I always buy this brand" "I would recommend this brand to my friends"
Constant Sum Scale	Measures the relative importance of different attributes in a product or brand	Please allocate 100 points among the following product attributes: "price," "quality", and "customer service"
Paired Comparison or Forced Choice Scale	Measures the relative preference for different brands or products	Which product do you prefer, A or B?
Stapel Scale	Measures perception of a concept on a scale from −5 to +5 with an adjective in the middle.	Please rate our product on a scale from " −5" to "+5" on the attribute "reliable"
Visual Analog Scale	Measures respondents' level of agreement or disagreement as indicated by them by placing a mark along a line	Please rate the level of pain you are experiencing on a scale from "no pain" to "worst possible pain"
Comparative Scale	Measures the respondent's preference for two or more options	Please rank the following products from most to least preferred: A, B, and C
Multiple Choice Scale	Measures knowledge or awareness of a subject	Which of the following ingredients is not found in our product? a) salt, b) sugar, c) pepper, d) cinnamon

AVOIDING COMMON BIASES

As with all human endeavors, our brand research projects aren't exempt from biases and it is in our best interests to be aware of them. It's important to find ways to minimize these common biases to ensure that our research is accurate and reliable.

Confirmation bias happens when we only look for information that confirms our pre-existing beliefs and ignore anything that contradicts them. To avoid this bias, we need to stay open-minded and actively seek out evidence that challenges our beliefs.

Another common bias is the **halo effect.** This is when we form an overall positive or negative impression of a brand or product based on a single positive or negative experience. To avoid this, we need to gather multiple sources of information and evaluate each source independently.

Social desirability bias is when people respond to survey questions in a way that is socially acceptable or expected, rather than truthful. We can avoid this by using anonymous surveys or minimizing social pressure.

Next, we have **response bias,** where people provide incomplete or inaccurate answers. We need to use clear and specific survey questions and ensure that respondents understand the question to avoid this bias.

Sampling or selection bias is when the sample of respondents is not representative of the population as a whole. We need to use random sampling methods and ensure that the sample size is sufficient to provide accurate results.

The Hawthorne effect is when respondents behave differently or answer questions differently when they know they are being observed. To avoid this, we can use covert or naturalistic observation methods.

Anchoring bias happens when we rely too heavily on the first piece of information we encounter when making a decision. To avoid this, we need to present information in a balanced and unbiased way.

Availability bias is when we rely too heavily on information that is readily available. We can avoid this by using multiple sources of information and avoiding making conclusions based on limited data.

Finally, **experimenter bias** is when researchers unconsciously influence the results of a study based on their expectations or preferences. We can avoid this by using double-blind studies or ensuring that experimenters are unaware of the study's hypotheses.

ON THE IMPORTANCE OF CONTINUOUS MEASUREMENT

When it comes to brand measurement scales, discrete scores are not as telling as continuous measurements and comparisons.

How are you faring now in relation to where you were six months ago? Has brand perception shifted since you last measured it? What are some potential explanations?

Brand managers must build an ongoing, periodic program around equity, relationship, and perception measurements. Only then can we make fair comparisons and determine, directionally, how the brand performs regarding our key indicators of choice.

Being healthy today is no guarantee of being healthy tomorrow. Large research projects are great sources of brand information, but smaller, higher-cadence measurements can open more paths for optimization and growth.

Countries run a full census every so many years, but they actively survey the population on pressing matters to keep a more updated source of truth to inform social interventions. This is also true for brand measurements: short and constant is better than complex and outdated.

TARGETING: BUILDING PERSONAS

The research techniques we just reviewed should ultimately allow you to learn more about the human being you're servicing and building a brand for.

At this point, it's important to make a distinction between buyers, customers, and consumers. With buyers, there's an expectation that something of value will be exchanged for what you offer. Customer, on the other hand, is a more general term describing someone who demands your product, idea, or service. "Customer" speaks to a need, but doesn't necessarily connote a purchase decision. "Customer" and "buyer" are used interchangeably in the marketing world.

Lastly, consumer points to usage. You won't always address consumers in brand communications because it is customers who participate and determine the decision to acquire what you offer—regardless of what the transaction looks like or who ends up enjoying the offering's value. "Consumer" is analogous to "user".

While you will often find these terms used interchangeably in this book, I will default to "**customer personas**" because this is the human profile we benefit from understanding more deeply. The label "customer" also captures non-monetary transactions that are typical of certain kinds of strategies, including political and cause branding. If it makes sense for your business model, feel free to refer to them as "user personas".

Customer **personas** are fictional representations of a brand's ideal customers, derived from both quantitative and qualitative insights collected through market segmentation research. They provide a comprehensive and humanized view of the target audience, thus aiding brand managers in targeting, which is the second step in the STP framework.

To build customer personas, start by analyzing any secondary research and quantitative insights from (primary) segmentation research you've completed, collecting demographics, geographic, and behavioral data. These insights will offer a broad understanding of who the customers are and what drives their purchasing decisions.

Next, explore qualitative insights to add depth and detail to the personas that are starting to surface. Qualitative research methods such as interviews, focus groups, and ethnographic studies can be employed to gather information about customers' emotions, motivations, and values. By combining both types of data, brand managers can create rich and vivid personas that reflect real-life customers.

For example, imagine a brand manager working for a sportswear company. The quantitative data might reveal that the target audience is predominantly women aged 25–40, living in urban areas, and interested in fitness. From qualitative research, the brand manager might find out that these women are motivated by self-improvement, seek a sense of community, and prefer eco-friendly products. By integrating these insights, the brand manager can create a persona like "Eco-conscious Emily", a 32-year-old urban professional who values sustainability and is passionate about maintaining a healthy lifestyle.

Personas are helpful for targeting because they enable us to better understand the audience we're branding to and tailor communications accordingly. Personas can also help align teams across the organization, ensuring that everyone is on the same page regarding the brand's goals and customer expectations.

Personas

Picture	TRAITS	PAINS	ASPIRATIONS	TO DOS	MOTIVATIONS	CHANNELS
	Gender:	-	-	-	-	-
	Income Level:	-	-	-	-	-
	Age:	-	-	-	-	-
Fictional name:	Marital Status:	-	-	-	-	-
	Children:	-	-	-	-	-
Occupation:	Education Level:	-	-	-	-	-
Location:						

Picture	TRAITS	PAINS	ASPIRATIONS	TO DOS	MOTIVATIONS	CHANNELS
	Gender:	-	-	-	-	-
	Income Level:	-	-	-	-	-
	Age:	-	-	-	-	-
Fictional name:	Marital Status:	-	-	-	-	-
	Children:	-	-	-	-	-
Occupation:	Education Level:	-	-	-	-	-
Location:						

Picture	TRAITS	PAINS	ASPIRATIONS	TO DOS	MOTIVATIONS	CHANNELS
	Gender:	-	-	-	-	-
	Income Level:	-	-	-	-	-
	Age:	-	-	-	-	-
Fictional name:	Marital Status:	-	-	-	-	-
	Children:	-	-	-	-	-
Occupation:	Education Level:	-	-	-	-	-
Location:						

FIGURE 6.4: Persona cards

NOTES

1. Kotler, P. (2011). Philip Kotler's contributions to marketing theory and practice. In *Review of Marketing Research: Special Issue–Marketing Legends.* Emerald Group Publishing Limited.
2. Meredith, G., & Schewe, C. (1994). The power of cohorts. *American Demographics, 16*(12), 22.
3. Noble, S. M., Haytko, D. L., & Phillips, J. (2009). What drives college-age Generation Y consumers? *Journal of Business Research, 62*(6), 617–628. https://doi.org/10.1016/j.jbusres.2008.01.020
4. Inglehart, R. (1997). *Modernization and Postmodernization: Cultural, Economic, and Political Change in 43 Societies.* Princeton University Press. https://doi.org/10.2307/j.ctv10vm2ns
5. Meredith, G., & Schewe, C. (1994). The power of cohorts. *American Demographics, 16*(12), 22.
6. Kupperschmidt, B. R. E. (2000). Multigeneration employees: Strategies for effective management. *Health Care Manager, 19*(1).
7. Jurkiewicz, C. L., & Brown, R. G. (1998). Generational comparisons of public employee motivation. *Review of Public Personnel Administration, 18*(4), 18–37. https://doi.org/10.1177/07343 71X9801800403
8. Wolburg, J. M., & Pokrywczynski, J. (2001). A psychographic analysis of Generation Y college students. *Journal of Advertising Research, 41*(5), 33–52.
9. Strauss, W., & Howe, N. (1991). *Generations: The History of America's Future, 1584 to 2069.* Morrow.
10. Twenge, J. M. (2014). *Generation Me - Revised and Updated: Why Today's Young Americans Are More Confident, Assertive, Entitled—and More Miserable Than Ever Before.*
11. Bolton, R. N., Parasuraman, A., Hoefnagels, A., Migchels, N., Kabadayi, S., Gruber, T., Komarova Loureiro, Y., & Solnet, D. (2013). Understanding Generation Y and their use of social media: A review and research agenda. *Journal of Service Management, 24*(3), 245–267. https://doi.org/10.1108/09564231311326987
12. Seemiller, C., & Grace, M. (2016). *Generation Z Goes to College.* John Wiley & Sons, Incorporated. http://ebookcentral.proquest.com/lib/unorte-ebooks/detail.action?docID=4305728
13. Turner, A. (2015). Generation Z: Technology and social interest. *The Journal of Individual Psychology, 71*(2), 103–113.

14. Singh, A. P., & Dangmei, J. (2016). Understanding the generation Z: The future workforce. *South-Asian Journal of Multidisciplinary Studies, 3*(3), 1–5.

15. Parment, A. (2013). Generation Y vs. Baby Boomers: Shopping behavior, buyer involvement and implications for retailing. *Journal of Retailing and Consumer Services, 20*(2), 189–199.

16. XPLANE. "Empathy Map Worksheet". https://xplane.com/worksheet/empathy-map-worksheet

17. Malhotra, M. (2011). *Basic Marketing Research.* Pearson.
Malhotra, N. K., Peterson, M., & Kleiser, S. B. (1999). Marketing research: A state-of-the-art review and directions for the twenty-first century. *Journal of the Academy of Marketing Science, 27*(2), 160–183.

CHAPTER 7

ASSOCIATIONS AND POSITIONING

DOI: 10.4324/9781003336693-9

Pasta
Rome
Wine
Parmigiano

If you're thinking "Italy", ***bravissimo.*** You are a human being whose brain has just connected the dots, identified a pattern, and retrieved its name. Your accumulated pieces of knowledge stored as notes have just lit up in recognition of something familiar.

You've recalled, deducted, and concluded in what probably felt like a fraction of a second.

This is the magic we play with. This is also the challenge we stand against: that mental impressions are instant and associations lasting.

As brand strategists we're given a rare opportunity to influence what these associations are and can become. Through our activities in messages, we get to impact the kinds of ideas linked to our brand.

In this chapter, we will review how human beings form brand associations, constructing maps we lean on to make sense of the options around us.

POSITIONING

When a brand generates strong associations with a given value story among its audience, we say that it has positioned itself. During positioning processes, brands align themselves with a specific use case, context, set of advantages, and industry.

Brands can also **reposition** themselves whenever a strategic business decision calls for it, redefining the place they occupy in the larger competitive landscape.

Essentially, *positioning is finding the right space in the consumer's mind and going for it before someone else does.*

In strategist Marty Neumeier's words, one can identify this core, distinctive position by completing the statement: "Our brand is the ONLY _____ that _____". He identifies this "only" statement as a brand's Zag: a unique differentiator that sets you apart in the marketplace. For brands struggling to define this Zag position, he recommends listing all competitors who share a claim and start pivoting from there[1].

In *Crossing the Chasm*, consultant Geoffrey Moore provides a helpful framework to define your brand's positioning statement clearly and succinctly[2]:

- **For** (target customers)
- **Who are dissatisfied with** (the current market alternative)
- **Our product is a** (product category)
- **That provides** (key problem-solving capability, benefit, compelling reason to buy)
- **Unlike** (the product alternative)
- **We have assembled** (key whole product features, statement of primary differentiation).

Let's review some examples of how this positioning statement template can be put to use. First up, an online learning platform for entrepreneurship education.

- **For** busy, self-motivated learners
- **Who are dissatisfied with** the high costs and rigid schedules of traditional education

- **Our product is** an online learning platform
- **That provides** affordable, flexible, and personalized entrepreneurship courses
- **Unlike** expensive universities and limited local options
- **We have assembled** a vast library of content, course recommendations, and a supportive learning community, making entrepreneurial education more accessible and tailored to individual needs.

For a physical product example, consider this eco-friendly cleaning product brand:

- **For** environmentally conscious consumers
- **Who are dissatisfied with** the harmful chemicals and waste generated by traditional cleaning products
- **Our product is** a range of eco-friendly cleaning solutions
- **That provides** effective, biodegradable, and non-toxic alternatives for a cleaner, greener home
- **Unlike** conventional cleaning products with harsh chemicals and single-use plastics
- **We have assembled** plant-based ingredients, reusable packaging, and a commitment to sustainability, setting a new standard for clean living

To get an idea of how this same template might apply to a service, review this example for a meal kit delivery service:

- **For** busy professionals and families
- **Who are dissatisfied with** the time-consuming process of meal planning, shopping, and preparation
- **Our product is a** meal kit delivery service
- **That provides** convenient, nutritious, and customizable meals with pre-portioned ingredients and easy-to-follow recipes

- **Unlike** dining out, fast food, or traditional grocery shopping
- **We have assembled** a diverse menu, locally sourced ingredients, and recyclable packaging, simplifying meal-time and promoting healthier eating habits

PERCEPTUAL BRAND POSITIONING MAPS

Perceptual maps are widely used tools to visualize multiple brands' positions with regards to a set of attributes of interest. You'll typically encounter two axes, one for each strategic attribute, and a set of brands mapped out according to how that attribute is perceived. Each axis represents two opposing ends (values) of an attribute. If the attribute is price, a y axis could go from cheaper (bottom) to more expensive (top). Brands positioned close to each other are also more tightly related in terms of said attributes.

There are many kinds of perceptual maps and a growing list of statistical analysis methods to put them together[3]. For the sake of this discussion, I'll refer to two-dimension perceptual mapscreated through a method known as factor analysis. As brand managers, we benefit from theoretically sound tools that are also practical.

Factor analysis is one of the most widely used approaches to building a perceptual map for brand positioning.. Put simply:

1. Ask a group of respondents to rate a number of brands, including yours, on specific attributes. You can identify these attributes beforehand with quantitative or

qualitative research techniques such as those reviewed in Chapter 6. A Likert-type scale is typically used to rate brands' performance on each attribute.

2. Combine any attributes that correlate strongly into factors. If two or more attributes make up a single factor, their values are combined.

3. Map brands in relation to each other on the grid based on their ratings for each of the two core factors. These two are usually the ones that explain the most variation in perceptions.

4. Analyze the map to understand the current brand positioning, identify gaps in the market, and develop marketing strategies to improve or adjust the brand's position.

For step 1, you can present a question like the following:

On a scale of 1 to 10, where 1 represents "poor performance" and 10 represents "excellent performance", please rate the following brands (Brand A, Brand B, Brand C, and Brand D) on each of the 5 key attributes listed below:

Product Quality:

a. Brand A: ____
b. Brand B: ____
c. Brand C: ____
d. Brand D: ____

Customer Service:

a. Brand A: ____
b. Brand B: ____
c. Brand C: ____
d. Brand D: ____

Pricing:

a. Brand A: ____
b. Brand B: ____
c. Brand C: ____
d. Brand D: ____

Innovation:

a. Brand A: ____
b. Brand B: ____
c. Brand C: ____
d. Brand D: ____

Sustainability:

a. Brand A: ____
b. Brand B: ____
c. Brand C: ____
d. Brand D: ____

Please provide your ratings based on your personal experience with or perception of each brand.

Feel free to replace the above with a set of evaluation attributes that reflect your category's main purchase drivers. Include your brand as one of the options to be rated. As recommended in step 2, you can combine two or more attributes into a single factor. This is so that, ultimately, you can map the two factors

Brand positioning map: example

SPREADSHEET APPS

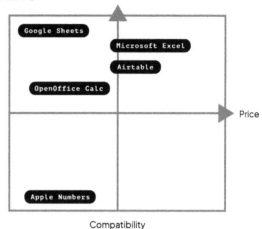

FIGURE 7.1: Brand positioning map

responsible for the most variation in perception, one for each axis. Statistical analysis methods like Maximum Likelihood (ML) can help you achieve this.

TOP-OF-MIND: ACHIEVING A DOMINANT POSITION

Ultimately, brands aim to secure dominant positions within their categories. When we think of a specific type of product or service, there's usually an **evoked set** of brands that comes to mind[4]. When it does, there can be a single brand that is recalled first. We say that a brand has achieved **top-of-mind awareness**: it is the strongest, most immediate alternative recalled within a given decision-making process—purchase or otherwise[5].

When you are truly unique, competition becomes less relevant. Customers perceive you as occupying that unique (mental) spot to the point where it doesn't matter how full the parking lot is. The challenge for brand strategists, then, becomes to create that unique position.

In *Positioning*, Al Ries shares a helpful technique to position yourself when you're not the first player in a given market and differentiation is difficult:

> To find a unique position, you must ignore conventional logic. Conventional logic says you find your concept inside yourself or inside the product. Not true. What you must do is look inside the prospect's mind. (Ries, 2001)[6]

Looking inside our prospective customer's mind for existing associations is what strong brand positioning is made of. While easier said than done, this challenge has been tackled by brand strategists for decades. In the forthcoming section, we'll learn some strategies to reveal our prospect's mental picture of our brands.

A LOOK INSIDE THE MIND: BRAND ASSOCIATIONS

Positioning is ultimately an exercise in strengthening desired associations. Marketing tradition has relied on the notion of an associative network memory model where **nodes** (information pieces) are connected by links. Nodes are our essential storage units for brand information, and they can activate related nodes when retrieved from memory.

Here are a few examples of brand associations you might be familiar with:

- Apple is associated with innovation, minimal design, and premium quality

- Coca-Cola is associated with happiness, nostalgia, and its signature red
- Nike is associated with sports, athleticism, and the "Just Do It" slogan
- Disney is associated with magic, fantasy, and childhood memories
- Harley-Davidson is associated with freedom, rebellion, and the rumble of engines

How did these associations come to be? Brand marketing activities play an instrumental role in linking ideas to specific brands. As you saw above, there's a wide range of association types, with some being closer to the product (central) and others more tangential (peripheral). Keller divides potential brand associations into three types of increasing scope: attributes, benefits, and attitudes[7].

Attributes are concrete features perceived as part of the brand's offering. **Benefits** are ideas we come to hold about a product's ultimate value for our wants and needs. Lastly, **attitudes** reflect our postures towards and judgments about a brand. This classification helps explain why a brand like Disney might be associated, simultaneously, with concepts as diverse in depth as a mouse, magic, and childhood memories.

The mind constructs an associative network to interpret new brand information in light of every other memory it has previously stored. Over time, these networks can expand and retrieval can become easier for brands whom we have richer relationships with.

According to French and Smith, strong brand associations are a result of "the number of associations, the strength of links between associations and the structure of the associative network, with those associations closest to the brand being the strongest".[8]

Brand managers must, then, identify second and third-order associations and attempt to upgrade them, work to increase the overall number of associations, and even build new connections between associations that are already present but sparse. Brand marketing activities like the following can all impact brand association strength (BAS):

- **Storytelling:** Engaging consumers with emotive, authentic stories helps to create a strong brand image by associating the brand with certain values, experiences, and emotions that resonate with the target audience
- **Partnerships and co-branding:** Collaborating with partners who share similar values as the brand can strengthen desired associations by leveraging each other's credibility, trust, and reach to reinforce the brand's image and message.
- **Content marketing:** Developing and distributing valuable, relevant, and consistent content can help to establish the brand as an authority in its industry, fostering trust and credibility, and strengthening desired associations in consumers' minds[9].
- **Experiential marketing:** Creating memorable, immersive experiences for consumers can help to build strong brand associations by engaging the senses, emotions, and cognitive processes, which can lead to lasting impressions and deeper connections with the brand[10].
- **User-generated content and social proof:** Encouraging consumers to create and share content related to the brand can foster a sense of ownership, engagement, and advocacy, which can further strengthen desired brand associations[11].

It is also essential to identify which ideas are most closely linked to the brand, as these first-order, core associations should be reinforced over time and consistently leveraged in marketing communications. Brand managers can lean on first-order associations for outward-facing language and infuse experiences that reinforce these core ideas throughout customers' journeys with the brand. We will dive deeper into brand experience mapping in Chapter 19.

To get an initial sense of the attributes, benefits, and attributes associated with the brand, you can apply Low and Lamb's Brand Image Scale[12]. This instrument asks respondents to rate brands on a set of predefined associations related to the dimensions of brand image, perceived quality, and brand attitude. The anchors can be modified to fit your brand's category and the proposed set of items is outlined below:

TABLE 7.1: Brand Image scale

Scale name	Brand Image
Authors	Low and Lamb (2000)
Type of scale	Semantic differential
Anchors	Different anchors per question, see below. Anchors can be customized to fit product category
Dimensions	Brand image, perceived quality, brand attitude
Items	**Brand image** I think that the (product Y) in this advertisement is/has: • friendly/unfriendly • modern/outdated • useful/not useful • popular/unpopular • gentle/harsh • artificial/natural **Perceived quality** I think that the advertised (product Y) is: • superior/inferior • excellent/poor • good quality/poor quality **Brand attitude** I think this brand is: • good/bad • pleasant/unpleasant • valuable/worthless

While providing options helps measure each association's intensity, it is highly recommended to use a qualitative technique (see Chapter 6) to unveil the wider network of ideas connected to the brand. Focus groups, in-depth interviews, and ethnography can all provide meaningful insights to inform a more structured questionnaire like the above. You can also try a combination of open and closed questions to remain open to emerging associations.

Strengthening desired associations is one part of the job, but the other part is preventing strategic associations from diluting. Sound brand extensions, cohesive service experiences, and coherent partnerships, are just some of the most strategic tools at our disposal.

Now, as you can imagine, a brand manager must be able to visualize these salient associations in order to impact them in any material way. To help us elucidate what consumers' brand concept maps look like, John et al. created a practical five-step process known as the Brand Concept Mapping (BCM) method[13].

BRAND CONCEPT MAPPING

The goal with this tool is to identify the most meaningful associations consumers hold around a brand and understand how they are linked in memory. By design, a brand concept map is a consensus tool: it must aggregate insights from individual consumers to arrive at a general association network.

The process starts with a **mapping stage** where a set of respondents are asked to write all of the associations they can think of in response to the prompt: *"What comes to mind when you think about [brand]?"* These elicited responses are collected in separate cards; John et al.'s original exercise gave them 25 cards to work with. To further assist respondents, you can also provide pre-written associations and ask them to select which ones apply based on their perspective.

Then, respondents are asked to develop their own brand concept map. They're given a blank piece of paper with the brand's name in the center and are encouraged to map out each of their association cards around it. The last step for them is to draw single, double, or triple lines to connect these cards based on how strong each association is. You can also show them what a (finished) brand concept map looks like before they start working to provide a reference.

At this point, our work with participants is over and it is time to build a consensus Brand Concept Map in an **aggregation phase**. There are five steps involved:

1. Organize the information respondents shared by logging:
   a. *All associations found*
   b. *How often each association was mentioned*
   c. *How often each association was connected to others*
   d. *How often each association was identified as a first-order one*
   e. *Calculate a ratio between the association's mention frequency (b) and how often that mention was a first-order one (d)*
   f. *How close each association was to the brand, specifying how many subordinate and superordinate associations it has below and above it, respectively*
   g. *How frequently links between specific associations occur across maps*
   h. *The average number of lines used by participants to connect each of these links (Round to the nearest integer: 1, 2 or 3)*

Brand Concept Map

SAMPLE CONSENSUS BCM FOR MAYO CLINIC, PATIENTS

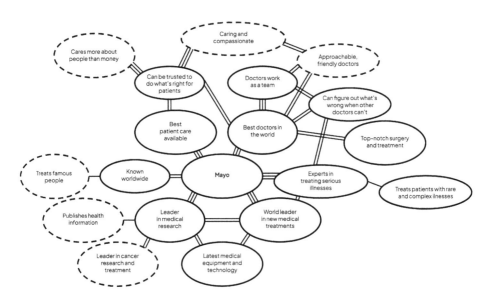

FIGURE 7.2: Brand Concept Map (John et al.)

2. Identify **core or first-order brand associations.** These will have the highest first-order mentions, a greater first-order mention ratio (e), and more superordinate than subordinate connections.
3. Map core or first-order brand association links.
4. Map non-core (second, third-order) brand association links.
5. Map single, double, or triple lines for each brand association link based on the average you found (h).

WHY ASSOCIATIONS MATTER

Consumers don't simply make choices based on a product's features. **Means–end theory** tells us consumers are swayed by what they believe the brand will do for them on a deeper level and how it resonates with their personal values[14]. Imagine a chain linking a product's utilitarian attributes, the benefit or consequence we get from them, and finally, the values we hold dear. A vibrant red color (attribute) leads to a delightful taste (consequence) and ultimately results in pure fun and enjoyment (value).

Understanding brand associations is key because they help us connect the dots between tangible product details and more abstract ideas, such as the psychological and social outcomes we seek.

But what is it that we seek? When faced with multiple options, what do we pursue first? In a seminal 1943 paper titled "A Theory of Human Motivation", Abraham Maslow proposed a **Hierarchy of Needs** as a list of five distinct categories of human needs, which he arranged in a hierarchy

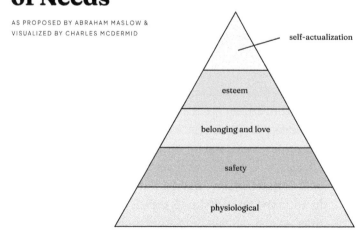

Maslow's Hierarchy of Needs

AS PROPOSED BY ABRAHAM MASLOW &
VISUALIZED BY CHARLES MCDERMID

self-actualization

esteem

belonging and love

safety

physiological

FIGURE 7.3: Maslow's hierarchy of needs

of prepotency[15]. Prior to focusing on needs that are higher up the hierarchy, he argued some needs are more basic or primary.

Whether aware or not, we are naturally propelled toward meeting these needs. In order of priority to us, basic needs like physiological and safety needs are addressed first, followed by social needs, and self-actualization. While Maslow didn't originally present these as a pyramid, it has become the go-to visualization for these principles[16].

Inevitably, individuals must satisfy their lower-order needs before they can focus on higher-order ones:

1. **Physiological needs:** These are the most basic, survival-related needs like food, water, air, sleep, and shelter. Only when these are addressed do we feel compelled to pursue higher-order needs.
2. **Safety needs:** These include the need for security, stability, and protection from threats, both physical and psychological.
3. **Love and belongingness needs:** After safety needs are met, individuals strive for social connections and relationships. These needs encompass friendship, intimacy, and a sense of belonging within various social groups, such as family, friends, and romantic partners.
4. **Esteem needs:** These needs revolve around an individual's desire for recognition, respect, and a sense of accomplishment. Esteem needs are divided into two categories: (a) the need for self-esteem, which includes self-confidence and achievement, and (b) the need for recognition from others, which involves reputation and status.
5. **Self-actualization needs:** Self-actualization refers to an individual's desire to realize their full potential, to grow and develop, and to become everything they

are capable of being. This includes pursuing personal growth, self-discovery, and creative expression. As we saw in Chapter 5, brands can facilitate self-affirmation, self-expression, and self-enhancement.

As an example, consider Headspace, a popular meditation app with an inviting, user-friendly interface (attribute). The app's design makes it easy for users to develop a meditation habit (consequence), fostering inner peace and mindfulness in their daily lives (value). These ultimate values would be classified as self-actualization needs in Maslow's hierarchy, meaning individuals would pursue them to the extent that other basic needs are addressed.

The user-friendly interface components might be one of the associations that comes to mind when we think of Headspace, but its real importance is it will likely activate deeper nodes reminding us of the benefits we derive from the brand and how it connects to our intentions.

As we just saw, associations can point to brand attributes, benefits, or attitudes. In becoming aware of their brand's associations, managers can make easier connections between their customers' deeper intentions and the products' attributes, enabling them to achieve their goals.

HOW TO ACT ON THESE ASSOCIATIONS

You've identified a set of salient brand associations and are ready to take action. Where should you focus first? How can you put brand initiatives in place to strengthen strategic associations and prevent them from diluting over time? How can you build new links to facilitate brand recall and eventual preference?

- **Reinforce first-order associations whenever possible.** Claim what you own. If there's a pattern between customers who identify certain associations as first-order that makes them different from another group in your analysis and there's an opportunity to segment this audience further. Learn what comes to mind first for different segments within your audience and own these positions in a differentiated way.
- **Connect** second and third-order associations with your core associations in your brand messaging to strengthen their links. Their mere proximity in brand verbal and visual communications can help establish relatedness. Remember brand strength is a function of the links between its associations[17]. The number of associations can also enhance recall.
- **Monitor** competing brands that are closely associated with yours. Something about these third-party brands is making customers recall them in relation to yours. They are references to watch.
- **Partner** with non-competing brands that emerge when customers think about you. Their products might be perceived as natural complements or enhancers of your own.

NOTES

1. Neumeier, M. (2006). *Zag: The Number One Strategy of High-Performance Brands*. Pearson Education.
2. Moore, G. A., & McKenna, R. (2006). *Crossing the Chasm: Marketing and Selling High-Tech Products to Mainstream Customers*. HarperCollins.
3. Kohli, C. S., & Leuthesser, L. (1993). Product positioning: A comparison of perceptual mapping techniques. *The Journal of Product and Brand Management, 2*(4), 10. https://doi.org/10.1108/10610429310047660
4. Howard, J. A., & Sheth, J. N. (1969). *The Theory of Buyer Behavior*. Wiley. https://bac-lac.on.worldcat.org/oclc/33508

5. Laurent, G., Kapferer, J.-N., & Roussel, F. (1995). The underlying structure of brand awareness scores. *Marketing Science, 14*(3), G170–G179.

6. Ries, A., Trout, J., & Kotler, P. (2001). *Positioning: The Battle for Your Mind* (1st edition). McGraw Hill.

7. Keller, K. L. (1993). Conceptualizing, measuring, and managing customer-based brand equity. *Journal of Marketing, 57*(1), 1.

8. French, A., & Smith, G. (2013). Measuring brand association strength: A consumer based brand equity approach. *European Journal of Marketing, 47*(8), 1356–1367. http://dx.doi.org/10.1108/03090561311324363

9. Pulizzi, J. (2012). The Rise of Storytelling as the New Marketing. *Publishing Research Quarterly, 28*(2), 116–123. https://doi.org/10.1007/s12109-012-9264-5

10. Schmitt, B. (1999). Experiential marketing. *Journal of Marketing Management, 15*(1–3), 53–67. https://doi.org/10.1362/026725799784870496

11. Daugherty, T., Eastin, M. S., & Bright, L. (2008). Exploring consumer motivations for creating user-generated content. *Journal of Interactive Advertising, 8*(2), 16–25. https://doi.org/10.1080/15252019.2008.10722139

12. Low, G. S., & Lamb Jr, C. W. (2000). The measurement and dimensionality of brand associations. *Journal of Product & Brand Management, 9*(6), 350–370.

13. John, D. R., Loken, B., Kim, K., & Monga, A. B. (2006). Brand concept maps: A methodology for identifying brand association networks. *Journal of Marketing Research, 43*(4), 549–563.

14. Gutman, J. (1982). A means–end chain model based on consumer categorization processes. *Journal of Marketing, 46*(2), 60–72. https://doi.org/10.2307/3203341
Reynolds, T. J., & Gutman, J. (1988). Laddering theory, method, analysis, and interpretation. *Journal of Advertising Research, 28*(1), 11–31.

15. Maslow, A. H. (1943). A theory of human motivation. *Psychological Review, 50*(4), 370.

16. McDermid, C. D. (1960). How money motivates men. *Business Horizons, 3*(4), 93–100. https://doi.org/10.1016/S0007-6813(60)80034-1

17. French, A., & Smith, G. (2013). Measuring brand association strength: A consumer based brand equity approach. *European Journal of Marketing, 47*(8), 1356–1367. http://dx.doi.org/10.1108/03090561311324363

CHAPTER 8

NAMING

DOI: 10.4324/9781003336693-10

Think about your name for a moment. Write it down on a piece of paper.

Is there a story behind it? Etymologically, what does it mean? Are there any objects, symbols, or values attached to it? How do you feel when you hear someone say it? Is it spelled in an atypical way?

Think about your acquaintances and loved ones next: what would you think comes to mind when they hear your name? A specific time or place?

Consider expectations tied to your name, as you've built it for yourself: is there something that wouldn't feel [your name] to do? To like? To say?

Over time, names become labels that encapsulate lived experiences, personality traits, lifestyle choices, and attitudes. They turn into symbols that, much like a headshot, can instantly bring associations to mind. Brand names become devices that facilitate retrieval from long-term memory[1].

Brand names, like human names, matter insofar as they capture associations. They are devices, mnemonics that encapsulate stories. As brand managers, we ascribe meaning to names through everyday positioning activities. While extrinsic to products themselves, brand names can influence perceptions of product quality, willingness to buy, and attitude toward the product[2].

Choosing the right name to begin with is also important. Aside from the associations we will build over time, words inherently come with their own layer of meaning. Consumers, for example, might be more likely to purchase a product if the brand name is comprised of common segments and sequences of segments rather than less common ones[3].

In this chapter, we will review some of the most widely used brand naming strategies, linguistic devices, and types of names. Along with a robust communication strategy, this brand name will go on to serve as a repository of meaning that differentiates your offering in the marketplace.

TYPES OF BRAND NAMES

Broadly speaking, Arora et al. found that brand names could be classified in two large buckets: word-based names and non-word based names[4].

Among word-based names, we can have concepts based on real words or invented ones. When pulling from real words, strategists choose either product related, product unrelated, or person/place related ideas.

When inventing words, they typically lean on either phonemes that make interesting sounds or base words they transform creatively through clipping, blending, compounding, affixation, or unusual spelling.

Brand names might also come to life in non-word structures like abbreviations, numbers, and acronyms. While abbreviations form with desired initials, irrespective of how they're pronounced, acronyms retain a word-like sound. That sound, in turn, can be loosely related to a word that is connected to the brand, related to a word with no direct connection to the brand, or entirely unrelated to any known words.

Brand Name Classification

ARORA-KALRO-SHARMA FRAMEWORK

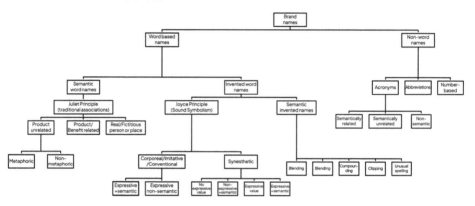

FIGURE 8.1: Types of brand names

BRAND NAMING: A PROCESS

Knowing which kinds of brand names are available is helpful, but it's just the start. The truth of the matter is that staring at a blank piece of paper or screen can paralyze even the most experienced brand strategist. Creating iconic brand names is, like most creative endeavors, *a matter of method.*

There's a process I've leaned on for years to generate memorable brand and sub-brand names. Like most, I wanted to rely on that serendipitous brainstorming scenario where ideas and divergent thinking run wild. I wanted that kind of free-flowing ideation session to work for me and my clients.

While there's value to that spontaneous lack of structure, I quickly found that **repeatable success leans on intentional processes.** To assist your own brand naming process,

FIGURE 8.2: Brand naming process

here are the three steps I've narrowed this down to over the years:

1. **Ideation:** a divergent thinking stage where *all ideas are entertained*. Using specific prompts, we build a long list of words that might eventually become naming options. At this stage, we're not judging these words on their potential to become a name, but merely allowing them to flow and capturing them as they do.

2. **Transformation:** taking the raw inputs from our ideation stage, we start shaping words and exercising convergent thinking. We select idea fragments and develop them into viable brand name concepts. Using a set of word transformation techniques, we arrive at various candidate options.

3. **Selection:** in the most objective phase of the process, we weigh our top options against a set of pre-defined criteria that serves the brand's mission. You can use the decision criteria and weights I'm outlining in the figure below or build your own based on the brand's priorities. The higher a name option's score in this matrix, the better fit it will be for the organization. If multiple team members are scoring options, you can average their scores for each name to arrive at a global indicator.

TABLE 8.1: Brand name ideation table: benchmarks

Benchmarks: defining what's out there	
SAME SHELF Brand names used by your **direct competitors**	**SAME CUSTOMER** Brand names your **target market loves**
SAME AISLE Brand names used in **substitute products**	**SAME STORE** Brand names used in **complementary products**

TABLE 8.2: Brand name ideation table: essence

Essence: Defining what's inside		
FEELINGS Emotions using your product should trigger	**VERBS** Actions your target customer will be able to do	**SYNONYMS** Product category **synonyms**
OUTCOMES Words that describe your product's core **benefit**	**SLANG** Casual expressions used by your **target customer**	**ADJECTIVES** Words that describe your product's qualities

TABLE 8.3: Brand name ideation table: metaphors

Metaphors: Engaging the imagination		
ANIMAL	PLACE	HISTORICAL FIGURE
FOOD OR INGREDIENT	COLOR	WILDCARDS

TABLE 8.4: Brand name transformation techniques

Transformation prompts	Example	Output
Extend with **synonyms**	*Start with "faith", extend to hope, trust, reliance*	
Drill down on subcategories	*Start with "color", extend to purple, blue, red, yellow*	
Mix and match words and fragments	*Frogurt, SpaceX, Skillshare*	
Translate to another language or cultural practice	*Alo Yoga, Asana, Panera*	
Alter spelling to enhance uniqueness	*Dribbble, Canva*	
Attach a prefix that conveys your product's qualities	*super-, over-, mega-, hyper-*	
Attach a suffix that conveys your product's qualities	*-able, -ful, -ous*	

TABLE 8.5: Brand name decision matrix

NAME EVALUATION CRITERIA	WEIGHT
Grammar and wording	**16%**
Is it easy to say?	8%
Is it easy to read?	8%
Differentiation	**24%**
Is it memorable?	8%
Is it different from what's already out there?	8%
Can it be legally registered and protected?	8%
Audience fit	**20%**
Would it resonate well with a professional audience?	10%
Is it related to the space we operate in?	10%
Symbolic meaning	**40%**
Does it evoke the type of product we sell?	8%
Does it trigger positive emotions?	8%
Does it align with the brand's vision?	8%
Does it carry positive connotations in other categories?	8%
Is it respectful of gender, race, religion, and diversity in general?	8%
	100%

Adapt this process to fit your organization's size and capabilities. It should support, not hinder, your brand naming exercise at all times. You might run into the same counterintuitive finding I did: **that creativity often benefits from constraints to let loose.**

CREATIVE NAME TRANSFORMATIONS

During the transformation phase of this process, strategists have a range of linguistic devices at their disposal. Our creative

Naming Techniques: Linguistic Devices

Characteristics	Definitions and/or Examples
Phonetic devices	
1. Alliteration	Consonant repetition (Coca Cola)
2. Assonance	Vowel repetition (Kal Kan)
3. Consonance	Consonant repetition with intervening vowel changes (Weight Watchers)
4. Masculine rhyme	Rhyme with end of syllable stress (Max Pax)
5. Feminine rhyme	Unaccented syllable followed by accented syllable (American Airlines)
6. Weak/imperfect/slant rhyme	Vowels differ or consonants similar, not identical (Black & Decker)
7. Onomatopoeia	Use of syllable phonetics to resemble the object itself (Wisk)
8. Clipping	Product names attentuated (Chevy)
9. Blending	Morphemic. "combination, usually with elision (Aspergum, Duracell)
10. Initial plosives	/b/, ic-hard/, /di, /g-hard/, /k/, /p/, /q/, /t/ (Bic)
Orthographic devices	
1. Unusual or incorrect spellings	Kool-Aid
2. Abbreviations	7-Up for Seven-Up
3. Acronyms	Amoco
Morphological devices	
1. Affixation	Jell-O
2. Compounding	Janitor-in-a-Drum
Semantic devices	
1. Metaphor	Representing something as if it were something else (Arrid). Simile was included with metaphor when a name described a likeness and not an equality (Aqua-Fresh).
2. Metonymy	Application of one object or quality for another (Midas).
3. Synecdoche	Substitution of a part for the whole (Red Lobster).
4. Personification/pathetic	Humanizing the nonhuman or ascription of human fallacy emotions to the inanimate (Betty Crocker)
5. Oxymoron	Conjunction of opposite (Easy-Off).
6. Paronomasia	Pun and word plays (Hawaiian Punch)
7. Semantic appositeness	Fit of name with object (Bufferin)

FIGURE 8.3: Creative linguistic devices for brand names

transformation toolkit includes phonetic, orthographic, morphological, and semantic devices[5].

Phonetic techniques play with brand name sounds to enhance impact. Some of the devices available include alliteration, assonance, and rhyme.

Orthographic devices alter how brand names are actually spelled, even turning to incorrect spellings and abbreviations at times to create linguistic interest around names. Closely related are **morphological** devices, which alter a name's physical form through affixation or compounding.

Lastly, **semantic devices** intervene name meanings creatively through figurative language like metaphors, oxymorons, and paronomasia.

NOTES

1. Jacoby, J., Szybillo, G. J., & Busato-Schach, J. (1977). Information acquisition behavior in brand choice situations. *Journal of Consumer Research, 3*(4), 209–216.
2. Gardner, D. M. (1971). Is there a generalized price–quality relationship? *Journal of Marketing Research, 8*(2), 241–243. https://doi.org/10.2307/3149770
3. Vitevitch, M. S., & Donoso, A. J. (2012). Phonotactic probability of brand names: I'd buy that! *Psychological Research, 76*(6), 693–698. https://doi.org/10.1007/s00426-011-0374-z
4. Arora, S., Kalro, A. D., & Sharma, D. (2015). A comprehensive framework of brand name classification. *Journal of Brand Management, 22*(2), 79–116. https://doi.org/10.1057/bm.2015.8
5. Bergh, B. V., Adler, K., & Oliver, L. (1987). Linguistic distinction among top brand names. *Journal of Advertising Research, 27*(4), 39–44.

CHAPTER 9

PRICING

DOI: 10.4324/9781003336693-11

How much would you pay for a cup of coffee *right now?*

If you're not a coffee drinker, your head is probably at "not a dime".

If you rely on coffee to get work done and have a huge, looming deadline, "it's an investment".

On the other hand, if you are a coffee connoisseur and happen to be after this *specific* cup from a typically unavailable place, roasted a certain way, your budget just got a lot more generous.

The message is simple: *perceived value drives our willingness to pay.* The minute you understand this, it is clear why personas had to come before pricing in this book.

When you're acutely in tune with someone's needs and aspirations, you understand what drives their intent, how far, and where your brand fits. You learn about their lifestyles, discretionary income, and priorities.

You also understand what you're up against: who is offering a comparable solution and how much they're asking for in exchange. In addition to basic production cost calculations, these insights form a sound foundation for pricing.

Throughout this chapter, we'll review some of the most popular cost and value-based pricing techniques to inform your brand's strategy. With this in mind, we'll also review the psychological principles at play in pricing and how consumers react to various offering designs.

Setting a price tag is not the end of the story. Prices are perceived contextually: placement cues, order, and priming all play a role.

POPULAR PRICING TECHNIQUES

Pricing techniques abound. The most experienced price strategists will describe the exercise as both an art and a science: the process of balancing financial considerations and customers' perceptions in a quantity (or set of quantities) they're willing to pay.

Price-setting approaches can be grouped into three categories based on their key driver[1]. You can define a price led by the product/service's cost (**cost-based pricing**), competitors' standards (**competition-based pricing**), and based on customers' perceptions and willingness to pay (**customer-based pricing**).

These strategies are not mutually exclusive and the most robust price-setting exercises often merge considerations from all three sources. Because of this book's focus on brand psychology, we will spend more time reviewing customer-based pricing strategies. These approaches more closely relate to perceived value, brand equity, cognitive dissonance, and other psychological principles at play when evaluating a brand's prices.

The nature of pricing is such that the following section will focus on paid products and services, referring to both interchangeably as "products". While brand development can position ideas,

TABLE 9.1: Popular pricing techniques

Cost-based pricing	Customer-based pricing	Competition-based pricing	Recurrence, presentation, & discounting
• Cost-plus pricing • Markup pricing • Gross-margin pricing • Dynamic pricing	• Parity pricing/ price matching • Penetration pricing • Zone pricing • Pay-what-you-want	• Value-based pricing • Premium pricing • Skimming • Freemium pricing • Odd-even pricing	• Decoy pricing • Bundling • Anchor pricing • Subscription pricing

causes, and freely available products, price-setting is only relevant for items that can be purchased at set amounts.

Cost-based pricing

Cost-plus pricing: This strategy involves calculating the cost of producing a product and *adding* a specific amount to determine the selling price[2]. This approach is commonly used by companies that manufacture physical goods, as it ensures that they cover their production costs and make a profit. Customers expect companies to earn a fair profit and are willing to pay a reasonable markup for a product.

Markup pricing: This technique involves setting a price based on how much items cost plus a standard percentage of that cost, known as its *markup*.

Gross margin pricing: Now imagine you're not calculating a product's price adding a certain percentage of its cost, but ensuring you keep a specific percentage of whatever price you land on as a set **margin.** I may decide that my fashion business will earn a 50% margin on every t-shirt sold. That means we'll keep half of each product's final price as a business gain, or margin.

Dynamic pricing: Dynamic pricing is a pricing strategy in which the selling price of a product changes based on various factors, such as demand, competition, and inventory levels. This approach is commonly used by companies that operate in industries where demand fluctuates regularly, such as airlines and hotels.

Customers are willing to pay more for products when demand is high and fluctuating prices can create a sense of urgency and scarcity. This strategy can help a brand maximize revenue and respond quickly to changes in the market.

Competition-based pricing

These types of strategies involve setting prices in relation to other options available in the market, therefore are competitor-based.

Parity pricing or price matching: This strategy involves matching the price of a competitor for the same product. The underlying assumption is that customers are more likely to purchase from a brand that offers price matching, as it creates a perception of fairness. This approach can help a brand remain competitive and retain customers.

Penetration pricing: Customers are attracted to low prices and are often more likely to try a new product if the price is low. Penetration pricing involves setting a low price for a product to gain market share and attract price-sensitive customers.

This approach is commonly used by companies that are entering new markets or launching new products and want to attract price-sensitive customers.

Zone pricing: This form of competitive pricing looks at a brand's competitive environment in divergent markets, setting different prices for the same product in different geographic regions.

Customers in different regions have different price sensitivities, which can be leveraged to optimize revenue. Offering a contextually attractive option is at the core of successful zone pricing. Tailoring prices to consider local income levels, purchasing power, and cultural dynamics is often the only way to compete with dominant players in new markets.

Zone pricing is a form of **price discrimination,** where brands charge different prices to different customers for the same product, based on their willingness to pay.

Customer-based pricing

Value-based pricing or economic value to the customer (EVC): Value-based pricing is a pricing strategy in which the selling price is determined by the product's perceived value to the customer.

Customers are willing to pay more for products whose perceived benefits outweigh any costs involved.

Premium pricing: Certain cues in advertising, packaging, and other marketing pieces can shift value perceptions and help justify a higher price.

Customers are willing to pay more for products that they perceive to be valuable[3]. This strategy is important for brand management as it can help a brand establish a reputation for providing high-value products and commanding premium prices[4].

Skimming pricing: Skimming pricing involves setting a high price for a product when it is first launched and then gradually lowering the price over time. This approach is commonly used by companies that offer innovative products that are not yet available in the market.

Early adopters are willing to pay a premium price for a new product and that high price can create an impression of exclusivity and quality.

Freemium pricing: This approach involves offering a basic version of a product for free and charging for premium features or upgrades. Freemium pricing is commonly used by companies that offer software products and want to attract users with a free version before converting them to paid subscribers.

Customers are attracted to free products and are more likely to try a product when there is no upfront cost. This strategy is important for brand management as it can help a brand attract new customers and create a loyal customer base.

When considering freemium pricing as your strategy, reflect on the following: *will customers be more willing to pay our price if they get a taste for the product, expand their usage, and require its most advanced features?*

Pay-what-you-want pricing: This strategy involves allowing customers to pay whatever they want for a product or service. It leans on the idea that customers value feeling a sense of autonomy and control over the price they pay, which can increase their satisfaction and loyalty. This strategy hinges heavily on each individual's perceived value and can lead to a range of pricing outcomes based on each person's perspective.

Odd-even or psychological pricing: This strategy involves setting prices that end in odd or even numbers, such as $4.99 or $5.00.

Several studies have found that customers perceive odd prices to be lower than even prices, and therefore, they may be more likely to make a purchase[5]. This phenomenon can be explained by the way our brains process numerical information. When we see a price that ends in an odd number, such as $4.99, our brains tend to round down to the nearest even number, which in this case would be $4.00. On the other hand, when we see a price that ends in an even number, such as $4.00, our brains tend to round up to the next even number, which in this case would be $5.00. This means that an odd price of $4.99 may seem like a better deal to customers than an even price of $5.00, even though the difference is only one cent.

This strategy is important for brand management as it can help a brand increase sales and create a perception of value.

STRATEGIC PRICE PRESENTATION, RECURRENCE, AND DISCOUNTING

Even after prices are set for individual products and services, brand managers can choose to *present* them in strategic ways.

Bundling: This strategy involves offering multiple products or services together as a package for a lower price than if the products were purchased separately. Customers are prone to perceiving bundled products as a "better deal" than purchasing products individually. This approach is commonly used by companies that want to increase the average order value and encourage customers to purchase more than one item. This strategy is important for brand management as it can increase sales and customer loyalty by creating a perception of value.

Anchor pricing: Also known as anchoring or price anchoring, anchor pricing is a cognitive bias-based pricing strategy that influences consumer perception of value by presenting an initial price (the anchor) to which subsequent prices are compared[6]. The anchor price establishes a reference point in the consumer's mind, making other prices seem more attractive or reasonable when compared to the initial anchor.

A strong example of anchor pricing can be found in the restaurant industry, specifically in menu design. A common tactic is to place a high-priced dish (the anchor) at the top of the menu, followed by more moderately priced dishes.

For instance, a restaurant might list an expensive steak dish priced at $50 at the top of the menu, followed by a range of entrees priced between $20 and $30. The $50 price tag serves as the anchor, making the subsequent entrees seem more reasonably priced and attractive by comparison. Customers may perceive the $20–$30 dishes as better value for money, as they instinctively compare these prices to the anchor.

The order in which prices are presented plays a crucial role in this strategy. If the lower-priced items were listed first, customers would not have the high-priced anchor in mind when evaluating the subsequent prices. As a result, the perception of value may not be as strong, and customers may be more inclined to focus on the absolute price rather than the relative value compared to the anchor.

This strategy is based on the **anchoring effect,** a cognitive bias that occurs when people rely too heavily on the first piece of information they encounter (the anchor) when making decisions. In the context of pricing, consumers may evaluate the value of a product based on its price relative to the anchor, rather than assessing the product's intrinsic value independently.

Decoy pricing: This strategy involves offering a third option that is less attractive than the other two, in order to make one of the other options appear more appealing. Customers are more likely to choose the option that appears to be the best value. **Framing** is the underlying mechanism at play here: we perceive one of the options to be more attractive by virtue of the context it is being presented in and not strictly based on its features.

An example of decoy pricing can be typically found in the subscription services industry. A company might offer a basic, standard, and premium plan. In comparison with the standard plan, the premium offers more features. However, the premium plan is priced much higher than the standard plan. This makes the standard plan appear to be the best value, and more likely to be chosen by customers.

By using decoy pricing, companies can not only increase sales, but also create a perception of value among customers. This perception of value can lead to customer loyalty and long-term brand success.

Subscription pricing: This strategy involves charging customers a recurring fee for access to a product or service over a set period of time. It can be applied in conjunction with competition, cost, or customer-based pricing techniques.

Customers tend to prefer the convenience and predictability of a recurring fee, rather than having to make repeated purchases. This strategy can help a brand generate predictable revenue and create a loyal customer base.

NOTES

1. Schindler, R. M. (2011). *Pricing Strategies: A Marketing Approach.* SAGE.
2. Kotler, P., & Keller, K. L. (2006). *Marketing Management.* Pearson Prentice Hall.
3. Dwivedi, A., Nayeem, T., & Murshed, F. (2018). Brand experience and consumers' willingness-to-pay (WTP) a price premium: Mediating role of brand credibility and perceived uniqueness. *Journal of Retailing and Consumer Services, 44*, 100–107. https://doi.org/10.1016/j.jretconser.2018.06.009
4. Han, Y. J., Nunes, J. C., & Drèze, X. (2010). Signaling status with luxury goods: The role of brand prominence. *Journal of Marketing, 74*(4), 15–30.
5. Schindler, R. M., & Chandrashekaran, R. (2004). Influence of price endings on price recall: A by-digit analysis. *The Journal of Product and Brand Management, 13*(7), 514–524. https://doi.org/10.1108/10610420410568453
6. Kahneman, D., & Tversky, A. (2013). Prospect theory: An analysis of decision under risk. In *Handbook of the fundamentals of financial decision making: Part I* (pp. 99–127). World Scientific.

CHAPTER 10

PERSONALITY AND VOICE

DOI: 10.4324/9781003336693-12

Personality traits are those flavor notes that make your favorite pizza sauce different from mine.

Is it spicier? Sweeter? Thicker, as in: can you feel actual tomatoes? Is it thin and watery? Is there a wine, vodka, or vinegar profile in it? Are there subtle hints of *pecorino* or *parmigiano*? Was it slow-cooked for hours where flavors are deep or does it feel like tomatoes were just cut from somebody's garden? Does it give oregano, thyme, basil, or laurel?

Personality makes a dent in our memory because, in a world of too much, too in-your-face, too quickly, only the remarkable is remembered.

True: companies are legal entities. Brands represent companies.

Also true: *companies are built by people for people. Brands represent these people.*

Quirks, style, peculiarities, and oddities matter. There is a place for humane nuance in brand strategy – a central one.

BRAND PERSONALITY DIMENSIONS

Brand personality, as conceptualized by Aaker[1], refers to the human-like attributes that are associated with a brand, giving it a unique identity. Aaker pinpointed five primary dimensions of brand personality: sincerity, excitement, competence, sophistication, and ruggedness.

Sincerity encompasses brands that exude an authentic, truthful, and wholesome aura. Warmth, a focus on family, and genuine emotions are traits commonly linked with such brands. *Dove*, for example, advocates for self-worth, natural

Brand Personality Framework

JENNIFER AAKER

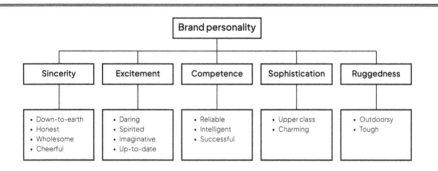

FIGURE 10.1: Dimensions of brand personality

allure, and genuineness, embodying sincerity through its marketing campaigns.

Excitement captures brands that are daring, vivacious, and full of spirit. They often captivate consumers who are thrill-seekers and crave novelty, adventure, and transformation. *Red Bull*, a purveyor of energy drinks, fosters an intrepid and adrenaline-charged lifestyle, supporting extreme sports events and unparalleled experiences.

Competence points to dependable, astute, and triumphant brands. Expertise, credibility, and effectiveness are among the traits that define such brands. Celebrated for its enduring and dependable vehicles, *Toyota* manifests competence through its dedication to quality and customer contentment.

Sophistication encompasses elegant, alluring, and polished brands. They often attract consumers in search of opulence, distinction, and elevated social standing. With its graceful, high-fashion, and timeless charm, *Chanel* radiates sophistication and refinement.

Ruggedness is associated with robustness, endurance, and an adventurous or outdoorsy disposition. These brands often appeal to consumers who value sturdiness and grit. Symbolizing ruggedness with its off-road prowess and resilient design, *Jeep* caters to adventurous consumers.

Aside from defining these dimensions, Aaker created a scale to characterize brands based on their most dominant personality traits. This scale, for use at managerial level, is described below.

TABLE 10.1: Brand personality scale

Scale name	Brand Personality Scale		
Author	Aaker 1997		
Type of scale	Five-point Likert		
Anchors	From "Not at all descriptive" (1) to "Extremely descriptive" (5)		
Scoring	Items within each dimension/factor can be added for a total score		
Dimensions	**5 factors/dimensions:** Sincerity, Excitement, Competence, Sophistication, Ruggedness **15 facets:** Down-to-earth, Honest, Wholesome, Cheerful, Daring, Spirited, Imaginative, Up-to-date, Reliable, Intelligent, Successful, Upper Class, Charming, Outdoorsy, Tough		
Items	Traits	Facet Name	Factor Name
	Down-to-earth	**Down-to-earth**	
	Family-oriented		
	Small-town		
	Honest	**Honest**	**Sincerity**
	Sincere		
	Real		
	Wholesome	**Wholesome**	
	Original		
	Cheerful	**Cheerful**	
	Sentimental		
	Friendly		

(Continued)

TABLE 10.1: (Continued)

Items	Traits	Facet Name	Factor Name
	Daring		
	Trendy	Daring	
	Exciting		
	Spirited		
	Cool	Spirited	Excitement
	Young		
	Imaginative	Imaginative	
	Unique		
	Up-to-date		
	Independent	Up-to-date	
	Contemporary		
	Reliable		
	Hard working	Reliable	
	Secure		
	Intelligent		
	Technical	Intelligent	Competence
	Corporate		
	Successful		
	Leader	Successful	
	Confident		
	Upper class		
	Glamorous	Upper class	
	Good-looking		Sophistication
	Charming		
	Feminine	Charming	
	Smooth		
	Outdoorsy		
	Masculine	Outdoorsy	
	Western		Ruggedness
	Tough	Tough	
	Rugged		

Another way to dive deeper into a brand's personality is through profiles known as **archetypes.** In these constructs, various personality traits come together to shape a distinctive mental image that is reminiscent of characters we've come to recognize as archetypical in society—hence the use of the term *archetypes.*

BRAND ARCHETYPES

A brand archetype encapsulates a universally discernible character or motif that symbolizes facets of human nature and conduct. Stemming from Carl Jung's theories and further popularized by Margaret Mark and Carol S. Pearson in their book *The Hero and the Outlaw*[2], these archetypes assist businesses in forging captivating, coherent, and emotionally evocative brand personas.

Much like Aaker's personality facets and dimensions, archetypes help represent a brand's distinctive identity. Unlike loose dimensions, an archetype consolidates multiple traits into a single narrative figure that brands can lean on for storytelling and communication purposes. Leaning on an archetype facilitates:

- Establishing the brand's fundamental values and purpose
- Steering the brand's narrative and communication
- Intensifying emotional bonds with the target demographic
- Boosting brand distinction and recognition
- Ensuring uniformity throughout all marketing channels

FIGURE 10.2: Brand archetypes

The 12 brand archetypes described by Mark and Pearson include:

The innocent

Symbolizing purity, virtue, and hope, brands exhibiting this archetype often tap into yearnings for simplicity and fond memories.

Coca-Cola's "Open Happiness" campaign perfectly encapsulates the innocent archetype by promoting a sense of joy, positivity, and togetherness. Coca-Cola's messaging frequently evokes nostalgia and encourages consumers to find simple pleasure in life's moments.

FIGURE 10.3: Coca Cola's "Open Happiness" campaign

The explorer

Representing the quest for liberty, exploration, and self-realization, these brands motivate individuals to escape limitations and embrace novel experiences.

Land Rover's "Above and Beyond" campaign embodies the explorer archetype, showcasing the brand's commitment to adventure, discovery, and pushing boundaries. Land Rover encourages customers to explore new terrains and challenge themselves, emphasizing the brand's off-road capabilities and rugged durability.

The sage

Emphasizing knowledge, acumen, and comprehension, sage brands typically offer expert guidance or niche information to support customers' well-informed choices.

Google's "Year in Search" campaign demonstrates the Sage archetype by highlighting the pursuit of knowledge and understanding. This annual campaign showcases trending searches, emphasizing the brand's role in answering questions and providing information to help individuals make informed decisions.

The hero

Championing bravery, resilience, and fortitude, heroic brands frequently portray themselves as advocates for a cause or catalysts for positive transformation.

Nike's memorable *Just Do It* campaign epitomizes the hero archetype by emphasizing determination, perseverance, and self-improvement. Nike inspires customers to overcome

FIGURE 10.4: Nike's Just Do It campaign

challenges and achieve their goals, positioning the brand as a catalyst for personal growth and empowerment.

The outlaw

Defying convention and bending rules, outlaw brands cater to those seeking defiance, disruption, or a sense of personal empowerment.

Harley-Davidson's "Screw It, Let's Ride" motto exemplifies the outlaw archetype by embracing a rebellious, rule-breaking spirit. Harley-Davidson encourages riders to defy conventions and assert their individuality, fostering a sense of freedom and personal empowerment.

The magician

Centered on metamorphosis, ingenuity, and wish fulfillment, Magician brands often pledge astonishing solutions or life-altering encounters.

Apple's *Think Different* campaign embodies the magician archetype by promoting innovation, creativity, and transformative experiences. This iconic campaign honored visionaries and challenged customers to embrace their own unique potential, positioning Apple as a brand that makes the impossible possible.

FIGURE 10.5: Apple's think different campaign

The regular guy/gal

Exemplifying relatability, genuineness, and a down-to-earth demeanor, these brands strive to foster a sense of community and rapport among consumers.

Walmart's iconic "Save Money, Live Better" positioning represents the regular guy/gal archetype by emphasizing relatability, affordability, and practicality. Walmart connects with everyday consumers by offering a wide range of products at low prices, promoting a sense of community and shared values.

The lover

Focusing on ardor, romance, and lavishness, lover brands frequently satisfy cravings for intimacy, delight, or sensory experiences.

The "Love Every Body" campaign by Victoria's Secret showcases the lover archetype by celebrating sensuality, self-love, and indulgence. Victoria's Secret encourages women to embrace their beauty and desire for intimate, luxurious experiences, evoking passion and romance.

The jester

Highlighting amusement, wit, and lightheartedness, jester brands aim to entertain, captivate, and enable customers to savor life.

Old Spice's "The Man Your Man Could Smell Like" campaign highlights the jester archetype by using humor, wit, and playfulness to entertain and amuse audiences. This memorable campaign engaged customers with its light-hearted, tongue-in-cheek approach, demonstrating the brand's commitment to making personal care enjoyable.

The caregiver

Concentrating on care, safeguarding, and empathy, caregiver brands typically offer solace, reassurance, or aid to those requiring support.

Volvo's "Vision 2020" campaign embodies the caregiver archetype by focusing on safety, protection, and well-being. Volvo's ambitious goal of ensuring no fatalities or serious injuries in their new cars showcased the brand's dedication to nurturing and safeguarding its customers.

The creator

Valuing self-expression, distinctiveness, and foresight, creator brands often inspire customers to innovate, craft, and establish an enduring impact.

LEGO's "Rebuild the World" campaign exemplifies the creator archetype by inspiring imagination, innovation, and self-expression. LEGO encourages individuals to explore their creativity and construct their own unique masterpieces, fostering a legacy of inventive play.

The ruler

Manifesting authority, leadership, and dominance, ruler brands usually entice those who crave stability, command, or opulence.

Mercedes-Benz and its longstanding "The Best or Nothing" campaign represents the ruler archetype by showcasing luxury, power, and prestige. Mercedes-Benz positions itself as a symbol of success and sophistication, appealing to consumers who desire the highest standards of quality and performance.

FIGURE 10.6: Mercedes:
The Best or Nothing
campaign

BRAND VOICE

Why does it matter that brands have a voice? When we reach customers, we do so within an environment of mistrust.

We are the organization, they are the individual. The presumed power dynamics are obvious.

A distinct voice and range of tones can surface the genuine humanity of every brand's builders: the people behind the product. In doing so, they reduce the sense of power distance, establishing enough proximity to relate.

Brand voice is an amalgamation of linguistic nuances, subtleties, and quirks that "sound like us":

- Signature expressions of emotion
- Vernacular or slang words
- Insider terms specific to our field of action
- Cultural references we've acquired from our context
- Filler words we use in natural language

Brand Voices

Adventurous	Classy	Disciplined	Futuristic	Kind	Obstinate	Rebellious	Sociable
Affectionate	Clean	Discreet	Generous	Knowledgeable	Old-fashioned	Refined	Solemn
Agile	Clever	Disruptive	Gentle	Laid-back	Optimistic	Reliable	Sophisticated
Agreeable	Coherent	Dramatic	Grumpy	Liberal	Outgoing	Religious	Soulful
Alert	Compassionate	Eager	Handsome	Lively	Outspoken	Reserved	Stable
Altruistic	Competent	Easy-going	Happy	Local	Passionate	Resolute	Strong
Ambitious	Competitive	Eccentric	Hard-working	Logical	Paternal	Resourceful	Studious
Analytical	Confident	Efficient	Helpful	Loud	Patient	Respectful	Subtle
Argumentative	Conservative	Emotional	Hip	Loyal	Patriotic	Responsible	Systematic
Artistic	Consistent	Empathetic	Humble	Masculine	Peaceful	Restless	Tactful
Assertive	Controlling	Energetic	Idealistic	Maternal	Pensive	Rowdy	Talented
Astute	Cooperative	Enterprising	Impetuous	Mature	Picky	Safe	Thoughtful
Balanced	Courageous	Enthusiastic	Impulsive	Methodical	Playful	Sarcastic	Tidy
Brave	Crafty	Exuberant	Incisive	Meticulous	Polite	Sassy	Traditional
Calm	Crazy	Fashionable	Independent	Mischievous	Popular	Scientific	Trustworthy
Candid	Creative	Fearless	Indiscreet	Modern	Practical	Sensitive	Unassuming
Capable	Critical	Feminine	Ingenious	Modest	Precise	Serene	Unconventional
Careless	Curious	Fervent	Innocent	Motivated	Proactive	Serious	Urban
Caring	Deep	Fiery	Innovative	Mysterious	Proficient	Sexy	Versatile
Cautious	Defiant	Flashy	Insightful	Natural	Profound	Sharp	Warm-hearted
Charismatic	Delicate	Flirtatious	Inspiring	Naughty	Proud	Silly	Watchful
Charming	Determined	Formal	Intellectual	Neat	Provincial	Sincere	Wealthy
Chatty	Devoted	Frank	Interesting	Nostalgic	Prudent	Sloppy	Wise
Chic	Diligent	Friendly	Joyful	Nosy	Punctual	Smart	Witty
Child-like	Diplomatic	Funny	Keen	Nurturing	Reassuring	Snobby	Young

FIGURE 10.7: Brand voices

Defining voice and tones

How does the brand's voice come to life across channels? A helpful way to present a unified voice is to create an inventory of touchpoints where the brand's voice must come to life. In Chapter 19, we will review how to create a comprehensive brand journey map; in the meantime, here is a set of touchpoints you can think of as opportunities to express brand voice internally and externally:

TABLE 10.2: Brand voice touchpoints

Public-facing Brand voice	Customer-facing Brand voice	Team-facing Brand voice
Company website and landing pages	Call to action	Employee handbooks
Social channels	Navigation	Onboarding process
Emails	Promotion	Success/error
Ads	Education	
Sales collateral	Success/error	
Press releases	Apology/regret	
Careers page and job sites	Reassurance/support	

Tone Development
WORKSHEET

Interested	Grateful	Confused	Funny
Regretful	Hopeful	Sad	Happy
Serene	Reassuring	Surprised	Excited

FIGURE 10.8: Tone development exercise

As you think strategically about these touchpoints, consider the range of occasion-based tones the brand should put forward. How does this brand sound when it is expressing interest, hope, serenity, surprise, or confusion?

NOTES

1. Aaker, J. L. (1997). Dimensions of Brand Personality. *Journal of Marketing Research, 34*(3), 347–356. https://doi.org/10.2307/3151897
2. Mark, M., & Pearson, C. S. (2001). *The Hero and the Outlaw: Building Extraordinary Brands Through the Power of Archetypes.* McGraw Hill Professional.

SECTION 2

SYMBOLS

DOI: 10.4324/9781003336693-13

INTRODUCTION

We rely on symbols to communicate ideas we hold dear. In Levy's* words, we are indeed "consuming symbols" for reasons that far transcend the utilitarian. The self-brand relationship we explored in Chapter 5 hinges on multiple brand touchpoints. Every interaction we have with a brand is a new opportunity to reinforce or dilute our associations, making brand positioning an ongoing project.

The sensory identity of a brand, as perceived through our senses and accumulating impressions of it, defines and improves many of these touchpoints. It is a strong messenger of the value a certain brand adds and the values it stands for. Design is instrumental in shaping these symbols our senses will perceive as representative of the brand.

Connecting the brand story elements we reviewed in the previous section, we'll gain a deeper understanding of design choices as enablers of this story.

Throughout this section, we will explore the implications of various design choices in bringing a brand to life. We will start with a broad overview of sensory branding, learning how to construct a Brandverse. Then, we will dive deeper into the field of visual perception, as well as specific components that make up a brand's visual identity. The following chapters will look into shapes, layout, type, color, imagery, and applications as effective devices to express brands.

---

* Levy, S. J. (1959). Symbols for sale. Harvard Business Review, 37(4), 117–124.

CHAPTER 11

THE BRANDVERSE

DOI: 10.4324/9781003336693-14

INTRODUCING THE BRANDVERSE

When a brand extends beyond its product's utilitarian benefits, it enters the realm of the symbolic.

In the previous section, we saw how strong **Brand Systems** are composed of layers that augment meaning in a brand's core value proposition, strengthening its resonance and memorability. A brand's core promise can be extended through an intentional value story, engaging sensory symbols, and an aligned communication strategy.

A **brand universe or Brandverse** is a unique set of sensory experiences that consumers can access and explore. It is built around a brand's story, values, and personality, capturing its essence in an immersive, multi-sensory way.

A **Brandverse** becomes a space that exists parallel to customers' daily lives and is perceived as an aspirational destination: a place to be. *A way to feel.*

Through the semiotic exercise that is creating a Brandverse, a brand is able to build a universe around a particular worldview, personality, and set of values.

Effective **brand symbols** engage the imagination. In many industry verticals, it simply isn't enough to present feature comparisons and extensive benefit lists: one must activate human beings' desires to create, belong, be inspired, express themselves, and aspire to more. In every other industry, where this level of innovation isn't already the norm, a brand can use this approach as a point of differentiation and disruption.

We are not programmed algorithms reacting to prompts. Human beings pursue aesthetic experiences that allow us to recognize and enjoy beauty—for the sake of beauty itself.

Throughout this chapter, we'll learn how to design a fictional, but fully immersible, brand universe that taps into our target customer's five senses.

ENGAGING THE SENSES

While most brand strategists and designers center their exercise around the sense of sight (logos, shapes, color, spacing, layouts, and type), there are infinite brand touchpoints one can strengthen with the remaining four senses.

Designing a Brandverse is not always about incorporating sensory experiences in their literal sense. Depending on the nature of your product, you may not be able to offer food, scents, or tactile experiences to your customers. However, you can draw inspiration from those kinds of sensory experiences to build a metaphorical space that indirectly incorporates them.

Multi-sensory brand experiences are not limited to physical spaces or packaging. For example, you could define "musk" as one of your brand's scents and convey that reference through photography. Seeing a candlelit scene can activate memories of scents, textures, and flavors without physically smelling anything. You could also decide on a set of sound effects that are linked to this brand universe you're building and incorporate them subtly into videos or online experiences.

Here are some ideas for teams building a Brandverse for an intangible product or service business:

- *Layer intentional textures into your graphics*
- *Develop brand photography by choosing venues that feel, smell, or look a certain way*

- *Be mindful of sound effects and genres and reinforce them in your brand videos*
- *Once you've selected sounds that align with your brand, express those in written and oral communications*

The more sensory cues you bring in, the richer your proposed universe becomes. Much like scriptwriters and film directors pulling references to design settings, we are constructing the scene our audiences will associate with this brand. As customers, these realistic Brandverses pull us in with associations that awaken all five senses.

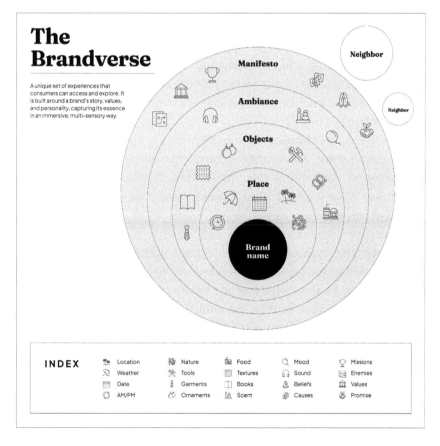

The Brandverse

A unique set of experiences that consumers can access and explore. It is built around a brand's story, values, and personality, capturing its essence in an immersive, multi-sensory way.

Neighbor

Neighbor

Manifesto
Ambiance
Objects
Place

Brand name

INDEX

Location	Nature	Food	Mood	Missions
Weather	Tools	Textures	Sound	Enemies
Date	Garments	Books	Beliefs	Values
AM/PM	Ornaments	Scent	Causes	Promise

FIGURE 11.1: The brandverse

BRANDVERSE: A FRAMEWORK

Creating this cultural entity that appeals to the senses and engages the imagination can feel daunting. To facilitate the process of designing a Brandverse, go through the following steps:

1. Define **place** in terms of location, time of day, weather, and historical period. When and where is this brand situated? Is it predominantly associated with mornings, afternoons, or nights? What is the weather like and does that affect how the brand is sensed?
2. Describe **objects** that can be found in this space. Consider items from material culture like books, tools, textures, food, garments, and ornaments that can represent and accentuate the brand. If you entered this brand's space, what kinds of props would you find?
3. Design an **ambiance** with specific details about its mood, scents, and sounds. What is the overarching emotion dominating this space? How is it aromatized? What sounds and audio can be perceived in the background?
4. Articulate the brand's purpose and values in a **manifesto**. The resulting perspective constitutes this entity's immaterial culture. This manifesto is a declaration of principles that helps root the Brandverse in deeper meanings that sway its target audiences. Refer to the figure below for some guiding statements that can help you shape your brand's manifesto.
5. Include **"neighbor"** brands that share spaces, objects, ambiances, or manifestos. They don't need to be competitors to serve as Brandverse references. You can find inspiring brands outside of your industry that have built similar sensory experiences.

YOUR BRAND
Manifesto

For others:

Our brand's name is _____
We are a _____
Every day we _____
We believe in _____
We work to / We're here to _____
We're interested in _____
We think that _____
Life is about _____
The key is to _____
We challenge _____

For yourself and/or your team:

Never forget _____
Free yourself from _____
Learn to _____
Focus on _____
Always choose to _____
Never stop _____
Take care of _____
Commit to _____
Create _____
Forget _____
Question _____
Let go _____
Fight against _____
Change _____
Be a _____
Enjoy _____

FIGURE 11.2: Brand manifesto

SENSORY BRANDING

Our senses are an essential device in brand communications. Over time, associating a specific sensation with a brand creates a mental pathway that strengthens recall and recognition.

Marketing researchers have long studied the impact of delivering messages leveraging more than one sense. **Dual coding,** the name given to this multi-sensory communication approach, has proven effective at strengthening brand memorability[1].

Dual coding theory proposes that information can be encoded in both visual and verbal forms, and suggests that when a brand is encountered through both of these forms, the information is held in memory more strongly[2].

When an organization uses a logo to represent its brand, it can also use language to explain and enhance the meaning of that logo. This dual coding of visual and verbal elements aids in brand recognition, as people are able to both form an overall impression of the brand and remember the individual elements that make up the brand[3]. This allows them to more easily recognize the brand in the future.

EMBODIED COGNITION

Why do these multi-sensorial brand experiences become so remarkably ingrained in memory? Part of the answer lies in a process known as **embodied cognition**. Essentially, human beings do not process and store information about the world in isolation. As we learn and reflect, we do so embedded in a specific physical environment that affects how we think.

Consider how specific spaces aid your reading, or how you're more prone to enjoying food in specific settings. **Embodied cognition** has immense implications for all kinds of learning, including consumer learning.

Many of us grew up within a paradigm where cognition, our ability to reason, was to remain untainted by feelings or emotions. This isolation is impossible. We take on the world as it presents to us, within the space we get to experience it, recalling our past experiences and values. These constructions shape brands.

As we elaborate increasingly complex thoughts about a brand, multisensory experiences can steer us. They can influence our perception of and relationship with this entity in ways that feature lists can't.

Sensory branding has the ability to evoke emotions and memories, create a sense of familiarity and connection, and allow us to explore a brand's story in a more holistic way. We'll review how these sensory Brandverses can be constructed below.

BUILDING A BRANDVERSE

Designing a brand's universe is, ultimately, about constructing a metaphorical, sensorial-defined place it calls its own. Having defined it, a brand welcomes its audiences into this space for a multi-sensory experience that strengthens their relationship.

Here are some questions to help you structure a Brandverse:

- *What time period are we on?*
- *Describe the location. Is it an indoor or outdoor setting?*
- *What season are we in? What is the weather like?*
- *What time is it: morning/afternoon/night?*
- *Describe the sounds in the background. Mention effects music, TV shows, movies, and any other piece of audio someone might perceive.*
- *Does this space feel luxurious or frugal?*
- *Is the overall ambiance formal or casual?*
- *Is there anything distinctive about the outfits people are wearing?*
- *How would you describe this scene's mood?*
- *What language is spoken here? Which local expressions are common?*

- *What does it smell like here?*
- *Are there any food or drinks present?*
- *Name any other props that fit naturally in this space:*
  - *Books*
  - *Signs*
  - *Posters*
  - *Electronics*
  - *Animals*
  - *Plants*
  - *Magazines*
  - *Newspapers*
- *What are some textures one can interact with here?*
- *Which brands do you see building similar universes and would fit right at home in yours?*
- *What are some rules people in this space live by?*

NOTES

1. Simmonds, L., Bogomolova, S., Kennedy, R., Nenycz-Thiel, M., & Bellman, S. (2020). A dual-process model of how incorporating audio-visual sensory cues in video advertising promotes active attention. *Psychology & Marketing, 37*(8), 1057–1067. https://doi.org/10.1002/mar.21357
2. Clark, J., & Paivio, A. (1991). Dual coding theory and education. *Educational Psychology Review, 3*, 149–210. https://doi.org/10.1007/BF01320076
3. Mitchell, A. A. (1986). The effect of verbal and visual components of advertisements on brand attitudes and attitude toward the advertisement. *Journal of Consumer Research, 13*(1), 12–24.

CHAPTER 12

VISUAL PERCEPTION

DOI: 10.4324/9781003336693-15

As you read these words, three sensitive cones in your eyes are weaving stems and serifs. Recognizing each letter's black figure against the page's white background. Hence, reading.

Your brain is now perceiving these words as related because they are part of a single paragraph and spaced against the next. Proximity tipped you off.

You were able to read "visual perception" above because your brain ignored the gaps to focus on the larger context. This text is feeling ordered and legible because there is a consistent baseline where all letterforms rest. *Alignment.*

All body copy in this book is set in a consistent font size and so are titles and that's how you are able to tell those two structures apart and pause as you read.

Cue by cue, shape by shape, 120 million light receptors in your eyes are sending signals to the brain. What feels instant is truly the work of millions of photoreceptors and a busy retina.

Not everything that meets the eye meets the mind. Our brains receive signals captured by our senses and select, organize, retrieve, interpret, and conclude. For all extents and purposes, everyday vision is a miracle.

Perception is selective by nature. Our eyes work as cameras that capture specific objects within our range. Our brain, the photographer, makes sense of the scene and interprets what exists. In short: the eyes *look*, but the brain *sees*.

And, as it turns out, **our eyes are pretty remarkable informants.**

Throughout this chapter, we will review some universal patterns in visual perception, how they translate into design composition principles, and how these influence brand graphics.

DEFINING VISUAL PERCEPTION

What exactly do we mean by visual perception? After studying the dynamics of perception from the lens of various disciplines, management researchers Kevin Sample, Henrik Hagtvedt, and S. Adam Brasel created an essential framework to understand how various layers of visual stimuli (piecemeal) are interpreted by our brains to shape the imagery we ultimately perceive[1].

Sample et al.'s definition of **visual perception** offers an integrative, marketing-relevant view of the process and we'll use it as a foundation throughout this chapter: "the processing and comprehension, via the eyes and the neural system, of holistic focal and non-focal stimuli, as comprised by their piecemeal components and as influenced by context and experience".

Synthesizing findings from perceptual psychology, engineering, graphic arts, architecture, and marketing literature, they propose that visual perception is an outcome of five layers or *piecemeal components* that our brain weaves to make sense of our surroundings:

1. Illuminance
2. Shape
3. Surface color
4. Materiality
5. Location

The authors argue that each of these components can be further broken down into facets, which are key in our discussion because they point to specific brand design choices one can make. These components and facets are summarized in the table below.

FACETS OF

Visual Perception

Construct	Definition	Symbolic Representation
Illuminance		
Brightness	The amount of lumens falling on a surface	
Illuminance Contrast	The differences that occur in the perception of light over space and/or time	
Directionality	The source of lighting in relation to the location of perception	
Illuminance Color	The temperature and hue of perceived light in an environment or projected onto an object	
Shape		
Dimensionality	An object's height, width, and/or length	
Unity	An object's perceived cohesiveness as allowed by segmentation and occlusion	
Demarcation	The outer boundary that contains the entirety of a perceived object	
Shape Contrast	The deviation of a perceived object from context or consumer experience	
Surface Color		
Hue	The facet of a perceived color that allows for classification as red, yellow, blue, or any mixture of these	
Saturation	The degree of deviation of a perceived hue from a gray of the same lightness	
Lightness	A surface color's range from black to white	
Materiality		
Visual Texture	The apparent consistency of a perceived object's surface	
Reflectance	An object's propensity to produce an image of the surrounding context on its surface	
Opacity	The lack of transparency in an object's surface	
Fluorescence	The propensity of an object's surface to emit light through reflection or internal lightning	
Location		
Positioning	The placement of a figure within the ground or in relation to another object	
Orientation	The angle of perception of an object	
Spacing	The distance between an intended focal object and additional information	
Movement	A change in the location of an object	

FIGURE 12.1: Components of visual perception

Illuminance, shape, surface color, materiality, and location can all be designed to convey a specific brand personality and identity.

Illuminance refers to the amount of light that is reflected or emitted from an object, which plays a critical role in how we perceive color and contrast[2].

As an example, you can choose to use brand photography that is dimly lit, building a darker, moodier ambiance that conveys a sense of mystery through reduced brightness and contrast (both facets of illuminance).

Another example of illuminance can be seen in how the brightness of a product can affect its perceived size. Bright objects tend to appear larger than dark objects, even if they are the same size[3].

Shape is another key component of visual perception, as it helps individuals recognize and distinguish different objects from one another. Studies have shown that humans are able to recognize objects even when they are presented in different orientations or sizes[4].

When it comes to shape, a brand can choose to use non-balanced demarcation shapes to emphasize a certain organic, free-flowing character.

Surface color refers to the color that is visible on the surface of an object, which can greatly impact how it is perceived by individuals. For instance, research has found that warm colors, such as red and orange, tend to evoke feelings of excitement and enthusiasm, while cooler colors, such as blue and green, tend to have a more calming effect[5].

The use of color in branding and marketing can also influence consumer behavior. For example, the color blue is often used in financial institutions because it is associated with trust and reliability. Brands might choose, for example, to leverage highly saturated, bright colors to exude a vibrant energy.

Surface color is one of the most influential design choices a brand strategist can make, warranting a separate chapter to dive deeper into its impact.

Materiality refers to the physical properties of an object, such as its texture, weight, and perceived quality. The materiality of an object can greatly impact how it is perceived by individuals, as it can evoke different emotions and associations. Materiality gives us a sense of a brand's textural value even if we can tangibly experience it.

For example, a product that is made of high-quality materials, such as leather or metal, can be perceived as more luxurious and upscale, while products made of plastic or other cheap materials may be perceived as low-quality or inexpensive.

Many brands leverage reduced opacity to create an ethereal, transparent feel that points to lightness and modernity. Visual texture can also point to aesthetic age, becoming a powerful cue for brands establishing themselves as vintage.

Finally, **location** is a vital component of visual perception, as it provides context information and helps individuals understand the relationship between different objects in their perceptual field. Location points to a brand object's relationship to its surroundings.

As an example, brands will often establish specific spacing rules around their logo to preserve a set amount of breathing room when displayed in context. Similarly, the location of an advertisement within a magazine or on a webpage can also impact its effectiveness in capturing the attention of viewers.

Up next, we will explore this idea of inter-object relationships and how it impacts brand assets through one of the most influential design theories of all time: *Gestalt*.

RECOGNIZING PATTERNS: GESTALT PRINCIPLES

We just saw how piecemeal components can inform our perception of individual objects. Let us now turn our attention to how multiple objects interact when perceived in relation to each other.

On a more practical level, Gestalt principles provide an explanation for how we interpret relationships, hierarchy, and grouping based on what is presented to us. These principles have deep implications for design composition: describing how laying out elements in relation to each other can dramatically affect our understanding.

We cannot possibly influence human perception with our designs if we don't understand the driving forces behind them. Creating effective brand graphics requires more than just selecting attractive colors, shapes, and textures—the piecemeal visual components and facets we just reviewed. It requires an understanding of how human beings perceive visual stimuli and how to leverage these perceptions to create effective designs.

This is where Gestalt psychology comes into play. The principles of **Gestalt,** a term used to describe the "effect of the whole", help us understand how humans perceive visual stimuli and how we can use these behavioral patterns to create visually appealing and effective designs that evoke the desired emotional response in our audience.

Throughout this section, we will explore how the principles of Gestalt psychology can be applied to brand design, reviewing examples of everyday branding activities that demonstrate each principle, and discuss how brand managers can leverage these principles to create effective brand graphics.

FIRST: A BIT OF HISTORY

The word Gestalt represents a unified pattern, figure, form, or structure. Gestalt Psychology, which began in Germany in the early 1900s, aims to understand the mechanisms at play in this interpretation: how our minds perceive whole things rather than their individual parts.

In 1912 psychologist Max Wertheimer published a paper titled "Experimental Studies of the Perception of Movement"[6], widely regarded as the first key event in the history of Gestalt psychology[7]. In it, Wertheimer explored the concept of apparent motion and introduced the phi phenomenon, a visual illusion in which multiple stationary stimuli are perceived as a single moving stimulus.

Later on, in 1923, Wertheimer would publish "Laws of Organization in Perceptual Forms", which consolidated the visual principles many associate with Gestalt today: proximity, similarity, closure, continuity, and figure-ground.

Max Wertheimer, Wolfgang Kohler, and Kurt Koffka continued to develop Gestalt theory's impact on visual perception. The main idea being that, during perception, we are exposed to a wide range of signals at once. As a way of organizing them, and to avoid being thrown into a state of disarray, we visualize our surroundings as unitary forms or groups.

The primary focus of Gestalt psychologists and designers for decades to come will be how we decide that some objects "go together".

COMMONLY APPLIED GESTALT PRINCIPLES

Take a moment to analyze how your mind automatically perceives the face of someone you know well. Although this specific face is made up of the same core features as every other human being's (nose, ears, eyes, etc) you will interpret its wholeness as belonging to and representing a single person you're acquainted with.

Gestalt psychology focuses on what your mind is doing here: *making sense of individual features as a unified, identifiable whole.*

Gestalt principles can help you create a strong brand identity that resonates with your customers and helps you stand out in a crowded marketplace. There are several Gestalt principles of perception, but the most commonly cited ones are proximity, similarity, closure, continuity, and figure-ground. However, some sources may include additional principles such as common fate, symmetry, and past experience.

In what follows, we'll combine the ideas proposed by Max Wertheimer[8], Stephen Palmer[9] as well as other contemporary Gestalt theorists. Let's review some of the most widely applied principles and how brand managers can put them into practice.

FIGURE 12.2: Gestalt proximity principle

Proximity

The eye perceives elements as belonging to the same group if they are placed close together[10]. For instance, proper kerning helps the eye distinguish between letters in individual words. It is sometimes difficult to determine when one word ends and when the next begins when there are excessive spaces between letters. In the examples below, notice how "proximity" is easier to read when letters are more closely placed (kerned) in relation to each other.

Consider the website of a travel brand that offers multiple destination options. By grouping the destination options together, the brand creates a visual hierarchy that makes it easier for customers to navigate the website. Similarly, a makeup brand may group together category-related products, such as skincare, to help customers navigate their offerings more easily.

Similarity

This principle suggests that objects that share visual characteristics are perceived as a group[11].

If elements look like each other, we consider them to belong to the same group. Color, size, orientation, texture, and font

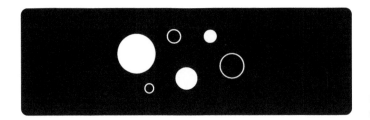

FIGURE 12.3: Gestalt
similarity principle

can all be used to trigger the principle of similarity. Creating a differentiated type hierarchy, for example, can help readers distinguish between captions, headlines, and body copy when reading a document. Your eye assumes headings set in a specific font size are titles and "reads" them as separators breaking up blocks of text.

In the image below, the similar-colored circles are not seen as individual objects, but rather as a separate group from those with a transparent filling. Our mind interprets their color as a signal of similarity and relatedness. As an example, this principle can come to life when certain button styles are applied across a website to indicate there's a call to action.

Closure

The principle of closure explains why we can still make sense of incomplete images. The problem-solvers we are, our minds tend to complete objects or shapes we encounter—or at least attempt the challenge. Unifying loose ends in this way helps us recognize patterns and make sense of the world around us.

The dotted circle below, for example, is still very much perceived as a circle. This principle lends itself well to creative, negative space-inspired logos where customers construct part

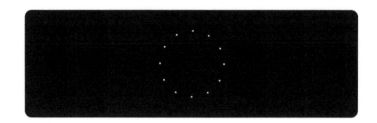

FIGURE 12.4: Gestalt closure principle

of the symbol in their minds. Consider the iconic FedEx logo with its "secret" arrow or NBC's not-so-hidden peacock.

Continuity

We tend to perceive elements arranged on a line or curve as more related to each other than those falling outside of a pattern. We're attracted by the sense of continuity and are guided by lines to look in a certain direction. Disruption and open paths affect our sense of relatedness between objects.

Continuity explains why designers preserve a baseline in typography: your eye is identifying these letterforms as part of unified sentences because they rest on a continuous line. Scattered letters would be harder to read and associate as part of single words. **Which of the two texts below are you finding easier to read?**

FIGURE 12.5: Gestalt continuity principle

Figure-ground

Our minds instinctively identify certain elements as being in the foreground (figures) and others as part of the background (ground). The figure-ground principle explains how we go about deciding which elements in a design are perceived as figures and which as grounds. This ability to discern what is closest to us (figure) is instrumental from a survival perspective: we're innately equipped to identify immediate dangers.

In brand design, we can leverage figure/ground relationships to create visual hierarchy, focus, and emphasis. As you read this, you're most likely identifying white (paper) as the background and these black forms (letters) as the figures to interpret. The "figure" is the focus, while the "ground" is the background that recedes behind the figure.

Symmetry

This Gestalt principle suggests that symmetrical elements are perceived as one unit by viewers. In our mind's search for organization and balance, we perceive symmetrical images as a collective whole and tend to prefer them.

When people encounter visual stimuli that have asymmetrical elements, they will try to group those elements in a way that creates a sense of balance and order. Symmetry can generate a feeling of harmony and stability, which enhances the overall perceptual experience.

In brand design, we rely on symmetrical layouts to create a sense of balance and harmony and leverage asymmetry to intentionally create visual tension and interest.

Common fate

Humans tend to perceive objects that move or change in a similar way as a group[12]. When we see several objects moving in the same direction and at the same speed, we're prone to perceive them as a collective, even if the individual elements are separate.

For example, a flock of birds flying in the same direction or a school of fish swimming together can be perceived as a cohesive group, even though they are composed of many individual elements. This principle is related to the concept of motion perception and can play a significant role in how people interpret dynamic visual scenes.

*Consider how
these words feel
like they're moving
away from the rest,
towards the right
side of the page.*

DESIGN AWAY!

Whether through consistent visual elements, creative use of negative space, or dynamic design, leveraging Gestalt principles can help brand managers create strong and recognizable brand identities that resonate with customers. By understanding and applying these principles, we can create brand graphics that effectively communicate the brand's identity and reinforce messaging with intentionally laid-out visual cues.

NOTES

1. Sample, K. L., Henrik, H., & Adam, B. S. (2020). Components of visual perception in marketing contexts: A conceptual framework and review. *Journal of the Academy of Marketing Science, 48*(3), 405–421. https://doi.org/10.1007/s11747-019-00684-4

2. Gibson, J. J. (1950). *The perception of the visual world* (pp. xii, 242). Houghton Mifflin.

3. Rock, I. (1983). *The Logic of Perception.* Cambridge: MIT Press.

4. Uttal, W. R. (2014). *A Taxonomy of Visual Processes.* Psychology Press. https://doi.org/10.4324/9781315769271

5. Bellizzi, J. A., & Hite, R. E. (1992). Environmental color, consumer feelings, and purchase likelihood. *Psychology & Marketing, 9*(5), 347–363. https://doi.org/10.1002/mar.4220090502

6. Wertheimer, M. (1912). *Experimentelle Studien über das Sehen von Bewegung.* J.A. Barth.

7. Behrens, R. R. (1998). Art, Design and Gestalt Theory. *Leonardo, 31*(4), 299–303. https://doi.org/10.2307/1576669

8. Max Wertheimer & Lothar Spillmann. (2012). *On Perceived Motion and Figural Organization.* The MIT Press.

9. Palmer, S. E. (1999). *Vision Science: Photons to Phenomenology.* Cambridge, Mass. : MIT Press. http://archive.org/details/visionsciencepho0000palm

10. Lidwell, W., Holden, K., & Butler, J. (2010). Universal Principles of Design, Revised and Updated: 125 Ways to Enhance Usability, Influence Perception, Increase Appeal, Make Better Design Decisions, and Teach Through Design. Rockport Pub.

11. Wagemans, J., Elder, J. H., Kubovy, M., Palmer, S. E., Peterson, M. A., Singh, M., & von der Heydt, R. (2012). A century of Gestalt psychology in visual perception: I. Perceptual grouping and figure-ground organization. *Psychological Bulletin, 138*(6), 1172–1217. https://doi.org/10.1037/a0029333

12. Koffka K. (1935). *Principles Of Gestalt Psychology (1935).* http://archive.org/details/in.ernet.dli.2015.7888

CHAPTER 13

LOGO DESIGN

DOI: 10.4324/9781003336693-16

It was the early twentieth century when linguist Ferdinand de Saussure made it his mission to study the life of signs within society, a science he called semiology (from semeion "sign" in Greek).

Saussure was curious about what constituted signs and the laws that govern them. Noting that what something genuinely *means* is separate from the way it is *labeled*, he proposed the notions of the *signifier* and *signified* as essential components of all signs[1].

A *signifier* is a form taken by the sign while *signified* refers to the concept our mind holds about it. Represented by signifiers, signs capture meanings known as "the signified".

Consider the red traffic light, an emblematic symbol of order and safety in our fast-paced world. This simple yet powerful signifier represents a call to halt, urging us to be mindful of others and the space we share on the road. The red light, as a sign, embodies the collective understanding that stopping is necessary to ensure the smooth flow of traffic and protect the lives of our fellow travelers. It is a reminder of the delicate balance between individual autonomy and communal responsibility, a lesson that transcends the context of traffic management and permeates various aspects of our lives.

Logos, as we've come to denominate the marks brands conduct trade under, are essentially **signifiers.**

In fact, the Greek word *logos* stands for meaning or reason. When brands design logos, they are creating signifiers that capture deeper meaning. When choosing shapes, colors, and layouts for these marks, we are constructing signs where form and function are equally important. Through form, we're creating a repository of trust, affect, and goodwill. Logos become shorthand for the qualities and values brands stand for.

On a practical level, logos have been defined as graphic design used by a company, with or without its name, to identify itself or its products[2]. For the purposes of this chapter, we will refer to the terms logo and brand mark interchangeably, defining them as design devices that signify and differentiate a brand's identity in the marketplace. We will look at the various kinds of logos further along, acquiring an expanded vocabulary to describe the specific types of marks we can create.

Semiology and semiotics give us a strong foundation to create logos mindfully[3]. Throughout this chapter, we will review tools from the fields of aesthetics, semiotics, and business to craft robust brand marks that blend form and function.

In the meantime, let's discuss some of the pillars sustaining strong logo designs.

WHY LOGOS MATTER

No discussion of brand strategy is complete without talking about logos, and yet, they are not—by any means—the extent of the branding conversation as so many believe.

When one understands the complex chain of symbols and symbolic touchpoints that impact brand perception, as well as customers' roles in redefining it, the relative importance of a single visual element is evident.

Yes, a logo can turn into a defining signifier for a brand. A powerful device to store associations in memory, and a shorthand for many of the brand's values and offerings. When strategically designed, it can differentiate the brand's offer in the marketplace. When seen in isolation, it can trigger recall and differentiated associations we've linked with the brand.

However, a logo isn't a replacement for customer-driven brand management. It isn't a hot fix for underlying brand relationship issues and it certainly won't lead to increasingly deep levels of attachment—not on its own. A logo is not a strategy.

That said, let's look at four valuable functions of a thoughtfully built logo:

Aesthetic pleasure: A logo's visual appeal can create positive associations and build an emotional connection with consumers. A well-designed logo can evoke emotions, such as happiness or satisfaction, leading to a more favorable perception of the brand. Take the Airbnb logo, for example, with its warm, inviting curves and a sense of belonging, it encapsulates the essence of the home-sharing experience.

Semiotic significance: Logos carry semiotic significance, meaning they act as symbols that convey a brand's identity and values. These visual representations help create meaning and establish a brand's position in the market. The Amazon logo, with its clever arrow pointing from A to Z and forming a smile, instantly communicates the company's mission to offer a vast array of products and a delightful customer experience.

Recall device: Logos serve as effective recall devices, aiding consumers in remembering and recognizing a brand. A memorable logo can facilitate faster recognition and retrieval of brand information from memory. The McDonald's golden arches, for example, are an instantly recognizable symbol that evokes associations with fast food and a consistent dining experience, helping consumers quickly recall the brand even in cluttered environments.

Business impact: A well-designed logo can enhance brand equity, generate awareness, and even affect consumers' willingness to pay a premium price for the brand's products or services. For example, the Coca-Cola logo, with its distinctive script and red color, has become synonymous with the brand, contributing to its high brand value and global recognition.

TYPES OF LOGOS

Not all logos are created equal. These essential brand marks can lean on different proportions of text and iconography to convey the desired identity. Consultant Alina Wheeler classified logos into five distinctive categories, ranging from the purely text-based to image-based graphics[4]:

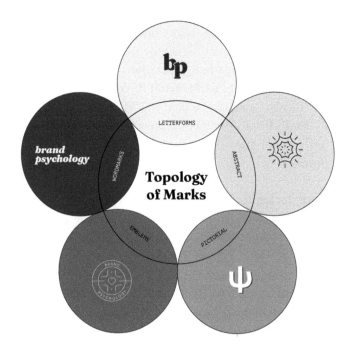

FIGURE 13.1: Types of logos

Wordmarks, also known as logotypes, are logo designs that utilize the entire name of a company or organization. These logos often use unique typography to make the brand name instantly recognizable. Three notable examples of wordmarks are Google, Coca-Cola, and FedEx.

Letterform logos, sometimes referred to as monograms or lettermarks, consist of one or more letters that represent a company's name. These designs are often more simplistic than wordmarks, but still convey a strong brand identity. Examples of well-known letterform logos include McDonald's "M", Chanel's interlocking "C"s, and Honda's "H".

Emblem logos are characterized by the incorporation of the brand name within a symbolic graphic element, often enclosed in a particular shape. Emblems are commonly used by organizations that wish to convey a sense of tradition or heritage. Examples of emblem logos are the Starbucks mermaid, Harley-Davidson's bar and shield, and the NFL's shield.

Pictorial marks, or brand symbols, are visually striking icons or images that represent a brand without the use of text. These logos often rely on strong visual associations to convey the brand's identity. Examples of famous pictorial marks include Apple's apple, Twitter's bird, and Nike's swoosh.

Abstract marks are geometric or non-representational shapes that symbolize a brand. These logos are versatile and can be particularly effective at conveying a brand's essence through unique visual language. Examples of abstract marks are Pepsi's circle, Adidas' three stripes, and BP's sunflower-like design.

THE PSYCHOLOGICAL IMPACT OF STRONG LOGOS

The semiotic devices they are, logos convey meanings far beyond their graphic qualities. Specifically, they support a mental mechanism known as **processing fluency**. Through processing fluency, we are able to interpret incoming information with ease[5]. Logos boost this processing fluency in at least two ways: helping us instantly associate the isolated image with a specific brand (perceptual fluency) and reminding us of the associations we've come to form around that brand (conceptual fluency).

Picture this: you're walking down the street and you come across a brand's logo that you've seen countless times before. Suddenly, your mind is filled with images, ideas, and associations related to that brand. You're actively experiencing perceptual and conceptual fluency.

Perceptual fluency is all about those visual features that get etched into our memories when we're exposed to a logo. The more we see it, the faster we can process and recognize it later on. One great example of this is the iconic Nike swoosh. Its simple design makes it easy for us to remember and identify the brand in a heartbeat.

On the other hand, **conceptual fluency** focuses on the meanings we attach to a logo, making it even more memorable and impactful. When we see a logo and associate it with certain qualities, we can't help but be reminded of those qualities when we see the logo again. Take the Starbucks mermaid, for instance. When we see her, we might be reminded of the aroma of coffee, the atmosphere of the stores, and the feeling that comes with sipping on our favorite beverage.

Logos enable brands to harness the power of perceptual and conceptual fluency, making a lasting impression on our minds.

THE ART AND SCIENCE OF DESIGNING STRONG LOGOS

Professors Pamela Henderson and Joseph A. Cote conducted one of the most thorough studies available on logo selection guidelines. They analyzed 195 logos on a set of design characteristics to get an understanding of how specific choices impact brand objectives like high recognition and high image perception. In doing so, they found that both of these objectives can be met through logo designs that are moderately high or highly **elaborate and natural.**

What do "elaborate" and "natural" mean in terms of visual choices? Let's look at each of the logo design characteristics they identified more closely:

While the design characteristics above are non-exhaustive, they provide a strong overview and objective language to make logo design decisions as a brand manager. Other findings suggest that logo shapes play a role in activating certain associations. **Circular and angular logo shapes** have been found to activate softness and hardness associations, respectively[6]. This tells us there's a relationship between a logo's visual facets and the attribute perceptions transferred to the brand it represents.

Asymmetry and symmetry are also effective ways to impact consumer perceptions of brand sophistication[7]. When brands take risks and play with asymmetry, it creates a sense of visual disruption that catches people's attention. The asymmetrical "Off the Wall" logo used by Vans is a bold visual that reflects the brand's focus on skateboarding and youth culture.

On the other hand, symmetry is often associated with beauty and harmony, and it can make brands appear more

Logo Design Factors

ADAPTED FROM HENDERSON AND COTE

High	Low	Factors
		### Natural
		Natural reflects the degree to which the design depicts commonly experienced objects. It is comprised of representative and organic.
		Representative and its opposite endpoint, abstract, capture the degree of realism in a design. Abstraction in a design occurs when the elements of an object are distilled down to the most typical features.
		Organic designs are those that are made up of natural shapes such as irregular curves. Alternatively, geometric designs tend to represent less natural, more synthetic-looking objects.
		### Harmony
		Harmony is a congruent pattern or arrangement of parts that combines symmetry and balance and captures good design from a Gestalt perspective.
		Symmetric designs appear as reflections along one or more axis. That is, the elements on one side of the axis are identical to the elements on the other side.
		Balance captures the notion that there is a center of suspension between two weights or portions of the design.
		### Elaborate
		Elaborate is not simply intricacy, but appears to capture the concept of design richness and the ability to use simple lines to capture the essence of something. It is comprised of complexity, activeness, and depth.
		Complexity can arise from many different design features such as irregularity in the arrangement of elements, increases in the number of elements, heterogeneity in the nature of elements, and how ornate the design is (Berlyne 1971; Schmitt, Simonson, and Marcus 1995).
		Active designs are those that give the impression of motion or flow. This flow is the basis for the design notion of rhythm (Bevlin 1989).
		Depth gives the appearance of perspective or a three-dimensional design (e.g., this design appears to have a raised triangular section that goes off into the distance).
		### Parallel
		Parallel designs contain multiple lines or elements that appear adjacent to each other.
		### Repetition
		Repetition of elements occurs when the parts of the design are similar or identical to one another. Conversely, identical elements that are simply part of a larger whole (e.g., needles on a pine tree) would be classified as one element (a pine).
		### Proportion
		Proportion is the relationship between the horizontal and vertical dimensions. One of the best known examples of proportion is the golden section.
		### Round
		Round designs are made of primarily curved lines and circular elements.

FIGURE 13.2: Logo design guidelines

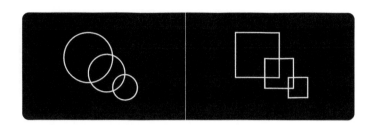

FIGURE 13.3: Circular and
angular logos

FIGURE 13.4: Vans "Off
the Wall"

sophisticated and prestigious. The symmetrical design of the
BMW logo conveys the brand's precision and luxury.

A logo's visual orientation can also convey messages about
brand performance. Upward (vs. downward) diagonals have
been found to get significantly higher ratings for success and
growth[8]. Upward diagonal direction can convey greater activity and effort than downward diagonals, given their underlying associations with ascending and descending motion.

A brand's choice of **metaphors** can also strengthen its viv-
idness, ability to differentiate itself, and consumer preference.
In comparison to human or non-metaphoric forms in brand
marks, animal-based metaphors have been found to impact

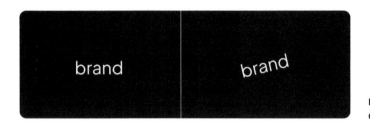

FIGURE 13.5: Upward diagonals in logo design

choice[9]. Unsurprisingly, visual metaphors also play an essential role in communicating a brand's cultural heritage. For instance, Asian-themed brand logos have been found to increase the perception of **cultural authenticity** and willingness to try the brand among consumers in a Western market[10].

How logos are framed can also make a perceptual difference. Understood as physical boundaries surrounding a logo, **frames** can be seen as protecting or confining depending on a customer's perceived level of risk[11]. When customers perceive a high level of risk at the moment of purchase, their inner need for security will guide their interpretation of a logo's frame as a protective device. Because this is consistent with their intent at the time, the frame has a positive effect on purchase intent. On the other hand, when their perceived risk is low, they may perceive the same frame as confining, negatively affecting purchase intent.

Let this be a reminder that logo perceptions are also consistent with human beings' **active needs and states.** Beyond aesthetic determinations, they are signifiers that interact with the interpretant's motives to acquire meaning. A meaning that is, by definition, subjective.

The extent to which customers can sensibly react to a logo is also mediated by aspects of their **personality**. When customers believe in a predetermined fate on a personal level, hence tend to be fatalists, they're less likely to feel any control over a brand's impact[12]. They may not be interested in interpreting symbols like a logo to abstract any meaningful effect to their lives, already determined by fate. On the other hand, people with more superstitious personalities are prone to interpreting and valuing a logo's deeper meanings.

THE IMPORTANCE OF CONSISTENCY AND CONGRUENCE

While making aesthetic changes can be visually stimulating, there's evidence in support of maintaining some level of brand consistency over time–especially as it relates to logos[13]. Simply put, the more consistent your brand's aesthetic design is, the easier it is for customers to transfer positive feelings about your brand to the products you offer.

Take the example of Herman Miller, a furniture manufacturer known for its pared-down, mid-century-inspired designs. The company's logo features a simple, sans-serif typography in black and white, which is carried through to its advertising and packaging. Herman Miller's products also feature consistent design elements, such as sleek lines, minimalist forms, and the use of high-quality materials, helping to reinforce the brand's identity and make it easily recognizable to customers. The unified feel of these visual elements helps customers carry over brand perceptions and feelings into individual products.

Aside from consistency, congruence between logos and other brand elements has been found to impact emotional engagement[14]. When brand components are visually aligned, hence congruent, customers may find it easier to interpret their association (processing fluency) and experience more positive emotions towards the set as a whole.

FIGURE 13.6: Herman Miller

Doyle and Bottomley found that certain fonts may be interpreted as appropriate for a brand when there is alignment between their associations, leading to perceptions of congruity and, ultimately, brand choice[15]. We will review the intricacies of typeface selection in Chapter 14.

NOTES

1. De Saussure, F. (2011). *Course in general linguistics*. Columbia University Press.
2. Henderson, P. W., & Cote, J. A. (1998). Guidelines for selecting or modifying logos. *Journal of Marketing*, *62*(2), 14–30. https://doi.org/10.2307/1252158
3. Berger, A. (2010). *The Objects of Affection: Semiotics and Consumer Culture*. Springer.
   Berger, A. A. (2019). Logos and visual signifiers. In A. A. Berger (Ed.), *Brands and Cultural Analysis* (pp. 75–85). Springer International Publishing. https://doi.org/10.1007/978-3-030-24709-6_8
   Mick, D. G. (1986). Consumer research and semiotics: Exploring the morphology of signs, symbols, and significance. *Journal of Consumer Research*, *13*(2), 196–213.

4. Wheeler, A. (2006). *Designing Brand Identity: A Complete Guide to Creating, Building and Maintaining Strong Brands.* Hoboken, N.J.: John Wiley. http://archive.org/details/designingbrandid0000whee

5. Alter, A. L., & Oppenheimer, D. M. (2009). Uniting the tribes of fluency to form a metacognitive nation. *Personality and Social Psychology Review, 13*(3), 219–235.
   Janiszewski, C., & Meyvis, T. (2001). Effects of brand logo complexity, repetition, and spacing on processing fluency and judgment. *Journal of Consumer Research, 28*(1), 18–32.

6. Jiang, Y., Gorn, G. J., Galli, M., & Chattopadhyay, A. (2016). Does your company have the right logo? How and why circular- and angular-logo shapes influence brand attribute judgments. *Journal of Consumer Research, 42*(5), 709–726.

7. Bajaj, A., & Bond, S. (2014). Effects of design symmetry on perceptions of brand personality. *ACR North American Advances, NA–42.* https://www.acrwebsite.org/volumes/1018034/volumes/v42/NA-42

8. Schlosser, A. E., Rikhi, R. R., & Dagogo-Jack, S. W. (2016). The ups and downs of visual orientation: The effects of diagonal orientation on product judgment. *Journal of Consumer Psychology, 26*(4), 496–509. https://doi.org/10.1016/j.jcps.2016.01.003

9. Noble, C. H., Bing, M. N., & Bogoviyeva, E. (2013). The Effects of Brand Metaphors as Design Innovation: A Test of Congruency Hypotheses. *Journal of Product Innovation Management, 30*(S1), 126–141. https://doi.org/10.1111/jpim.12067

10. Southworth, S. S., & Ha-Brookshire, J. (2016). The impact of cultural authenticity on brand uniqueness and willingness to try: The case of Chinese brands and US consumers. *Asia Pacific Journal of Marketing and Logistics, 28*(4), 724–742. https://doi.org/10.1108/APJML-11-2015-0174

11. Fajardo, T. M., Zhang, J., & Tsiros, M. (2016). The contingent nature of the symbolic associations of visual design elements: The case of brand logo frames. *Journal of Consumer Research, 43*(4), 549–566.

12. Jian Wang, Y., Hernandez, M. D., Minor, M. S., & Wei, J. (2012). Superstitious beliefs in consumer evaluation of brand logos: Implications for corporate branding strategy. *European Journal of Marketing, 46*(5), 712–732.

13. Liu, Y., Li, K. J., Chen, H. (Allan), & Balachander, S. (2017). The Effects of Products' Aesthetic Design on Demand and Marketing-Mix Effectiveness: The Role of Segment Prototypicality and Brand Consistency. *Journal of Marketing, 81*(1), 83–102. https://doi.org/10.1509/jm.15.0315

14. Salgado-montejo, A., Velasco, C., Olier, J. S., Alvarado, J., & Spence, C. (2014). Love for logos: Evaluating the congruency between brand symbols and typefaces and their relation to emotional words. *Journal of Brand Management, 21*(7–8), 635–649. https://doi.org/10.1057/bm.2014.29

15. Doyle, J. R., & Bottomley, P. A. (2006). Dressed for the Occasion: Font-Product Congruity in the Perception of Logotype. *Journal of Consumer Psychology, 16*(2), 112–123.

CHAPTER 14

TYPOGRAPHY

DOI: 10.4324/9781003336693-17

In 1984, a nervous young entrepreneur turned on a 9-inch black and white display to demo the original Macintosh. Immediately visible was a rare selection of text styles named after cities: Chicago, Monaco, Toronto, Geneva. Were these options? Could they be? Would we all now decide how our words display on pages?

Yes, on all three counts. This was the origin of an era of democratization of typography. Since then, type designers haven't stopped creating: there are now hundreds of thousands of commercially available typefaces.

As the options get virtually limitless, well-founded judgment becomes essential. With great power comes great responsibility.

Typesetting, a discipline reserved to a select few, had now entered the larger creative vocabulary. Today, we can all edit a font's spacing, line height, and weight within almost any basic office app. Type education became a practical topic for everyone, not just those who devoted their careers to it.

The psychological implications of type have been put to the test once and again. We now have a robust body of research to inform brand design decisions: one that combines findings from fields as diverse as vision, psychology, architecture, human–computer interaction, and education.

This chapter will present some of the most meaningful insights we have around typography and its role in brand psychology. We will cover the impact of spacing, weight, letterform, layout, and typeface selection decisions on brand messaging.

When you hear a word, it activates a mental image of the concept behind it. In semiotic terms, the signifier triggers a set of signified meanings. When you read a word, aside

FIGURE 14.1: Typographic effect

from consulting memory to retrieve these encapsulated ideas, you are perceiving visual cues as signals. What you know, what you see, and what you interpret based on both are allowing you to form a snap judgment of the words in front of you.

This is why the two expressions in the figure above feel different:

Typography is an incredibly powerful design element that adds layers of shape, opacity, and color to the texts we perceive. In doing so, it augments what is said, reinforcing desired associations or downplaying those we wish to mute.

It all comes down to purposely-built letterforms: type designers make conscious decisions about weight, shape, and spacing to convey a specific style. Those of us using fonts, then, can mindfully typeset our text to enhance readability, sophistication, hierarchy, and contrast.

TYPE ANATOMY

Unless you're close to the world of typography, you may not have noticed the small, intricate, seemingly subtle decisions involved in designing a single letterform. Because these shapes impact logo and brand messaging interpretations, an essential awareness of their structure is helpful.

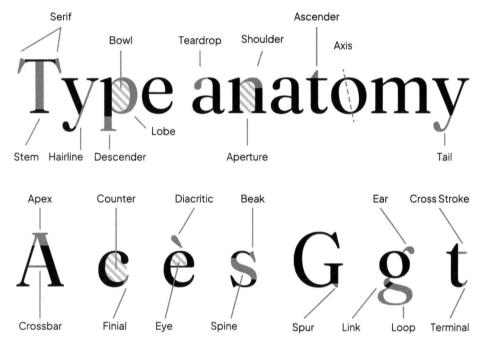

FIGURE 14.2: Type anatomy

Let's review the essential components of typography:

1. **Aperture:** The open area in a letterform
2. **Apex:** The top point of a letterform
3. **Ascender:** The part of a letterform that extends above the x-height
4. **Axis:** The imaginary line that runs through the middle of a letterform
5. **Beak:** The extended stroke in certain letterforms
6. **Bowl:** The curved or round part of a letterform
7. **Counter:** The enclosed space in a letterform
8. **Cross-stroke:** The horizontal or diagonal stroke that intersects the stem in certain letterforms

9. **Crossbar:** The horizontal stroke in certain letterforms
10. **Descender:** The part of a letterform that extends below the baseline
11. **Diacritic:** A mark or symbol that indicates a specific pronunciation or accent, which can suggest cultural or linguistic associations.
12. **Ear:** The small stroke or flourish that extends from the upper part of a letterform,
13. **Eye:** The enclosed oval or circular shape in a letterform
14. **Finial:** The finishing stroke or flourish at the end of a letterform
15. **Hairline:** The finest stroke found in a letterform
16. **Link:** The stroke that connects the bowl and stem in certain letterforms
17. **Lobe:** A rounded projection in a letterform
18. **Loop:** The curved or circular stroke in certain letterforms
19. **Shoulder:** The curved part of a letterform that connects the stem and the serif
20. **Spine:** The main curved or diagonal stroke in a letterform
21. **Spur:** A small projection or serif in a letterform
22. **Stem:** The main vertical or diagonal stroke in a letterform
23. **Tail:** The downward extension of a letterform
24. **Teardrop:** The curved, teardrop-shaped stroke ends in certain letterforms
25. **Terminal:** The end of a stroke in a letterform

Given the unique features designers can imprint on any given font, It should come as no surprise that some brands actually commission custom fonts for their exclusive use. In 2018, Airbnb commissioned the custom font "Airbnb Cereal" to improve the readability and consistency of its brand across different languages and regions[1]. Netflix also worked with typographic foundry Dalton Maag to develop their custom "Netflix Sans" in 2018[2].

TYPE CLASSIFICATION

Having seen the range of design options available in crafting a single letter, it's also important to understand that typefaces (font families) come in a variety of styles that are the result of typography's historical evolution.

Within the context of the typography discussion, it's important to understand the fundamental difference between serif and sans serif typefaces. **Serifs** are small lines or flourishes that are added to the ends of strokes in typefaces. They are designed to help guide the reader's eye across the page and improve legibility. Serifs are often used in printed materials like books and newspapers because they are easier to read in long passages of text.

Sans-serif typefaces, on the other hand, do not have these small lines or flourishes. They have a more modern, clean look and are often used in digital media and advertising. Sans-serif typefaces are also believed to be easier to read on smaller screens because they have a simpler design.

Design researcher Ellen Lupton created one of the most widely adopted frameworks for type classification[3]. Let's review an

FIGURE 14.3: Serifs vs. sans serifs

adaptation of her framework and some freely available examples from Google Fonts below.

- **Humanist or old-style:** These typefaces date back to the fifteenth and sixteenth centuries and are intended to evoke classical calligraphy. Humanist typefaces have a warm, organic feel with a slightly slanted axis and subtle variations in stroke width. They often feature a calligraphic influence with slightly curved or angled serifs. Sabon is a great example of a humanist typeface.
- **Transitional:** Introduced in the mid-eighteenth century, they feature sharper serifs and a more vertical axis than humanist typefaces. They have a more mechanical feel and

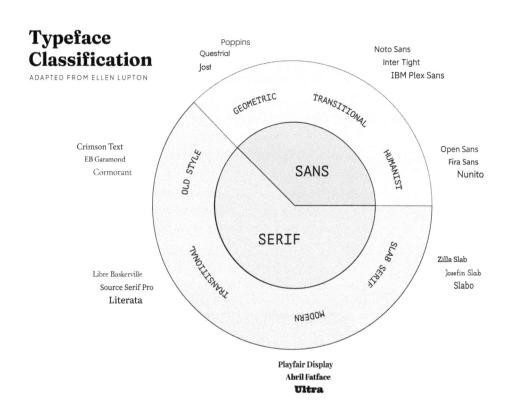

FIGURE 14.4: Typeface classification

the higher contrast between thick and thin strokes and sharp angles makes them easier to read in smaller sizes. Times New Roman is an example of a transitional typeface.

- **Modern:** Modern typefaces were designed in the late eighteenth and early nineteenth centuries and feature extremely thin, straight serifs, and a vertical axis with sharp contrast between thick and thin strokes. Modern typefaces have a very clean, geometric look that makes them ideal for display use. Bodoni is a great example of a modern typeface.

- **Egyptian or slab serif:** Originally used in advertising, these typefaces were introduced in the nineteenth century. They feature thick serifs known as slabs that are bold, eye-catching, and work well in large sizes. Rockwell is a well-known example of an Egyptian typeface.

- **Humanist sans-serif:** Sans-serif typefaces became popular in the twentieth century, and humanist sans-serifs have a similar organic feel to humanist serif typefaces. They have rounded terminals and an angled axis, with a slightly curved or angled stroke. Humanist sans-serif typefaces are often used for body text, as they are easy to read and have a warmer feel than other sans-serifs. Gill Sans is a classic humanist sans-serif typeface.

- **Transitional sans-serif:** These typefaces are similar to transitional serif typefaces, with a more mechanical feel compared to humanist sans-serifs. They have a uniform, upright character and are often used for display purposes. Helvetica, one of the most widely used typefaces in the world, is a great example of a transitional sans-serif typeface.

- **Geometric sans-serif:** As the name suggests, these typefaces are built around geometric forms. They are simple, clean, and often feature perfect circles and triangles. Geometric sans-serifs are popular in modern design, as they have a clean, minimalistic look. Futura is an example of a geometric sans-serif typeface.

THE PSYCHOLOGICAL IMPACT OF TYPOGRAPHY

Naturally, typographic decisions have been an area of interest for marketers, psychologists, and designers. We have learned plenty about how font and typesetting choices affect consumer psychology and decisions. Let's turn our attention to some of these findings.

When we look at a brand's name or marketing copy, the typefaces in which they're set are sending concurrent messages of their own. Typefaces convey their own special meanings, distinct from the content of the written words they clothe[4]. When we use them in marketing messages, they act as standalone elements that speak volumes to consumers.

People pick up on these subtle cues and store them in memory, associating them with their existing knowledge about the brand. The font used to display a brand's name affects how its personality dimensions are perceived (see Chapter 10 for a full overview). Grohmann et al. identified some guidelines for font selection based on the personality dimension one desires to highlight[5]:

- To emphasize sincerity, select typefaces that are high in harmony, natural, and flourish
- To create excitement, increase elaborate, natural, and flourish
- To elicit ruggedness, increase weight and flourish
- To convey sophistication, increase harmony, natural, and flourish, but decrease weight
- To evoke competence, increase harmony, natural, weight, and flourish, but reduce elaborate

Typefaces create distinct impressions that add to our overall perception of the brand they embody. Based on our reaction

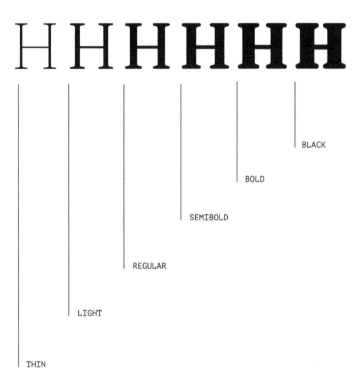

FIGURE 14.5: Font weights

to typefaces, they can be described as pleasing, engaging, reassuring, or prominent[6]. Their design characteristics can either enhance or reduce these effects. For example, typefaces that are natural and harmonious have been found to feel more pleasing. Bolder weights make typefaces come off as more prominent and more elaborate fonts are perceived as unsettling.

In a related study, Henderson et al. provide six **dimensions of typeface design** that can help steer the decision-making process for brand managers:

- Elaborateness (e.g. ornate, depth, and distinctive)
- Harmony (e.g. balance, smoothness, and symmetry)

- Naturalness (e.g. active, curved, and organic)
- Flourish (e.g. serifs and ascenders)
- Weight (e.g. heavy and fat)
- Compression (e.g. condensed)

Beyond typeface selection, there are important design decisions that can affect perception. **Typesetting** is the intentional configuration of spacing, sizing, and other character settings to enhance typeface readability and convey desired impressions.

Regarding the impact of **upper and lowercase** characters, studies have found that consumers feel closer to lowercase wordmarks[7]. This sense of closeness is due to reduced psychological distance: the idea that we've been exposed to lowercase characters so much that we feel a certain familiarity.

Lowercase wordmarks have been perceived as friendlier, while their uppercase counterparts exude higher strength and authority. Another study found that subjects were able to judge sentences and identify words correctly faster when they were set in lowercase[8].

Although subject to much debate, **serif and sans serif typefaces** can also trigger different responses. One study found that serif typefaces were more closely associated with elegance and beauty while sans serifs conveyed power and vitality[9].

FIGURE 14.6: Upper vs. lowercase

FIGURE 14.7: Incomplete typefaces

Less controversial is the impact of letterform **roundness** on certain key brand associations. In a study of hedonic product advertising and packaging in China, Wang et al. found a significant effect of a typeface's curvature on consumers' preferences for these kinds of products[10]. The linkage between round shapes and indulgence, flow, and organic motion is likely related to this effect.

Brand designers can also choose to modify or stylize typefaces to add a unique character when building logos. Professor Henrik Hagtvedt found that **solid typefaces** contribute to a company's perceived trustworthiness, while incomplete ones hurt that impression[11]. On the other hand, these incomplete typefaces that "force" the eye to connect segments can come off as interesting and positively impact a company's perceived innovativeness.

NOTES

1. Airbnb. *Introducing Airbnb Cereal*. Airbnb.Design. Retrieved March 26, 2023, from https://airbnb.design/introducing-airbnb-cereal/
2. Brewer, J. (2018). *Netflix unveils Netflix Sans, a new custom typeface developed with Dalton Maag*. It's Nice That. Retrieved from https://www.itsnicethat.com/news/netflix-sans-typeface-dalton-maag-graphic-design-210318
3. Lupton, E. (2010). *Thinking with Type, 2nd Revised and Expanded Edition: A Critical Guide for Designers, Writers, Editors, & Students* (Expanded edition). Princeton Architectural Press.

4. Childers, T. L., & Jass, J. (2002). All dressed up with something to say: Effects of typeface semantic associations on brand perceptions and consumer memory. *Journal of Consumer Psychology*, *12*(2), 93–106.

5. Grohmann, B., Giese, J. L., & Parkman, I. D. (2013). Using type font characteristics to communicate brand personality of new brands. *Journal of Brand Management*, *20*, 389–403.

6. Henderson, P. W., Giese, J. L., & Cote, J. A. (2004). Impression management using typeface design. *Journal of Marketing, 68*(4), 60–72.

7. Xu, X., Chen, R., & Liu, M. W. (2017). The effects of uppercase and lowercase wordmarks on brand perceptions. *Marketing Letters*, *28*(3), 449–460. https://doi.org/10.1007/s11002-016-9415-0

8. Laham, N., & Leth-Steensen, C. (2023). The effect of letter-case type on the semantic processing of words and sentences during attentive and mind-wandering states. *Language and Cognition, 15*(1), 106–130. https://doi.org/10.1017/langcog.2022.28

9. Tantillo, J., Di Lorenzo-Aiss, J., & Mathisen, R. E. (1995). Quantifying Perceived Differences in Type Styles: An Exploratory Study. *Psychology & Marketing, 12*(5), 447.

10. Wang, L., Yu, Y., & Li, O. (2020). The typeface curvature effect: The role of typeface curvature in increasing preference toward hedonic products. *Psychology & Marketing, 37*(8), 1118–1137.

11. Hagtvedt, H. (2011). The impact of incomplete typeface logos on perceptions of the firm. *Journal of Marketing, 75*(4), 86–93.

CHAPTER 15

COLOR

DOI: 10.4324/9781003336693-18

A newborn opens her eyes. There is black, white, and shades of gray. Suddenly, here's a darker shape getting bigger as your parent's voice gets louder. For the first couple of days, there she is: just making her way in this odd world of loosely defined objects and shadows.

A week has gone by and she starts reacting to red. This bright primary hue catches a sensitive retina and developing nerves. All of a sudden, there they are: shades of green. Skin, lips, faces ... living things.

Five months later, a full spectrum of colors has become visible, lighting up a world she's about to discover. As soon as our chromatic possibilities open up, so does an additional sign to connect with our growing set of ideas: a blue sky, a green tree, neon yellow highway signs.

You may not think of your ability to discern color as a skill. But it is undoubtedly one of the most exceptional functions of our body.

If you are able to see a range of colors, please understand the gift you possess.

Various factors including gender, age, and disability impact how human beings are able to discern varying amounts of colors within this wide range. Your role as a brand strategist is to remain aware of this fundamental truth and serve customers in the most inclusive manner possible.

Throughout this chapter, we will explore the meaning of color for brand strategy: how it amplifies our visual perception, the associations each hue triggers, and how to construct mindful combinations based on the ideas we're trying to evoke.

THE ART AND SCIENCE OF COLOR

The last 20 years of research have been enlightening for color. We now know that color can generate a cognitive, emotional, and even physical response in human beings. Color is also personal: people feel attached towards hues that affirm aspects of their self or allow the expression of them in social contexts.

Colors also help shape brand perceptions, becoming a clue we interpret in conjunction with the messaging we're exposed to. Consumers lean on commonly held color associations to attribute personality traits to brands[1]. As a cue, color can prime us to recognize a certain level of quality, which in turn informs our willingness to pay[2]. Aside from pricing signals, a color can point us to core product attributes like taste and ingredients, as well as benefits of usage[3].

We've also realized how color associations vary according to cultural contexts. As we explore color psychology findings further, it's important to underline that meanings aren't universal, but situated. For each study, there's a specific population being analyzed—one that has been exposed to relatively similar cultural conditioning. This principle holds true for every other brand design and strategy decision you make; brand managers must remain acutely aware of contextual differences in the markets they serve. More on the idea of brand globalization in Chapter 20.

If you are developing brands for an Asian, South American, European, or North American market, be mindful about the generalizations made around color. For every study you review, make a note of the region in which it was made to better inform your decisions.

That said, let's review some of the most relevant scientific findings around color psychology of the last few decades.

COLOR ASSOCIATIONS

Color influences us in such a natural way that we can't always articulate its impact, but it's there—silently shaping our experiences and swaying our emotions. Color has been found to shift perceptions of brand personality and amplify likeability and familiarity[4]. The findings you're about to read about come from researchers who have unearthed powerful behavioral and attitudinal triggers in certain hues.

Red, orange, and yellow have been found to evoke active emotions, the kind that get our hearts racing. On the flip side, passive emotions tend to make us feel more relaxed and subdued[5].

Red can make men perceive women as more attractive and desirable[6]. Yellow, with its bright disposition, is linked to happiness and excitement, reminiscent of warm summer days[7].

Blue is the epitome of tranquility, associated with low anxiety levels, calm, and comfort. Considering what we've just discussed about arousal and activation, it's no surprise that red stirs up more anxiety than blue, influencing how users perceive wait times. Gorn et al. found that users waiting for a download on a blue background perceived it as faster than those with a red background[8]. In a similar vein, Mehta and Zhu discovered that **red** can trigger avoidance motivation, improving performance on detail-oriented tasks, while blue boosts creativity[9].

Blue may also boost perceived competence and performance-related brand personality traits[10], while red brings out perceived excitement. In a separate study on color's impact, a brief glimpse of red was found to undermine intellectual performance[11]. Studies show more positive outcomes in blue retail environments, including increased purchases, reduced postponements, and a stronger desire to shop and browse[12]. It's no wonder that websites with blue hues and medium brightness or saturation consistently receive high aesthetic ratings[13].

Black, on the other hand, often comes across as rebellious and doesn't mingle well with words like tender, calm, or cheerful[14]. It can also emphasize a brand's perceived sophistication[15]. Research from the University of Illinois suggests that **yellow, white, and grey** lean towards weakness, while red and black exude strength[16].

Interestingly, **red** was found to enhance attractiveness through perceived sexual receptivity, while **black** did so through fashionableness[17]. Aaronson's classic study on color and affective stereotypes revealed intriguing associations: red, orange, and yellow with outgoing exuberance; red, yellow-green, and purple with hostility; and purple, gray, and black with asocial despondency[18].

Green, the color of nature's embrace, elicits positive emotions like relaxation and comfort[19]. In a study on brand personality and logo colors in fashion, blue logos exuded competence (confidence, corporate, reliability), while green logos projected ruggedness (outdoorsy, rugged, masculine)[20]. However, green-yellow was the outcast, linked to feelings of sickness and disgust due to its association with vomit. Also worth noting is that deviating from the colors that would be typical of a certain category has been found to attract attention, an especially interesting insight for brand launches[21].

Color also plays a role in how we perceive faces, with French researchers discovering that red backgrounds led to more negative face perceptions than green backgrounds, regardless of the gender of the person being viewed[22].

In the world of fashion, purple logos are the epitome of sophistication, exuding qualities like "feminine," "glamorous," and "charming"[23]. Many subjects in a study on the bio-psychological effects of color felt soothed by purple[24].

Brown, on the other hand, brings stability to the table. When asked to match brand qualities with colors, respondents linked stability with blue/brown, fun and energy with yellow, and excitement with red/purple[25].

COLOR'S MANY FACETS

As we saw in our review of visual perception facets, surface color doesn't act in isolation. Each color we see has a specific **hue, chroma, saturation, value, and opacity**, and can be transformed into a **tone, shade, or tint.** In today's world where brands must render equally on print, screens, and surfaces, the same color can also be defined using different languages: RGB, CMYK, Pantone, and HEX being the most widely used. So no: "red" isn't enough direction to build a brand system around – not anymore.

Color associations

- Attractiveness
- Sexual desire
- Arousal
- Excitement

- Arousal
- Excitement
- Fun

- Happiness
- Excitement
- Summer
- Arousal

- Calm
- Comfort
- Efficiency
- Low anxiety
- Competence

- Defiance
- Strength
- Fashionableness
- Despondency

- Relaxation
- Comfort
- Ruggedness
- Masculinity
- Positive face perception

- Sophistication
- Charm
- Glamour
- Femininity
- Calm

- Stability
- Formality

FIGURE 15.1: Color psychology

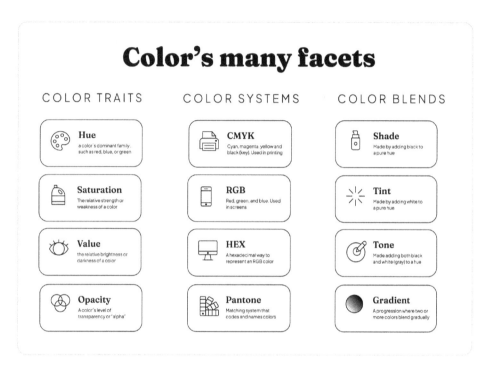

Color's many facets

COLOR TRAITS

Hue
a color's dominant family, such as red, blue, or green

Saturation
The relative strength or weakness of a color

Value
the relative brightness or darkness of a color

Opacity
A color's level of transparency or 'alpha'

COLOR SYSTEMS

CMYK
Cyan, magenta, yellow and black (key). Used in printing

RGB
Red, green, and blue. Used in screens

HEX
A hexadecimal way to represent an RGB color

Pantone
Matching system that codes and names colors

COLOR BLENDS

Shade
Made by adding black to a pure hue

Tint
Made by adding white to a pure hue

Tone
Made adding both black and white (gray) to a hue

Gradient
A progression where two or more colors blend gradually

FIGURE 15.2: Color Basics

Because so much of brand design involves being comfortable with a common language around color, let's review what each of these terms means and how you can increase or reduce them to achieve certain visual effects.

Hue refers to the dominant color family that a particular color belongs to, such as red, blue, or green. When it comes to hue, designers might select a signature color that embodies the brand's personality. Choosing an unconventional hue within the industry can differentiate a brand and create a lasting impression in consumers' minds.

Saturation is the purity or intensity of a color. When a color is saturated, it is as intense as possible, while when it is less saturated, it appears muted or washed out. Saturation represents the vibrancy and vivacity of a brand's colors, making them truly come alive. Opt for highly saturated colors to convey energy and excitement, or lean on a more muted palette to create an aura of sophistication or calmness. Also expressed as "Chroma".

Value is the relative lightness or darkness of a color. Using different shades of a single hue in a design creates a sense of depth and hierarchy, ensuring that critical brand components take center stage. Also expressed as "Brightness".

Opacity is the degree to which a color allows light to pass through it, with higher opacity indicating a more solid or dense color, and lower opacity resulting in a more transparent appearance. It is common for brands to use various levels of opacity in their user interfaces to guide users' attention to key elements. Also expressed as "Alpha".

Aside from a color's inherent facets, we can also transform hues by adding white, black, or grey. These transformations are what we call tones, shades, and tints.

Tones are created by adding both black and white (gray) to a hue, resulting in a more subdued and complex version of the original color. Tones can be used to add sophistication and balance to a brand, making it appear more grounded and mature.

Shades, on the other hand, are derived by adding black to a hue, making it darker and more intense. Designers might utilize shades to evoke feelings of power, depth, or elegance. Shades can lend a sense of mystery and richness to brands.

Tints are achieved by adding white to a hue, creating a lighter, airier version of the original color. Brands may use tints to convey a sense of softness, openness, or approachability. By strategically incorporating tints, designers can craft a brand image that feels welcoming and gentle.

We can leverage a combination of tones, shades, and tints to create a cohesive color palette. By selecting a base hue and generating a range of tones, shades, and tints from it, we can create a toolkit with a wide spectrum of options. This is especially important for brand illustrations, where having a range of colors at our disposal facilitates depth and texture. This is also true for user interface palettes, where having an array of tints and shades can help signal different states, button types, and typographic hierarchies.

COLOR COMBINATIONS

Single colors can encapsulate meaning. However, color combinations play into each hue's associations and express entirely novel ideas. It is not an overstatement to say individual colors connote emotions, but a strong color palette can tell a story. While powerful in isolation, this symbolic character of color also interacts with other design elements to create specific mental images that coincide with our vision for the brand.

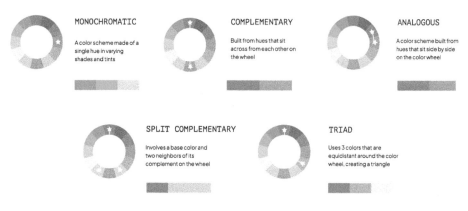

MONOCHROMATIC

A color scheme made of a single hue in varying shades and tints

COMPLEMENTARY

Built from hues that sit across from each other on the wheel

ANALOGOUS

A color scheme built from hues that sit side by side on the color wheel

SPLIT COMPLEMENTARY

Involves a base color and two neighbors of its complement on the wheel

TRIAD

Uses 3 colors that are equidistant around the color wheel, creating a triangle

FIGURE 15.3: Color combinations

When you take multiple colors' inherent qualities and mix them to convey a visual narrative, you're developing a brand palette. Basic color theory points us to different kinds of harmonies we can develop with two or more colors. Let's review what those combinations can look like.

- **Monochromatic:** As the name suggests, a monochromatic color scheme consists of a single hue in various shades, tints, and tones. This scheme creates harmony and unity within a design by employing a single color family. For example, a monochromatic blue color scheme might include navy, sky blue, and baby blue.
- **Complementary:** This color scheme is derived from hues that sit directly opposite each other on the color wheel. The high contrast between these colors generates visual interest and energy within a design. An example of a complementary color scheme would be the pairing of red and green, or blue and orange.
- **Split complementary:** This combination technique involves selecting a base color and pairing it with two neighboring colors of its complement on the color wheel. This scheme offers a balance of contrast and harmony, allowing for a visually stimulating yet cohesive design. For instance, a split complementary color scheme might involve yellow as the base color, paired with blue-violet and red-violet.
- **Analogous:** Crafted from hues that sit adjacently on the color wheel, an analogous color scheme exudes a sense of harmony and fluidity. This scheme often captures a specific mood or emotion, as the colors are closely related. An example of an analogous color scheme might include the serene combination of blue, blue-green, and green.
- **Triad:** This color scheme incorporates three colors that are equidistant from one another on the color wheel, forming a perfect triangle. The triadic combination strikes

a balance between contrast and harmony, creating a visually dynamic design. An example of a triad color scheme might involve the vibrant trio of red, blue, and yellow.

NOTES

1. Ridgway, J., & Myers, B. (2014). A study on brand personality: Consumers' perceptions of colours used in fashion brand logos. *International Journal of Fashion Design, Technology and Education, 7*(1), 50–57. https://doi.org/10.1080/17543266.2013.877987
2. Sliburyte, L., & Skeryte, I. (2014). What we know about consumers' color perception. *Procedia-Social and Behavioral Sciences, 156,* 468–472.
3. Kauppinen-Räisänen, H., & Luomala, H. T. (2010). Exploring consumers' product-specific colour meanings. *Qualitative Market Research: An International Journal, 13*(3), 287–308. https://doi.org/10.1108/13522751011053644
4. Labrecque, L. I., & Milne, G. R. (2012). Exciting red and competent blue: The importance of color in marketing. *Journal of the Academy of Marketing Science, 40*(5), 711–727. https://doi.org/10.1007/s11747-010-0245-y
5. Clarke, T., & Costall, A. (2008). The emotional connotations of color: A qualitative investigation. *Color Research & Application, 33*(5), 406–410. https://doi.org/10.1002/col.20435
6. Elliot, A. J., & Niesta, D. (2008). Romantic red: Red enhances men's attraction to women. *Journal of Personality and Social Psychology, 95*(5), 1150–1164. https://doi.org/10.1037/0022-3514.95.5.1150
7. Kaya, N., & Epps, H. H. (2004). Relationship between color and emotion: A study of college students. *College Student Journal, 38*(3), 396–405.
8. Gorn, G. J., Chattopadhyay, A., Sengupta, J., & Tripathi, S. (2004). Waiting for the web: How screen color affects time perception. *Journal of Marketing Research (JMR), 41*(2), 215–225.
9. Mehta, R., & Zhu, R. (Juliet). (2009). Blue or red? Exploring the effect of color on cognitive task performances. *Science, 323*(5918), 1226–1229. https://doi.org/10.1126/science.1169144
10. Labrecque, L. I., & Milne, G. R. (2012). Exciting red and competent blue: The importance of color in marketing. *Journal of the

Academy of Marketing Science, 40(5), 711–727. https://doi.org/10.1007/s11747-010-0245-y

11. Elliot, A. J., & Maier, M. A. (2007). Color and psychological functioning. *Current Directions in Psychological Science, 16*(5), 250–254.

12. Bellizzi, J. A., & Hite, R. E. (1992). Environmental color, consumer feelings, and purchase likelihood. *Psychology & Marketing, 9*(5), 347–363. https://doi.org/10.1002/mar.4220090502

13. Seckler, M., Opwis, K., & Tuch, A. N. (2015). Linking objective design factors with subjective aesthetics: An experimental study on how structure and color of websites affect the facets of users' visual aesthetic perception. *Computers in Human Behavior, 49*, 375–389. https://doi.org/10.1016/j.chb.2015.02.056

14. Murray, D. C., & Deabler, H. L. (1957). Colors and mood-tones. *Journal of Applied Psychology, 41*(5), 279–283. https://doi.org/10.1037/h0041425

15. Labrecque, L. I., & Milne, G. R. (2012). Exciting red and competent blue: The importance of color in marketing. *Journal of the Academy of Marketing Science, 40*(5), 711–727. https://doi.org/10.1007/s11747-010-0245-y

16. Adams, F. M., & Osgood, C. E. (1973). A Cross-cultural study of the affective meanings of color. *Journal of Cross-Cultural Psychology, 4*(2), 135–156. https://doi.org/10.1177/002202217300400201

17. Pazda, A. D., Elliot, A. J., & Greitemeyer, T. (2014). Perceived sexual receptivity and fashionableness: Separate paths linking red and black to perceived attractiveness. *Color Research & Application, 39*(2), 208–212. https://doi.org/10.1002/col.21804

18. Aaronson, B. S. (1970). Some affective stereotypes of color. *International Journal of Symbology.*

19. Kaya, N., & Epps, H. H. (2004). Relationship between color and emotion: A study of college students. *College Student Journal, 38*(3), 396–405.

20. Ridgway, J., & Myers, B. (2014). A study on brand personality: Consumers' perceptions of colours used in fashion brand logos. *International Journal of Fashion Design, Technology and Education, 7*(1), 50–57. https://doi.org/10.1080/17543266.2013.877987

21. Kauppinen-Räisänen, H., & Luomala, H. T. (2010). Exploring consumers' product-specific colour meanings. *Qualitative Market Research: An International Journal, 13*(3), 287–308. https://doi.org/10.1108/13522751011053644

22. Gil, S., & Le Bigot, L. (2015). Grounding context in face processing: Color, emotion, and gender. *Frontiers in Psychology, 6.* https://doi.org/10.3389/fpsyg.2015.00322

23. Ridgway, J., & Myers, B. (2014). A study on brand personality: Consumers' perceptions of colours used in fashion brand logos. *International Journal of Fashion Design, Technology and Education, 7*(1), 50–57. https://doi.org/10.1080/17543266.2013.877987

24. Kido, M. (2000). *Bio-psychological Effects of Color.* http://www. qigonginstitute.org/abstract/1938/bio-psychological-effects-of-color

25. Hynes, N. (2009). Colour and meaning in corporate logos: An empirical study. *Journal of Brand Management, 16*(8), 545–555. https://doi.org/10.1057/bm.2008.5

CHAPTER 16

APPLICATIONS, PACKAGING, AND SYSTEMS

DOI: 10.4324/9781003336693-19

A logo is one among the vast collection of symbols representing our brand's story. As we saw in Chapter 11, Brandverse, there's an ever-growing set of sensory signals at our disposal to convey brands' most fundamental values and desired associations.

BUILDING BLOCKS

When it comes to brand applications, there's an endless amount of physical and digital formats to think about. All executions, however, are based on a few strategic design decisions. Here are the building blocks, or core components, we typically rely on when developing brand applications:

- *Main logo and alternates*
- *Color palette*
- *Typography scheme*
- *Supporting imagery: iconography, photography, textures and patterns, illustrations (brand and technical)*
- *Motion principles*
- *Sound*
- *Scent*

We've covered logo, color, and typography development at length in previous chapters. To nurture our understanding of these building blocks, let's focus on supporting imagery, motion, sound, and scent next.

BRAND IMAGERY

Beyond logos, letterforms, and color, one can get a more comprehensive feel for a brand's essence through supporting graphics like photographs, icons, illustrations, textures, and patterns. These kinds of assets offer something isolated design components can't: *context*.

The story-driven beings we are, our minds seek these more complex symbols as challenges to be deciphered. We are drawn to the faces, scenes, and implicit narratives in great brand photography. We lean on technical illustrations to simplify what product instructions can't. Our minds reinforce the verbal with the iconographic. No matter how conditioned to screens, our eyes still crave imperfect textural cues. The grit, the tactile feel of something real—situated.

This is what brand imagery brings to the table: the possibilities of an engaged imagination.

Within the category of imagery, we have various kinds of graphics that range from the abstract to the realistic:

- Iconography
- Illustrations
- Patterns
- Textures
- Photography

WHY A BRAND IMAGE IS WORTH A THOUSAND WORDS

From a purely utilitarian perspective, visual imagery helps customers interpret information more efficiently than verbal elements. Townsend and Kahn found that there's a "visual preference heuristic" at play in consumers' selection process suggesting that they prefer visual to verbal depiction of information when making sense of a product assortment[1].

Images can transport customers to a specific Brandverse (see Chapter 11), offering an escape from mundane environments into a high-art experience. In a study with fashion advertisement imagery, Phillips et al. found that images with grotesque (or bizarre) instead of idealized (pretty) scenes can offer a superior narrative performance that immerses and transports customers, stimulating them intellectually.

In line with this insight, Jeong found that advertisements with visual metaphors may be more persuasive compared to advertisements with literal (non-metaphorical) images[2]. Part of the reason is metaphors offer more implicit persuasive arguments that we find ourselves working harder to decode; this additional investment in constructing meaning out of this image makes us, in turn, more prone to adopting its proposition.

DEFINING IMAGERY GUIDELINES

The sensory decisions involved in building a Brandverse (Chapter 11) are vital when defining brand imagery guidelines. The place, object, and ambiance layers, in particular, can help answer some of the essential questions around brand imagery:

- What is the general atmosphere like?
- Do we apply any color guidelines consistently? What are the levels of saturation and temperature in our images?
- For photography: are there depth of field, composition, and lighting guidelines?

- Which textures reinforce aspects of the brand's personality?
- For illustrations: how are strokes, shadows, and volume treated?
- What is the proportion of negative space used?
- What objects are commonly present in this Brandverse?
- What subjects do we depict and how, if any?
- What themes do we express and why?
- Which values do we reinforce in our choice of visuals and what do we stay away from?

MOTION PRINCIPLES

Still within the visual realm, a brand's approach to motion can convey important messages about its identity and the ideas it holds dear. The following considerations may come in handy when defining a brand's motion style:

- What kind of speed is evident in the brand's video content?
- What kinds of transitions are put in place, if any?
- If/when we rely on human voiceovers, what kind of tone do we look for?
- If/when we rely on soundtracks, what kind of moods and genres do we look for?
- How is text interwoven with visuals in brand video assets? How are subtitles and headings treated?
- Is there any specific colorization or filtering in place?
- What is the proportion of white space in video compositions?
- Is there a signature intro and outro for brand videos?
- Are there any animation guidelines?
- Are there any special effects we apply consistently?

AUDIOBRANDING

At the beginning of this section, we saw how a brand's sensory realm, its Brandverse, can turn into an aspirational destination for customers: a place to be. When brands engage more than one sense in their communications, they're appealing to various paths within our memory. **Audiobranding,** also known as sonic branding, is the use of signature sounds to express a brand's identity and capture customers' sense of hearing.

While audiobranding can comprise a full sound library, the **audio logo** is perhaps the central, most identifiable asset in this collection. An audio logo is a brand's audio signature or "identifier", fulfilling a powerful sonic mnemonic function tied to a visual logo[3].

Beyond this sonic signature, brands can design a range of audio assets in support of the associations they intend to strengthen. Audiobranding expert Karsten Killian summarized a list of asset types that can help us build an aural brand identity: sound logos, brand songs, jingles, brand soundscapes, and Brand themes[4].

- **Sound logo:** the sonic equivalent of a visual logo. It's a short, memorable sound that identifies a brand, and it can be made up of vocals, sound effects, or music.
- **Brand song:** The brand song is a longer piece of music that expresses the values and identity of the corporate brand. It often relies on vocals with understandable meaning and spans several minutes.
- **Jingle:** a melody created specifically for the brand that is shorter than a brand song; typically only a few seconds in length. It's meant to be easy to remember and helps consumers identify and remember the brand.

- **Brand soundscape:** a sonic ambiance created to represent the brand's character (see Brandverse in Chapter 11) by combining sound objects, sound textures, brand themes, and other acoustic traits of a brand.
- **Brand theme:** An extended piece of music that defines and samples the brand's aural identity. This is related to Jackson's idea of a *brand score*, which is an (often) internal reference piece that includes elements like vocal, instrumental, and ambient sounds[5].

In addition to the above, we can also leverage a specific brand voice and signature product sounds. A brand's voice is the vocal element used to communicate the brand's personality orally. It can be part of the audio logo or used in advertising creatives, and some brands use the same spokesperson's voice for years and across multiple channels[6].

Product sounds are audible parts of the product in use that become reminiscent of its identity and are widely recognized by consumers. Examples include the pop of a tube of Pringles.

Each piece of audio has a set of attributes that can enhance desired brand responses. Melzner and Raghubir found that timbral sound quality in audio logos (i.e., roughness/ smoothness) helps customers judge analog aspects of a brand's personality (i.e., ruggedness/sophistication)[7]. In a separate study on audio logo attributes, Bonde and Hansen found that pitch can be recognized more readily than rhythm and melodic distinctiveness assists logo and brand recognition[8].

While custom audio helps differentiate the brand's sonic fingerprint, there's also value in leveraging well-known music. Studies have shown that pairing brands with recognizable music can increase brand choice[9].

OLFACTIVE BRANDING

Like sound, scent is a powerful cue to reinforce brand associations. When designing a brandverse (Chapter 11), there are specific scents and aromas associated with the mental scenery we are building. Scent can convey seasons, eras, moods, and, in what is perhaps its primary survival function, danger. **Olfactive branding** aims to express a brand's identity leveraging the powerful sense of scent.

Bradford and Desrochers identified three distinct ways in which scent can be utilized in marketing strategies[10]:

1. The first type of scent, which we refer to as **"marketer scent"**, is a promotional tool used by marketers to enhance brand recognition and create an immersive customer experience. This sensory tactic is part of a specific promotional campaign, helping reinforce the brand's message.

2. The second type of scent, known as **"product scent"**, is the actual product itself. Perfumes, air fresheners, and scented candles are all examples of products that customers buy to use on themselves or in their homes to create a preferred scent. For instance, the perfume industry is built on the concept of creating unique and appealing fragrances that consumers want to wear as a form of self-expression.

3. The third and final type of scent is **"ambient scent"**, which is a general odor that is present in a retail environment and is not derived from a specific product. In this category, there are two types: objective and covert objective scents. Objective scents are used in a retail environment with the intention of affecting the attitudes and behavior of consumers. For instance, a grocery store might use the scent of freshly baked bread to

create a warm and inviting atmosphere. Covert objective scents, on the other hand, are infused to motivate an action or influence consumer behavior, but they are not openly acknowledged or displayed. These scents are below the consumer's threshold of consciousness, such as a subtle scent of citrus to encourage shoppers to make quick purchases in a store.

Signature scents can help us remember brands, the messages they've shared with us, and specific product attributes[11]. In one study, product scent was found to enhance memory for product information more effectively than ambient scent[12]. Used as a memory aid in this way, scent is even more effective when it is congruent with brand image vs. unrelated[13].

Aside from assisting memory, a pleasant scent can better prepare us to interpret incoming product information. Bone and Ellen found evidence that more pleasant scents led customers to experience a better mood, which in turn affected their evaluative responses to products[14].

For service brands, specifically, scent offers a powerful means of making offerings feel more tangible and differentiated[15]. Scent's impact transcends pleasantries: specific aromas can activate memories of certain emotions in customers, which in turn can connect those emotional states with the brand[16].

BRAND APPLICATIONS

Brand applications extend the building blocks we just reviewed and apply them to physical and digital brand assets that reach our end customers.

TABLE 16.1: Digital and physical brand applications

Digital Brand Applications *Intangible brand assets designed to be rendered on a screen*	Physical Brand Applications *tangible brand manifestations one can interact with in person*
• Digital collateral: whitepapers, proposals, ebooks • Digital advertising • Presentation styling • Social marketing graphics • Avatars & signatures • Web styles (layout and spacing, user interface components, interaction patterns, key user views & states, user experience guidelines)	• Print collateral: brochures, proposals, line sheets, flyers, proposals, reports • Print advertising • Packaging • Merchandising • Stationery: letterhead, business cards, stamps • Signage: outdoor and indoor • Uniforms

Also known as brand elements, **applications** are artifacts built by the brand to generate awareness, affinity, and desired behaviors.

Brand applications are digital and physical artifacts that communicate meaning. Well-designed, they become messengers of a brand's ethos and value. Signs that remind us of what it is we're getting out of this relationship.

Beautiful applications do not imply brand success very much like a show-stopping engagement ring can't guarantee happiness. In both cases, these artifacts stand as symbols that remind others who we are, what we're about, and what we're not.

As meaning devices, brand applications must be developed and deployed strategically. To be clear: *ordering 55 t-shirts with your logo, on a whim, because others do it, is not a strategy.*

When designing brand applications consider the following:

- How does this object or experience represent the brand?
- Is there anything about the way this is built that reinforces brand values? Is there anything that contradicts them?

- Knowing my customers' contexts, does this make sense for them to use?
- Is this object or experience consistent with the brand promise we make?
- What kinds of emotions does it trigger for customers upon interaction?
- What kinds of desired associations does it trigger?
- What kind of messaging, if any, do we need to project through this?

Once you've defined this, go ahead and order the t-shirts. And caps and mugs to top that too. The difference? You're now acutely aware of how this brand application is an effective token of meaning. It sends a message, stands for something, *matters*.

BRAND PACKAGING

While the typography and color effects we've reviewed also apply, there are scientific findings to learn from specifically around packaging design.

Color, in particular, can play a fundamental role in three key packaging functions: attention, aesthetics, and communication[17]. Studies also show that including product images in packaging might boost attitudes toward the package and improve beliefs about the brand[18].

Well-designed packaging can also turn into an aesthetically stimulating experience for customers, motivating desired behavioral effects. Reimann et al. found that attractive packages significantly boost consumers' choice responses and are selected over products with well-known brands in standardized packages, despite higher prices[19].

FIGURE 16.1: Brand packaging design

Overall package shape can also reinforce brand attributes and associations. In a study with milk dessert packaging, Ares and Deliza found that both package shape and color influenced people's expectations of product flavor[20]. For brands without a physical retail location, packaging is also a rare opportunity to engage customers through the senses of touch and scent. One study found that marketing materials can be more persuasive when the experience of touch, as in packaging, trigger an emotional response. This effect was strong in people who enjoy touch as a hedonic experience[21].

BRAND BOOKS AND STYLE GUIDES

Brand books or style guides serve as the ultimate source of truth for a brand's verbal and visual identity. They contain guidelines and constraints to maintain a cohesive presence

FIGURE 16.2: Brand book

over time, across channels. When updated consistently, they can create a powerful sense of alignment within teams.

Your brand is the story that customers recall when they think about you. When you capture that story in writing, your team can work together to uphold and safeguard those values consistently. There are multiple benefits to building and maintaining a thorough brand book:

- **Cohesion:** It keeps your brand's presence cohesive and harmonious.
- **Access:** It enables teams to use assets consistently. Collaborating across diverse functions becomes easier with a shared language.

- **Flexibility:** This ever-evolving system ensures that your team always has access to the most current and accurate information.
- **Speed:** Having essential building blocks at your fingertips makes everything easier to create. No need to reinvent the wheel when robust components can be repurposed.
- **Ethos:** Capturing your brand's core values inspires the team to cherish, defend, and expand upon them. This inner consistency is noticed and appreciated by your users.
- **Scalability:** Whether you're considering a brand extension or building a franchise, keeping a record of the brand's differentiators is key to scaling its identity.

It doesn't matter if you have the resources to build a multi-page, interactive brand book that feels like a bible or a simpler style guide. Distilled even further, you can also turn this tool into a quick brand-at-a-glance. The more succinct and accessible these principles are, the more naturally they'll become a part of your team's shared language.

We don't develop brand systems for *storage*, we design them for *appropriation*.

The effort to document a Brand System is a valuable exercise in synthesis: at the end of the day, what are the components that make this brand memorable?

Beyond symbols, brands may also choose to document elements of their story and strategy to facilitate understanding and appropriation. The most complex brand books include a complete overview of the brand's past, present, and future and are often used as a go-to repository of the brand's identity.

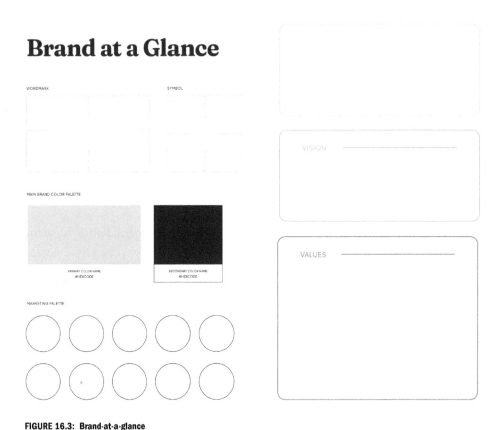

FIGURE 16.3: Brand-at-a-glance

To make this cohesion easier to maintain, you can document your Brand System and share it with everyone helping build it. This template will facilitate that process:

AN INTERNAL BRANDING RESOURCE

A thorough, well-documented brand system can help onboard new team members. It serves as a reference guide to understand the brand's past, present, and future perspectives[22].

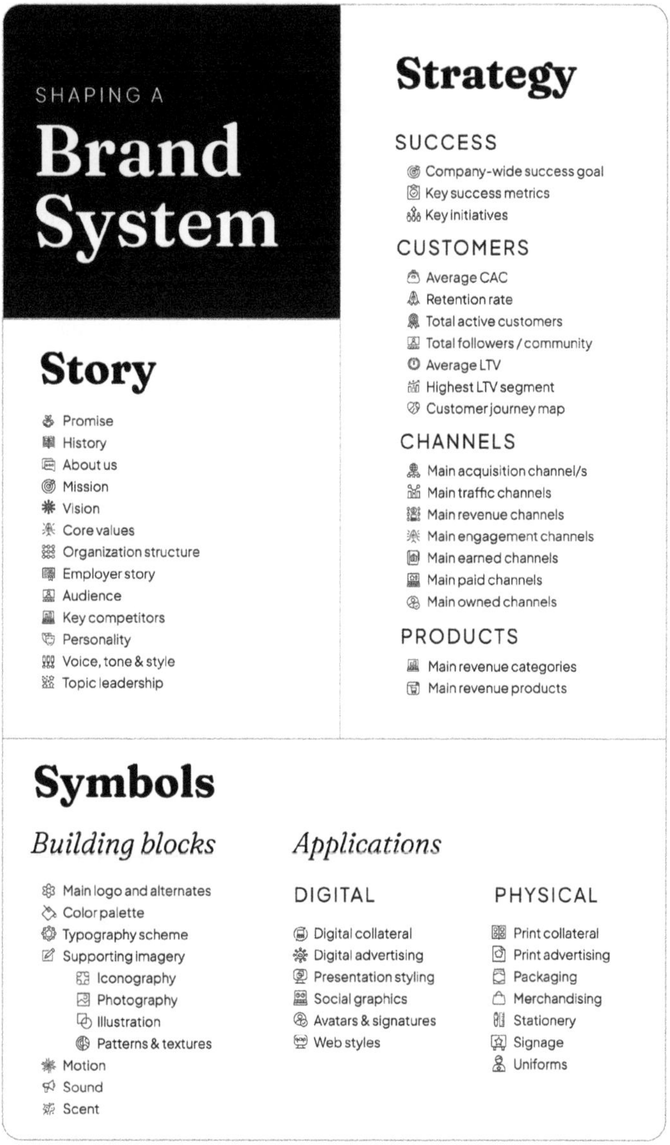

SHAPING A

Brand System

Strategy

SUCCESS

- Company-wide success goal
- Key success metrics
- Key initiatives

CUSTOMERS

- Average CAC
- Retention rate
- Total active customers
- Total followers / community
- Average LTV
- Highest LTV segment
- Customer journey map

CHANNELS

- Main acquisition channel/s
- Main traffic channels
- Main revenue channels
- Main engagement channels
- Main earned channels
- Main paid channels
- Main owned channels

PRODUCTS

- Main revenue categories
- Main revenue products

Story

- Promise
- History
- About us
- Mission
- Vision
- Core values
- Organization structure
- Employer story
- Audience
- Key competitors
- Personality
- Voice, tone & style
- Topic leadership

Symbols

Building blocks

- Main logo and alternates
- Color palette
- Typography scheme
- Supporting imagery
  - Iconography
  - Photography
  - Illustration
  - Patterns & textures
- Motion
- Sound
- Scent

Applications

DIGITAL

- Digital collateral
- Digital advertising
- Presentation styling
- Social graphics
- Avatars & signatures
- Web styles

PHYSICAL

- Print collateral
- Print advertising
- Packaging
- Merchandising
- Stationery
- Signage
- Uniforms

FIGURE 16.4: Shaping a brand system

STORY

The key question in this section is: What does your brand solve, for whom, and why?

- **Promise:** What is this brand's core value proposition?
- **History:** What does its history look like? Include a timeline and key milestones.
- **About us:** How do you summarize both of the above in an "About us" blurb?
- **Mission:** What is the brand's mission as it relates to its target customers? How about the team itself and society at large?
- **Vision:** How does the brand see itself evolving in the future?
- **Core values:** What are the brand's core values and pillar beliefs? What propels this team forward?
- **Organization structure:** How is the team organized to meet the brand's goals?
- **Employer story:** How does this brand add value to team members' lives?
- **Audience:** Who is the audience? Who are the main personas being addressed and what are these individuals trying to get done?
- **Key competitors:** Who are we up against and how is our product different?
- **Personality:** What is this brand's personality like?
- **Voice, tone, and style:** What defines the brand's voice? How does it adopt different tones in specific situations? Grammar and spelling-wise, does this brand adhere to a specific style manual? What are some common words and expressions users can expect from this brand?
- **Topic leadership:** What topics should this brand aim to be a thought leader at?

SYMBOLS

What does the brand look and feel like? As discussed above, this is a strictly sensory representation of the brand, leaning on symbolic assets that express the brand's identity. As we just reviewed, there will be a set of building blocks and some physical and digital brand applications developed from them.

STRATEGY

How does the brand succeed at serving its customers? There are four defining aspects to this section: the brand's definition of **success**, a clear understanding of its **customer** base, and an overview of top-performing **channels** and **products** aimed at achieving that success.

Success

- **Company-wide success goal:** How does this brand define success? What must be achieved by when? These are goals the entire team aligns around.
- **Key metrics:** What growth metric does the team focus on to track performance? (GMV, revenue, EBITDA, sales, etc).
- **Key initiatives:** What initiatives or themes is the brand focusing on to meet that wider success goal?

Customers

- **Average CAC:** What is the average customer acquisition cost (CAC), blended across channels? Which channel offers the lowest CAC, on average?

- **Retention rate:** How well does this brand build loyal, repeat customers? (More on loyalty in Chapter 17)
- **Total active customers:** How many customers currently fuel this brand's business or sustainability model, actively using its offer?
- **Total followers/community:** How large is the brand's community of followers, who may or may not turn into customers?
- **Average LTV:** What is the average customer lifetime value (LTV)?
- **Highest LTV segment:** out of every segment targeted, which one is the most valuable to the brand over customers' lifetimes? Which of the buyer personas defined in the "Story" section brings the most revenue?
- **Customer journey map:** how does the typical customer's experience with the brand unfold? What are some key touchpoints (see Chapter 19)? What does the conversion funnel look like? How does this brand acquire, activate, and retain customers?

Channels

- **Main acquisition channels:** Which channels generate the highest volume of customers?
- **Main traffic channels:** Which channels bring the largest amount of traffic?
- **Main revenue channels:** Which channels drive the most revenue, if applicable?
- **Main engagement channels:** Where is our brand most actively engaged?
- **Main earned channels:** Out of the brand's borrowed channels, which one is most performant in terms of traffic, revenue, and acquisition? For a definition and list of earned, paid, and owned channels, see Chapter 18.

- **Main paid channels:** In which paid channels have we seen the most traffic, revenue, and acquisition success?
- **Main owned channels:** which of our brand's owned channels perform best in terms of traffic, revenue, and acquisition?

Products

- **Main revenue categories:** Which product categories drive the most revenue? Traffic?
- **Main revenue products:** Which individual products drive the most revenue? Traffic?

REBRANDING

Far too many times, I've seen companies take on rushed logo redesign projects calling them rebrands.

Changing one of the *thousands* of elements consumers associate with you is **not** a rebrand.

What is a rebrand, then? **A genuine rebrand is a Brand System shift** (see Chapter 1). For strategic reasons, this company has decided to pivot into a new positioning, redesigning building blocks like promise, personality, yes symbols, but also: user experience, loyalty programs, communication channel strategy, and even internal brand development.

NOTES

1. Townsend, C., & Kahn, B. E. (2014). The "visual preference heuristic": The influence of visual versus verbal depiction on assortment processing, perceived variety, and choice overload. *Journal of Consumer Research*, *40*(5), 993–1015. https://doi.org/10.1086/673521

2. Jeong, S. (2008). Visual metaphor in advertising: Is the persuasive effect attributable to visual argumentation or metaphorical rhetoric? *Journal of Marketing Communications*, *14*(1), 59–73. https://doi.org/10.1080/14697010701717488

3. Renard, S. (2017). What defines an audio logo? Composition and eaning. *College Music Symposium*, *57*. https://www.jstor.org/stable/26574465

4. Kilian, K. (2008). From brand identity to audio branding. In *Audio Branding* (pp. 36–51). Nomos Verlagsgesellschaft mbH & Co. KG.

5. Jackson, D. M. (2003). *Sonic Branding* (P. Fulberg, Ed.). Palgrave Macmillan UK. https://doi.org/10.1057/9780230503267

6. Fraile, E. B., Jiménez, A. M. E., Veloso, M. L. B., & Payet, A. F. (2021). Sonic identity and audio branding elements in Spanish radio advertising. *Anàlisi*, *65*, 103–119.

7. Melzner, J., & Raghubir, P. (2022). The Sound of Music: The effect of timbral sound quality in audio logos on brand personality perception. *Journal of Marketing Research*, 00222437221135188. https://doi.org/10.1177/00222437221135188

8. Bonde, A., & Hansen, A. G. (2013). Audio logo recognition, reduced articulation and coding orientation: Rudiments of quantitative research integrating branding theory, social semiotics and music psychology. *SoundEffects*, *3*(1–2). https://doi.org/10.7146/se.v3i1-2.15644

9. Anglada-Tort, M., Schofield, K., Trahan, T., & Müllensiefen, D. (2022). I've heard that brand before: The role of music recognition on consumer choice. *International Journal of Advertising*, *41*(8), 1567–1587. https://doi.org/10.1080/02650487.2022.2060568

10. Bradford, K. D., & Desrochers, D. M. (2009). The use of scents to influence consumers: The sense of using scents to make cents. *Journal of Business Ethics*, *90*, 141–153.

11. Lwin, M. O., & Morrin, M. (2012). Scenting movie theatre commercials: The impact of scent and pictures on brand evaluations and ad recall. *Journal of Consumer Behaviour*, *11*(3), 264–272. https://doi.org/10.1002/cb.1368

12. Krishna, A., Lwin, M. O., Morrin, M.. (2010). Product scent and memory. *Journal of Consumer Research, 37*(1), 57–67. https://doi.org/ 10.1086/649909

13. Errajaa, K., Legohérel, P., & Daucé, B. (2018). Immersion and emotional reactions to the ambiance of a multiservice space: The role of perceived congruence between odor and brand image. *Journal of Retailing and Consumer Services, 40,* 100–108. https:// doi.org/10.1016/j.jretconser.2017.08.016
Bosmans, A. (2006). Scents and sensibility: When do (in)congruent ambient scents influence product evaluations? *Journal of Marketing, 70*(3), 32–43.

14. Bone, P. F., & Ellen, P. S. (1999). Scents in the marketplace: Explaining a fraction of olfaction. *Journal of Retailing, 75*(2), 243–262.

15. Goldkuhl, L., & Styvén, M. (2007). Sensing the scent of service success. *European Journal of Marketing, 41*(11/12), 1297–1305. https:// doi.org/10.1108/03090560710821189

16. Davies, B. J., Kooijman, D., & Ward, P. (2003). The sweet smell of success: Olfaction in retailing. *Journal of Marketing Management, 19*(5–6), 611–627. https://doi.org/10.1080/02672 57X.2003.9728228

17. Kauppinen-Räisänen, H. (2014). Strategic use of colour in brand packaging. *Packaging Technology and Science, 27*(8), 663–676. https://doi.org/10.1002/pts.2061

18. Underwood, R. L., & Klein, N. M. (2002). Packaging as brand communication: Effects of product pictures on consumer responses to the package and brand. *Journal of Marketing Theory and Practice, 10*(4), 58–68.

19. Reimann, M., Zaichkowsky, J., Neuhaus, C., Bender, T., & Weber, B. (2010). Aesthetic package design: A behavioral, neural, and psychological investigation. *Journal of Consumer Psychology, 20*(4), 431–441.

20. Ares, G., & Deliza, R. (2010). Studying the influence of package shape and colour on consumer expectations of milk desserts using word association and conjoint analysis. *Food Quality and Preference, 21*(8), 930–937. https://doi.org/10.1016/j.foodqual.2010.03.006

21. Peck, J., & Wiggins, J. (2006). It just feels good: Customers' affective response to touch and its influence on persuasion. *Journal of Marketing, 70*(4), 56–69.

22. Busche, L. *The Case For Brand Systems: Aligning Teams Around A Common Story.* Smashing Magazine. https://www.smashingmagazine .com/2019/06/case-brand-systems-align-teams/

SECTION 3

STRATEGY

DOI: 10.4324/9781003336693-20

INTRODUCTION

Branding is a verb. A permanent exercise. An ongoing attempt to express a set of values in connection with a product, service, or idea.

The human brain is in a permanent state of meaning-making, information processing, and emotion-triggering. We are active perceivers and sense-makers of the world around us and no experience escapes our mind's eye.

Whether you're actively involved in messaging or not, your brand is being constructed every minute.

Objects, ideas, and services are all branded. This has nothing to do with your price tag or lack thereof. If you're out in the world, someone is branding you. The goal of brand management is to participate proactively in that conversation and influence it.

Throughout this section, we'll see how brand managers can use owned, earned, and paid communication channels to exert an active role in their product's branding.

Having designed a story and symbols to express your brand, it is now time to amplify these messages strategically. As in previous chapters, we will review science-backed findings in the fields of psychology, business, and design to build a robust brand strategy that stands the test of time.

Instead of investing our time in trending, ephemeral tactics, we'll focus on the timeless principles at play in brand communications. Tools and fads will come and go, but human beings' deeper intentions, behavior patterns, and ulterior motives are largely consistent.

That is what we'll study and those are the lasting strategies we'll put in place.

You'll find that understanding the fundamentals of human behavior is a much better use of your time and effort than chasing the next shiny object. The best part? Principles open doors to understanding all else. Yes, these fundamentals will also give you a strong playbook to find any and all shiny objects.

I wrote this book to put that playbook in everyone's hands. It's been buried in databases for too long.

CHAPTER 17

BUILDING STRONG BRAND RELATIONSHIPS

DOI: 10.4324/9781003336693-21

What this market needs is more brands willing to treat their customers like friends. We might and will have our differences. We do each other favors. Long-term, we build a relationship that serves us both. We're all better for it.

You can't growth-hack your way into brand affinity just like you can't bulldoze your way into a healthy long-term relationship.

Human beings respond to consistent care, reciprocity, and attention. Brands that invest in authentic relationships with their customers are strengthening the bridge they'll cross to reach them once and again. The key word here is investment—an investment with a strategic, stable return: loyalty.

Brands are built by humans for humans and we all better start marketing accordingly. Throughout this chapter, we will learn how to build meaningful brand relationships with varying levels of engagement, going from basic affect and affinity all the way to highly involved loyalty behaviors.

From least to most intense, we will review the following brand relationship effects:

- Awareness
- Familiarity
- Image
- Association
- Sentiment
- Attachment
- Differentiation
- Preference
- Perceived Quality
- Trust
- Loyalty
- Advocacy

BRAND RELATIONSHIPS: RESPONSE MODELS

The strongest relationships develop over time—this is true for human beings and certainly also true for their interactions with brands. You can't microwave trust, affect, or loyalty. These affinities build up over a series of consistent touchpoints where customers grow progressively fond of the brand.

This sense of progression is at the core of what we call **response models:** the idea that one meaningful interaction sets a foundation for the next. A *crawl-walk-run* perspective on branding that understands brand equity as a currency that you build over time; as a value that compounds or compresses as a result of our strategy as brand managers and its resonance with target audiences.

Originally created to explain advertising impact, response models can also be used to understand the process customers go through as they get increasingly closer to the brand. They typically start with some form of cognitive awareness, are followed by varying levels of emotional attachment, and may lead to a behavioral response (actions like purchasing or recommending).

One of the simplest and most well-known response models in marketing is AIDA: shorthand for a series of steps that include Attention, Interest, Desire, and Action. The model is attributed to advertiser St Elmo Lewis, who allegedly crafted it to explain how personal selling works in 1898[1]. To actually buy a product, customers must go from being aware of its existence to being fascinated enough to pay attention to its benefits and advantages, to having a desire to use it.

In 1961, Lavidge and Steiner built upon the foundation of AIDA to shape a more detailed framework known as the

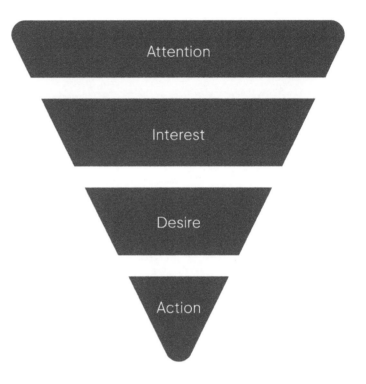

FIGURE 17.1: AIDA model

Hierarchy of Effects model[2]. This is the model we'll use to explore the various levels of affinity one can experience towards a brand. The model is illustrated in the figure below, which displays Lavidge and Steiner's six effects in a customer's movement toward purchase: *awareness, knowledge, liking, preference, conviction, and purchase.*

The Hierarchy of Effects starts with an **awareness** phase, where the brand enters our consciousness. The more we learn about it, the more we progress into a **knowledge** phase that, properly nurtured, can lead to a **liking** phase where we can experience affect and a growing affinity towards the brand.

Hierarchy of Effects

ROBERT J. LAVIDGE AND GARY A. STEINER

Related behavioral dimensions	Movement toward purchase	Examples of types of promotion to various steps	Examples of research approaches related to steps of greatest applicability
CONATIVE The realm of motives. Ads stimulate or direct desires.	**PURCHASE** ↑ **CONVICTION** ↑	• Point-of-purchase • Retail store ads • Deals • Last-chance offers • Price appeals	• Market or sales tests • Split-run tests • Intention to purchase • Projective techniques
AFFECTIVE The realm of emotions. Ads change attitudes and feelings.	**PREFERENCE** ↑ **LIKING** ↑	• Competitive ads • Argumentative copy • "Image" ads • Status, glamor appeals	• Rank order of preference for brands • Rating scales • Image measurements, including checklists and semantic differentials
COGNITIVE The realm of thoughts. Ads provide information and facts.	**KNOWLEDGE** ↑ **AWARENESS**	• Announcements • Descriptive copy • Classified ads • Slogans • Jingles • Sky writing • Teaser campaigns	• Information questions • Play-back analyses • Brand awareness surveys • Aided recall

FIGURE 17.2: Hierarchy of Effects model

Should this sense of **liking** expand, we might find ourselves **preferring** this brand above similar competitors. These middle steps, liking and preference, involve incrementally positive attitudes or feelings towards the brand. Lastly, the stages of **conviction** and **purchase** capture the behavioral impact of our (now) involved relationship with this brand.

It's important to recognize that not every brand's purchase process will involve all six of these steps. Depending on the customers' level of involvement with the purchase, they might jump from awareness into conviction and proceed with an **impulse purchase**. More complex purchase decisions, such as those in the B2B (business-to-business) space, might take longer to progress through these hierarchical effects.

The impulse buying theory was a landmark idea in marketing that continues to be relevant today. Impulse decisions are primarily driven by external factors, like encountering a captivating advertisement, and have little to do with the traditional decision-making processes[3].

According to Stern's theory, impulse buying unfolds on four levels:

- The first level is the spontaneous, **pure impulse purchase,** like grabbing a candy bar while waiting in line at the grocery store.
- The second level, known as the **"reminded" impulse purchase,** creates a connection between two products, nudging you to buy both. Imagine finding chips and salsa side by side in an aisle; you planned to buy one but are reminded that the other would be a perfect pairing.
- The third level is the **suggested impulse purchase,** akin to adding a warranty offer to your cart when buying electronics or power tools. It's a gentle nudge that encourages you to make an additional purchase based on the initial item.
- The fourth level is the **planned impulse decision,** where consumers have a clear intention to buy a particular type of product but haven't settled on the specifics just yet.

In Chapter 18, when we review available brand communication channels, we'll explore the concept of "elaboration likelihood" to determine the most efficient path to persuasion based on someone's level of involvement.

BRAND EQUITY DIMENSIONS AT EACH LEVEL

Researchers have examined several dimensions of brands and how managers can influence them in different phases through intentional marketing activities. Different brand relationship variables are involved in every phase of the process.

At the most basic stage, **brand awareness** can be used as an indicator of initial familiarity. Further along in a customer's journey with the brand, one might start seeing **brand associations** and a brand image develop.

In subsequent effects, brand **sentiment** and affinity might activate as customers become attitudinally and emotionally connected to the brand. Higher-order behavioral responses like **brand preference** and **loyalty** may naturally follow.

Because of their relevance for brand management, let's dive deeper into each of these dimensions and how a brand manager can effectively impact them. We will review these response levels using the *Hierarchy of Effects* as a foundation.

Throughout the next few pages, we'll also explore practical measurement scales to explore brand attachment (Park et al. 2010) and brand loyalty (Odin et al. 2001). Complement these with the Multidimensional Consumer-Based Brand Equity Scale and Brand Associations Scale covered in Chapters 3 and 7 for a full overview of customers' responses to your branding efforts.

AWARENESS

Brand awareness

The starting point for any brand relationship is having it enter the customer's radar. Awareness is the realization that the brand exists, solves a specific want/need, and is available.

Although often deprioritized in "high-growth" organizations, nothing happens unless someone is cognizant of your brand's existence. Devesting in brand awareness efforts entirely sabotages any long-term growth plan. Failing to expand the brand' base proactively is a form of slow, seemingly harmless, death.

Brand familiarity

Increasing levels of awareness can lead to familiarity. Even if you've never interacted with or purchased anything from this brand, you've perceived it enough times so that, should your need for its offerings activate, it would be part of your evoked and consideration sets.

KNOWLEDGE

Brand image

As we've seen throughout this book, brand image is a revealing construct that captures customers' general body of knowledge about the brand. As our awareness and familiarity grow, so do our cognitive elaborations of what this brand is and does. Our mental brand image reflects these constructions, leading many to define this very dimension as "the brand". The brand image scale covered in Chapter 7 can clarify which image components are most salient.

Brand association

We reviewed brand associations at length in Chapter 7. For the sake of this discussion on brand relationships, forming a rich network of meanings around a brand is an indicator that one is internalizing more information about its offerings and identity.

LIKING

Brand sentiment

Classic psychology divides behavior into cognitive, affective, and motivational components. **Brand sentiment** taps into the emotional dimension of our relationships with brands. Over time, we develop specific feelings over certain brands that also end up informing our higher-order actions (preference, conviction, and purchase).

Brand attachment

Brand attachment points to "the strength of the affective and cognitive bond between consumers' self and the brand"[4].

Attachment is an essential construct in our discussion about brand relationships. After all, it is the foundational bond between customers and the brands they come to associate with: the starting point for more complex interactions.

Attachment expands as affective and cognitive connections strengthen between brands and the customers they serve.

Park et al. designed a set of items to shed light on brand–self connections and the prominence of brand thoughts and feelings[5]. Their four-item scale is described below.

A related measure, **brand affinity** also reflects an attitudinal posture towards a brand, but is related to its level of congruence with one's self, beliefs, and motivations. How well do *brand X* and I resonate?

PREFERENCE

Brand differentiation

What is it about this brand that sets it apart from other available options? These distinctive traits enrich our overall brand image, giving us information about how the brand performs in relation to others.

TABLE 17.1: Brand Attachment Scale (Park et al.)

Scale name	Brand Attachment Scale
Authors	Park et al. (2010)
Type of scale	11-point Likert
Anchors	From "Not at all" (0) to "Completely" (10)
Dimensions	*Brand–self Connection, Brand Prominence*
Items	**Brand–self Connection** • To what extent is [Brand Name] part of you and who you are? • To what extent do you feel that you are personally connected to [Brand Name] **Brand Prominence** • To what extent are your thoughts and feelings toward [Brand Name] often automatic, coming to mind seemingly on their own? • To what extent do your thoughts and feelings toward [Brand Name] come to you naturally and instantly?

Brand preference

Among a range of alternatives, the **knowledge** and **liking** we've developed towards this brand start influencing our preferences and decision-making process. As we evaluate brands in our consideration set, the brand's unique differentiators are now informing preference.

CONVICTION

Perceived quality

One of the most influential associations we store about a brand is its perceived level of quality. Note that the variable of importance here is not a factual quality marker. The influential factor at play here is, regardless of objective truths, what the brand's perceived level of quality is. This difference is key because it underlines the importance of brand communication in messaging accurate quality messages.

Yoo and Donthu's Multidimensional Consumer-based Brand Equity Scale[6] measures this dimension through two essential items customers must rate from "Strongly disagree" (1) to "Strongly agree" (5):

- The likely quality of (brand X) is extremely high
- The likelihood that (brand X) would be functional is very high

Brand trust

Here comes the leap of faith that turns prospects into customers. Do I trust this brand enough to exchange whatever measure of value is required in exchange for its offer? Do I have reasons to believe it will reliably deliver on its promise?

Marketing professors Munuera-Alemán, Delgado-Ballester, and Yagüe-Guillén drew insights from social psychology, sociology, management, and marketing to define brand trust as "the confident expectations of the brand's reliability and intentions in situations entailing risk to the consumer"[7].

To operationalize this idea, they developed an eight-item **Brand Trust Scale** that rests on two dimensions: **reliability** and **intentions**. The scale is summarized below.

PURCHASE

Brand loyalty

It is widely known that acquiring a new customer is several times more expensive than retaining one[8]. **Brand**

TABLE 17.2: Brand Trust Scale (Munuerá-Aleman et al.)

Scale name	Brand Trust Scale
Authors	Delgado-Ballester, Munuera-Alemán & Yagüe-Guillén, 2003
Type of scale	5-point Likert
Anchors	From "Completely disagree" (1) to "completely agree" (5)
Dimensions	*Reliability, Intentions*
Items	**Reliability** • (X) is a brand name that meets my expectations • I feel confidence in (X) brand name • (X) is a brand name that never disappoints me • (X) brand name guarantees satisfaction **Intentions** • (X) brand name would be honest and sincere in addressing my concerns • I could rely on (X) brand name to solve the problem • (X) brand name would make any effort to satisfy me • (X) brand name would compensate me in some way for the problem with the (product)

loyalty is a mediating factor in our ability to stimulate repeat purchases or some other desired action from existing customers.

Jacoby and Kyner provided one of the most widely cited definitions of **brand loyalty,** defining it as a "nonrandom behavioral response (i.e. purchase) expressed over time by some decision-making units with respect to one or more alternative brands, out of a set of such brands". They also propose brand loyalty is a function of psychological (decision-making) processes[9].

Brand loyalty, then, involves consistently choosing to buy products from the same brand over a period of time. If you always choose to buy a certain brand of jeans or a particular type of phone, you're exhibiting brand loyalty. This is not just a random decision, but rather a result of a decision-making process that involves factors such as your personal preferences, values, and past experiences.

How can we size the extent of our customer's loyalty to the brand? Odin et al. offer an answer: a four-item Brand Loyalty Scale we can apply to get a sense of its intensity[10]. Item and scoring details are available below.

TABLE 17.3: Brand Loyalty Scale (Odin et al.)

Scale name	Brand Loyalty Scale
Authors	Odin et al. (2001)
Type of scale	6-point Likert
Anchors	From "Totally disagree" (1) to "Totally agree" (6)
Items	1. I am loyal to only one brand of (category)
	2. During my next purchase, I will buy the same brand of (category) as the last time
	3. I always buy the same brand of (category)
	4. Usually, I buy the same brand of (category)

Brand advocacy

Brand advocacy occurs when customers recommend a brand out of their conviction that it is worthwhile. Advocacy is important because it generates organic, credible awareness for the brand, which can lead to increased sales and customer loyalty.

The concept of **brand advocacy** has been defined as a set of behaviors that are aimed at maintaining the relationship between the brand and the customer as well as promoting the brand to others, including proactively recommending the brand and defending it against its detractors[11].

One way that companies measure brand advocacy is through the Net Promoter Score (NPS) metric proposed by Frederick Reichheld[12]. NPS is a metric that looks at the level of brand advocacy by asking a simple question:

"How likely is it that you would recommend our company to a friend or colleague?"

Based on their responses on a scale of 0 to 10, customers are classified as promoters (9–10), passives (7–8), or detractors (0–6). The NPS is calculated by subtracting the percentage of detractors from the percentage of promoters, resulting in a score that can range from −100 to +100. The higher the score, the more likely it is that customers will recommend the brand to others, which is a key indicator of brand advocacy.

BUILDING RELATIONSHIPS THAT LAST

Professor Susan Fournier's theory of Brand Relationship Quality (BRQ) has become one of the most widely applied ideas in the brand development space. Fournier's conception of brand relationships is founded on the reciprocity principle on which all (human) relationships are grounded[13].

Emphasizing the importance of meaningful interactions between brands and consumers, Fournier's model identifies six key components that contribute to the overall quality, depth, and strength of a brand relationship. When it comes to keeping any relationship alive, as you may have experienced, there is more to it than just positive feelings:

- **Love/passion:** This component refers to the emotional bond that a consumer has with a brand, fostering loyalty and advocacy. The Ritz-Carlton, for example, is renowned for its exceptional customer service, luxurious accommodations, and attention to detail. The brand offers indulgent experiences that evoke a strong sense of love and passion among customers.
- **Self-connection:** The extent to which a brand represents a consumer's self-concept, values, or identity. For example, Lush's commitment to ethically sourced, cruelty-free, and environmentally friendly cosmetics resonates with consumers who value sustainability and social responsibility. Brands and customers have a strong connection when their values align.
- **Interdependence:** This facet concerns the degree to which a consumer relies on a brand to fulfill specific needs or goals. Amazon, for example, is a go-to source for a wide range of products, making consumers dependent on its convenience.

- **Commitment:** This element involves a consumer's dedication to maintaining a long-term relationship with a brand. Emirates, an international airline, has cultivated commitment among its customers by offering exceptional inflight experiences, a diverse route network, and a loyalty program that rewards frequent flyers. Travelers trust and love the brand because it's committed to innovation and customer service.

- **Intimacy:** This component refers to the level of understanding and trust between a consumer and a brand. Spotify's personalized playlists, like Discover Weekly and Daily Mixes, show that it understands individual customer preferences, fostering intimacy and trust.

- **Brand partner quality:** This aspect evaluates the overall perception of a brand's competence, trustworthiness, and attractiveness. BMW's commitment to engineering excellence, luxurious design, and advanced technology leads to a perception of high brand partner quality. A BMW customer can trust the brand to give them a great driving experience.

Fournier argues that some of the positive outcomes of durable brand relationships are similar to what you would expect from a healthy, strong inter-human relationship. They include:

- Accommodation, or our willingness to work with a partner to maintain the relationship even when they're not being constructive
- Tolerance and forgiveness when things go wrong
- Positively biased perceptions of our partner
- Devaluation of alternatives, out of preference for our partner
- Positive attribution biases, consistently casting our partner's actions in a positive light

In Professor Fournier's own words:

> Brands cohere into systems that consumers create not only to aid in living but also to give meaning to their lives. Put simply, consumers do not choose brands, they choose lives.

Brand Relationship Quality & Stability

SUSAN FOURNIER

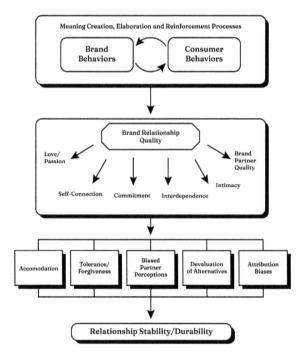

FIGURE 17.3: Brand Relationship Quality and stability (Fournier)

INTERNAL BRANDING

Having reviewed brand relationships as they develop between customers and the brands they prefer, let's now turn our attention toward internal customers: the team members bringing it all to life. Increasingly, this set of stakeholders has garnered the attention of the academic and practitioner world because of their unique position to bring brand values to life.

Internal branding is about reinforcing a brand's essence among the human beings in charge of bringing it to life. It is a crucial exercise in walking the talk—*branding from the inside out.*

When organizations live by their values, the people they're made of experience a sense of alignment and coherence that propels brands forward.

Like customers, team members are active perceivers of brand expressions. They contrast what the brand says *externally* against what the brand does *internally* and draw their own conclusions about its authenticity.

This perceived coherence can enhance or hurt service moments. Marketing researchers have explored how brand *endorsement* and *allegiance* impact employees' ability to enact their roles. Conclusively, one cannot separate a brand's inward dynamics from its builders' outward-facing dispositions. How a brand is built inevitably impacts what it turns out to be.

When brand values are in alignment with internal practices, trust, and loyalty are reinforced. When they're not, the dissonance steers us away from connecting with the brand and leveraging that sense of purpose to strengthen the touchpoints we're in charge of.

But how can we explore the way team members perceive the brand? How can we identify outstanding brand associations among the very people communicating its message? King, Grace & Funk designed an instrument called the **Employee Brand Equity (EBE) Scale** to provide answers[14].

The scale evaluates brand equity strength among employees looking at three dimensions: *brand endorsement, brand allegiance, and brand-consistent behavior.* Its 11 items and scoring details can be found below.

Because team member perception is such an instrumental part of B2B service brands, Coleman et al. took on the challenge of developing a measurement tool specifically for this

TABLE 17.4: Employee Brand Equity Scale (King et al.)

Scale name	Employee Brand Equity (EBE) Scale
Authors	King, Grace & Funk (2012)
Type of scale	7-point Likert
Anchors	From "Strongly disagree" (1) to "Strongly agree" (7)
Dimensions	*Brand Endorsement, Brand Allegiance, Brand-consistent Behavior*
Items	**Brand endorsement** • I say positive things about the organization (brand X) I work for to others • I would recommend the organization (brand X) I work for to someone who seeks my advice • I enjoy talking about the organization (brand X) I work for to others • I talk positively about the organization (brand X) I work for to others **Brand allegiance** • I plan to be with the organization (brand X) I work for, for a while • I plan to be with the organization (brand X) I work for 5 years from now • I would turn down an offer from another organization (brand X) if it came tomorrow • I plan to stay with the organization (brand X) I work for **Brand-consistent behavior** • I demonstrate behaviors that are consistent with the brand promise of the organization I work for • I consider the impact on my organization's brand before communicating or taking action in any situation • I am always interested to learn about my organization's brand and what it means to me in my role

use case[15]. Their B2B Service Brand Equity Scale evaluates five dimensions that contribute to delivering compelling service as a business-to-business brand: employee and client focus, corporate visual identity, brand personality, consistent communications, and human resource initiatives.

TABLE 17.5: B2B Service Brand Equity Scale (Coleman et al.)

Scale name	B2B Service Brand Equity Scale
Authors	Coleman et al. (2011)
Type of scale	7-point Likert
Anchors	From "Disagree Very Strongly" (1) to "Agree Very Strongly" (7). Midpoint of "Not Sure" (4)
Dimensions	*Employee and Client Focus, Corporate Visual Identity, Brand Personality, Consistent Communications, Human Resource Initiatives*
Items	**Employee and client focus** • Our organization treats each employee as an essential part of the organization • Our employees will help clients in a responsive manner • Our organization makes an effort to discover our clients' needs • Our organization responds to our clients' needs • Our top management is committed to providing quality service **Corporate visual identity** • Our organization treats each employee as an essential part of the organization • Our employees will help clients in a responsive manner • Our organization makes an effort to discover our clients' needs • Our organization responds to our clients' needs • Our top management is committed to providing quality service **Brand personality** • Our organization treats each employee as an essential part of the organization • Our employees will help clients in a responsive manner • Our organization makes an effort to discover our clients' needs • Our organization responds to our clients' needs • Our top management is committed to providing quality service **Consistent communications** • The people managing the communications program for our organization have a good understanding of the strengths and weaknesses of all major marketing communications tools • Our organization's advertising, PR and sales promotion all present the same clear, consistent message to our stakeholders **Human resource initiatives** • Our employee training programs are designed to develop skills required for acquiring and deepening client relationships • Our organization regularly monitors employees' performance

Instead of focusing strictly on corporate visual identity, Coleman et al. encourage B2B service brand managers to ask more systemic questions like "Are we focusing adequately on our employees' and clients' needs? What type of brand personality do we wish to develop?" and "What human resource initiatives do we have in place to support our desired service brand identity?".

Put simply, you can't expect magic at the moment of truth in service and make it a nightmare for your team members to deliver it.

Marketing professor Phillip Kotler phrased this idea well:

> Employees are the most intimate consumers of the company's practices. They need to be empowered with authentic values. Companies need to use the same storytelling approach with their employees that they use with their consumers.[16]

Why? For one, passion is contagious. Enjoying something equips you to talk about and sell it with more confidence. On the other hand, a brand's bold, signature promises to customers should also hold for its very first customers: the team of human beings building it all. Internally aligned, genuine brands will find it easier to attract and retain top talent. This coherence is the foundation of all successful internal branding.

Brands don't carry souls, but the humans building them do.

Because self-affirmation matters to us, we seek positions and brands that reflect our ethos. This is especially true for employees and contractors: the association with a certain brand must feel additive to our journey and properly representative of who we are.

NOTES

1. Oxford Reference. AIDA. *Oxford Reference.* Retrieved 30 March 2023, from https://www.oxfordreference.com/view/10.1093/oi/authority.20110803095432783

2. Lavidge, R. J., & Steiner, G. A. (1961). A model for predictive measurements of advertising effectiveness. *Journal of Marketing, 25*(6), 59–62. https://doi.org/10.2307/1248516

3. Stern, H. (1962). The significance of impulse buying today. *Journal of Marketing, 26*(2), 59–62.

4. Japutra, A., Ekinci, Y., & Simkin, L. (2018). Tie the knot: Building stronger consumers' attachment toward a brand. *Journal of Strategic Marketing, 26*(3), 223–240. https://doi.org/10.1080/0965254X.2016.1195862

5. Park, C. W., MacInnis, D. J., Priester, J., Eisingerich, A. B., & Iacobucci, D. (2010). Brand attachment and brand attitude strength: Conceptual and empirical differentiation of two critical brand equity drivers. *Journal of Marketing, 74*(6), 1–17.

6. Yoo, B., & Donthu, N. (2001). Developing and validating a multi-dimensional consumer-based brand equity scale. *Journal of Business Research, 52*(1), 14.

7. Munuerá-Aleman, J. L., Delgado-Ballester, E., & Yagüe-Guillén, M. J. (2003). Development and validation of a brand trust scale. *International Journal of Market Research, 45*(1), 1–18. https://doi.org/10.1177/147078530304500103

8. Gallo, A. (2014, October 29). The value of keeping the right customers. *Harvard Business Review.* https://hbr.org/2014/10/the-value-of-keeping-the-right-customers

9. Jacoby, J., & Kyner, D. B. (1973). Brand loyalty vs. repeat purchasing behavior. *JMR, Journal of Marketing Research (Pre-1986), 10*(000001), 1.

10. Odin, Y., Odin, N., & Valette-Florence, P. (2001). Conceptual and operational aspects of brand loyalty: An empirical investigation. *Journal of Business Research, 53*(2), 75–84. https://doi.org/10.1016/S0148-2963(99)00076-4

11. Wilder, K. M. (2015). *Brand Advocacy: Conceptualization and Measurement.* Dissertation.

12. Reichheld, F. F. (2003). The one number you need to grow. *Harvard Business Review, 81*(12), 46–55.

13. Fournier, S. (1998). Consumers and their brands: Developing relationship theory in consumer research. *Journal of Consumer Research, 24*(4), 343–353. https://doi.org/10.1086/209515

14. King, C., Grace, D., & Funk, D. (2012). Employee brand equity: Scale development and validation. *Journal of Brand Management, 19.* https://doi.org/10.1057/bm.2011.44

15. Coleman, D., de Chernatony, L., & Christodoulides, G. (2011). B2B service brand identity: Scale development and validation. *Industrial Marketing Management, 40*(7), 1063–1071. https://doi.org/10.1016/j.indmarman.2011.09.010

16. Kotler, P., Kartajaya, H., & Setiawan, I. (2010). *Marketing 3.0: From Products to Customers to the Human Spirit.* John Wiley & Sons, Incorporated.

CHAPTER 18

UNDERSTANDING CHANNELS

DOI: 10.4324/9781003336693-22

Brand building is, at its core, an exercise in learning—consumer learning. Brand concepts require ongoing expansion, positioning, and reinforcement. But how can we convey a set of ideas that define our brand to a group of individuals, i.e. target audience, that might be entirely unfamiliar?

That's the key to success: **we bridge the gap between the unknown and the familiar.** We identify the events and memories our brand *does* relate to and start building a relationship with this customer by virtue of those links.

It is not enough to just create a brand; we must also foster an emotional connection between the customer and the brand. Thus, we must strive to create meaningful learning experiences for our target audience. The world of constructivist psychology calls this kind of interconnected, personally rooted process meaningful learning.

Meaningful learning encourages customers to actively engage with the brand, thereby creating a deeper and more profound bond. Thus, we must strive not only to create a brand but also to create meaningful learning experiences for our customers and foster an emotional connection between the customer and the brand.

Meaningful learning and brand building are, above all, acts of effective communication. Linguists have studied and distilled the complexities at play during every act of communication. As brand strategists, we'd do well to put these principles into practice when we attempt to message key brand ideas:

- Medium
- Sender
- Receiver
- Message

- Channel
- Noise

Make no mistake, just like every message in a communication process is a result of receivers' inputs, brand concepts are constructions where customers play a creative role. It is, ultimately, them storing this information about a brand in a way that feels coherent with their experience, undoubtedly permeated by their point of view—as is everything else we learn.

Even noise plays a crucial role in the communication process, especially in today's environment of permanent information overwhelm.

Full attention is utopia.

Finding moments of peace or undivided attention is no longer realistic. Instead, we must be mindful of the constant dialogue between what we say, what others do, and what is happening around us. As brand builders, understanding the context is now more vital than ever.

There are hundreds of tactical manuals full of the latest tricks to dominate existing and emerging brands channels. *That is not what this is.* Throughout this chapter, we'll review the brand psychology principles at play in some of the most strategic channels brands can own, earn, and pay for.

INTRODUCING EARNED, PAID, AND OWNED CHANNELS

Brands have different kinds of communication channels at their disposal, with varying levels of control.

Earned channels confer the right to present your message in exchange for non-monetary rewards like partnership, reciprocity, or simple presence. Regardless of how much perceived creative freedom is available, earned channels remain within a third party's control.

What does this control mean and how can you identify it? Here are three distinctive features:

- **Content control:** If a third party could effectively edit or delete your brand's messages without your permission
- **Access control:** If a third party could unilaterally decide that your use of the channel requires payment
- **Experience control:** If a third party determines most of the channel's look, feel, and infrastructure. Your message's container is largely within this third party's control.

Owned channels are quite the opposite. These are channels wholly owned and controlled by your brand, where all changes take place with your direct intervention. The elements of channel control we just reviewed are within your domain.

This predictability and flexibility make owned channels the most reliable long-term investment for any brand. Email lists and websites are two standout examples of owned channels that brands benefit from investing in over time.

Lastly, paid channels offer brand exposure in exchange for a monetary reward. They are available as long as one commits to specific fees and set their own rules with regards to creative and formatting.

These types of channels come in handy as message amplifiers; in an ideal scenario, a brand is relying on earned and paid channels to funnel qualified leads into owned channels where they can convert and nurture them over time.

An easy way to think about earned, paid, and owned channels is the difference between a public park, a theme park, and your backyard.

Public parks are free to use but you must abide by a set of rules. There are schedules, allowances, and prohibitions to be mindful of. For the most part, the government will determine what the park looks like and how it's maintained, similar to how an earned channel would operate.

Theme parks come with a ticket price attached. You pay to enter and enjoy rides, behaving in accordance with rules set by the park's owners. You can't expect to return on a different day and enter for free: there is always a pay for play. This is how paid channels work.

In your backyard, on the other hand, the sky is the limit. You are free to build and organize the space however you see fit. You get to choose what entertains you and have permanent access to the space. While you may have to pay to maintain underlying infrastructure, just like you do with most owned channels, everything you build is ultimately yours to own and control. In specific cases, even sell.

Regardless of their costs and benefits, these three kinds of channels come with their own dynamics and underlying psychological principles. Throughout this chapter, we will review the human behaviors and intentions at play in each of these channel types. Features that determine how brands and their messages can succeed in each platform.

TABLE 18.1: Examples of paid, earned and owned channels

Paid channels	Earned channels	Owned channels
• Paid search advertising • Display advertising • Social media advertising • Native advertising • Influencer marketing • Affiliate marketing • Podcast advertising • Sponsored content • Product placement • Out-of-home advertising • Print advertising • Direct mail • Event sponsorship • Trade shows • Celebrity endorsements • Branded content partnerships • Content discovery platforms	• Word-of-mouth referrals • Customer reviews • Social media shares • Press coverage • Guest blog posts • Influencer mentions • Award recognition • Industry recognition • Backlinks • Affiliate referrals • Brand advocacy • Brand-related hashtags • Public speaking engagements	• Website • Blog • Social media profiles* • Mobile apps • Email • Podcasts • Webinars • Online courses • Customer support forums • Branded online communities • Loyalty programs

Earned, paid, and owned channels

A simple way to think about earned, paid, and owned channels is the difference between a public park, a theme park, and your backyard.

public park

Public parks are free to use but you must abide by a set of rules. There are schedules, allowances, and prohibitions to be mindful of.

They resemble **earned channels.**

theme park

Theme parks come with a ticket price attached. You pay to enter and enjoy rides, behaving in accordance with rules set by the park's owners.

They resemble **paid channels.**

your backyard

In your backyard, the sky is the limit. You are free to build and organize it. You get to choose what entertains you and have permanent access to the sample.

They resemble **owned channels.**

FIGURE 18.1: Brand communication channels

Before we jump into channel executions, let's review some basic principles of persuasion to make the best possible use of those mediums.

BRAND COMMUNICATIONS AND THE ART OF PERSUASION

Petty, Cacioppo, and Schumann's **Elaboration Likelihood Model** (ELM) provides a clear, actionable framework to create persuasive brand messages depending on our audience's level of involvement[1].

The main idea of the ELM is that the best way to convince someone depends on how likely they are to think deeply about the message or issue at hand. When they're more likely to invest time thinking about it, the **central route of persuasion** works well. But, if they're not likely to put much thought into it, the **peripheral route** is the way to go.

For example, if you want to convince someone with the **central route**, you could:

- Present solid facts and statistics to support your argument
- Use logical reasoning to make a compelling case
- Share expert testimonials to boost credibility

On the other hand, if you're using the **peripheral route**, you might:

- Use a celebrity endorsement to grab attention
- Create a memorable slogan that's easy to remember
- Appeal to their emotions with a heartwarming story

Central route persuasion focuses on the merits of the argument, utilizing logical reasoning, evidence, and expert opinions. In contrast, the peripheral route to persuasion relies on superficial cues and emotional appeal to influence attitudes without requiring deep thought.

PRINCIPLES OF PERSUASION

Dr. Robert Cialdini, who worked with Petty & Cacioppo to understand the mechanisms behind attitude change, developed a set of principles of persuasion[2]. These principles are widely used in the field of marketing to create compelling brand messaging.

Reciprocity: People tend to return favors when they receive them. Brands, for example, can offer their customers discounts or freebies to encourage them to purchase their products. For example, Sephora offers a free makeup sample to customers who visit their stores and complete a survey. This not only increases customer satisfaction but also encourages repeat purchases.

Scarcity: We tend to perceive scarce items as more valuable. Brands can create a sense of scarcity by using limited edition products, time-limited offers, and exclusive access. For example, Louis Vuitton creates a sense of exclusivity by producing a limited number of its handbags, making them highly sought-after by customers.

Authority: People are often influenced by authoritative figures and follow their advice. Brands can leverage this principle by using celebrity endorsements, expert opinions, or certifications. For example, Nike uses professional athletes such as LeBron James and Cristiano Ronaldo to promote their products and establish their authority in the athletic industry.

Consistency: Individuals tend to follow through on their previous commitments and actions. Brands can use this principle by encouraging customers to make small commitments to their brand, which will lead to larger commitments in the future. For example, Fitbit motivates users to make small commitments to their fitness goals by tracking their daily activity levels, leading to larger commitments to healthy living and the brand.

Liking: This principle suggests that people tend to be persuaded by people they like. Brands can use this principle by creating likable brand personalities, using attractive models, and creating emotional connections with their customers. For example, Coca-Cola's "Share a Coke" campaign used personalized labels to create an emotional connection between customers and the brand.

Consensus: In uncertain situations, people tend to seek guidance from others. Brands can use this principle by highlighting the popularity of their products, social proof, and endorsements from satisfied customers. For example, Expedia uses customer reviews to establish consensus among potential travelers about the quality of hotels and travel experiences.

Unity: A more recent addition by Cialdini in 2016, this principle suggests that people tend to be more persuaded by those who share commonalities with them[3]. Brands can use this principle by creating a sense of community among their customers, using shared values and experiences to connect with them. For example, Whole Foods creates a sense of togetherness by promoting its stores as a place for people to connect.

PUTTING BRAND CHANNELS TO WORK

Having reviewed the nature of the channels available to us based on our level of control, let's look at how we can best leverage them for effective brand communications. Two ideas are essential here: the difference between peripheral and central cues and the Hierarchy of Effects model we saw in Chapter 17.

ELM tells us that some customers will elaborate our messages through a central route: they'll rely on the quality and strength of the arguments being presented to process them cognitively. It also tells us that some customers will take the peripheral route: exerting minimal cognitive effort while being influenced by cues unrelated to the message's content or quality such as attractiveness, credibility, or emotion.

These divergent paths to persuasion carry deep implications for brand communications. Specifically for something I'll herein refer to as the **brand messaging mix**.

BRAND MESSAGING MIX

As you likely remember, customers experience increasingly more involved effects towards the brand as their cognitive, emotional, and behavioral responses are triggered. As brand managers, then, it is in our best interest to provide a variety of messages that cater to this range of consumer states. Specifically, we should build a communications strategy with the following building blocks:

- Messages to explain
- Messages to engage
- Messages to convince

Let's look at each of these types of messages in greater detail:

319

TABLE 18.2: Brand messaging mix

Messages to	Explain	Engage	Convince
Appeal	Cognitive	Emotional	Behavioral
Type of cue	Central	Peripheral	Both
Sample message types	Product efficacy through clinical trials	Celebrity or influencer endorsements	Promotions
	Feature comparisons	Emotional storytelling	Personalized recommendations
	Cost savings calculations	Catchy jingles	Loyalty programs
	Infographics	High-quality aesthetics	Cross-selling
	Case studies	Sense of exclusivity	Upselling
	Product demos	Sense of scarcity	Pre & post-purchase support
	Expert certifications	Cause marketing	Referral programs
		Humor and entertainment	Live chat
		Aspirational lifestyle	Social proof
			Risk-free trials
			Money-back guarantees

Messages to explain

These kinds of messages appeal to our cognitive ability, offer-ing rational data points that increase awareness and interest around a brand. We are guided to understand the brand's ben-efits through a rational presentation of facts centered around efficacy, savings, and utilitarian value derived from its products.

Messages to engage

When we message to engage, we're speaking to human beings' emotions, attitudes, and feelings. We rely on periph-eral cues to generate liking and ultimate preference. These kinds of messages trigger an affective response. As discussed, you might find that certain customers lean directly on this peripheral route to dictate their decisions. Even if someone's preferred persuasion style is closer to the cognitive cues we just discussed (in Messages to explain), they might find their engagement and conversion intent strengthened through this layer of emotional involvement[4].

Messages to convince

Lastly, our messaging to convince is focused on triggering the desired conversion action, whether that's a purchase, vote, signup, or some other form of commitment. These messages are direct, time-sensitive incentives designed to prompt behaviors. A brand marketer's resource at the moment of truth.

USING THIS MIX FOR BRAND COMMUNICATIONS

Owned, earned, and paid channels can all amplify these three types of messages. There are blog posts, for example, that can cater to a customer's logical analysis of product features (cognitive), others that leverage humor (emotional), and others that might directly introduce testimonials to induce purchase (behavioral).

You can set up a partnership where an influential figure describes your brand's benefits (cognitive), leans into their celebrity status to set an aspiration (emotional), or directly offer a discount code to incentivize the audience (behavioral). Or all three at once!

The **brand messaging mix** is more of a strategic approach to messages than it is a firm line drawn to categorize them. What is most important is understanding that customers find themselves at different points along their awareness journey with the brand, reacting more effectively to the message types that speak to their state. As described by the Elaboration Likelihood Model, some might even skip cognitive cues altogether and make their purchase decisions based on purely emotional drivers.

An effective brand manager understands that human beings differ in their motivations, involvement, and persuasion triggers, and creates a diverse communications program to cater to these differences.

Having reviewed the generalities of a brand messaging mix, let's look at some of examples of how different kinds of channels can support each message type:

TABLE 18.3: Brand messaging mix examples

Channel	Messages to explain	Messages to engage	Messages to convince
Blog	Grammarly's blog post explains the benefits of using their checker to improve the effectiveness of written communication.	Airbnb shares stories of people who have had life-changing experiences through travel, such as a woman who traveled the world to overcome grief and find herself.	Buffer presents customer success stories on its blog encouraging readers to sign up for a free trial to get the same results.
Social	Canva, a graphic design platform, demonstrates newly released product features through social media videos	Supreme features limited-edition collaborations on social media	Sephora's social media posts highlight limited-time sales events to encourage immediate action
Email	Asana shares details about new feature releases and how they enhance productivity	Patagonia shares its environmentally conscious initiatives with subscribers	Starbucks emails rewards program members to incentivize purchase
Website	L'Oréal skincare product pages mention clinical trial results as proof of efficacy	Ralph Lauren's website features photos portraying a luxury lifestyle	Warby Parker offers a low-risk, home try-on program
Partnerships	Samsung partnered with Instagram to promote its new Galaxy S21 Ultra camera, highlighting the cognitive appeal of the smartphone's advanced camera technology.	Glossier's products feature endorsements from makeup artists	Uber partnered with Spotify to allow users to link their accounts and play their favorite songs during their Uber rides, incentivizing immediate signups.
Advertising	LG explains its OLED TV technology at depth in ads	Calvin Klein represents an aspirational lifestyle featuring certain models in its underwear campaigns	Bumble, a dating and networking app, empowers women to make the first move and download the app

BRAND PARTNERSHIPS

As brands take on the challenge of crafting these different types of messages, they often explore alliances with compatible organizations and individuals. Brand partnerships can be an effective strategy to transfer desirable associations among complementary allies. By agreeing to leverage each other's platforms to expand audiences, one brand's owned channels essentially become another one's earned channels.

There are many ways to structure partnerships with varying levels of commitment and types of exchanges. A partnership can involve some sort of monetary reward, be paid, or it can be a win-win collaboration where both parties commit to a set of actions in each other's favor (unpaid).

You'll find a basic typology of brand partnerships below, outlining six popular approaches:

- **Unpaid co-creation:** two or more brands join forces to design a new product or service under both of their names
- **Unpaid co-promotion:** two or more brands commit to promoting each other's offerings leveraging owned channels
- **Paid creation:** brands commission the creation of specific assets (images, video, content, products, etc) in exchange for a fee
- **Paid placements:** a brand's product is placed within another's channel/s so that a third-party's audience is made aware of the offering. Can range from subtle placements (implicit) to entirely explicit mentions.
- **Paid sponsorships:** a brand decides to support a third-party's event or campaign in exchange for a mention or opportunity to reach the event's audience
- **Paid endorsements:** a brand pays for a direct recommendation from an influential figure or brand.

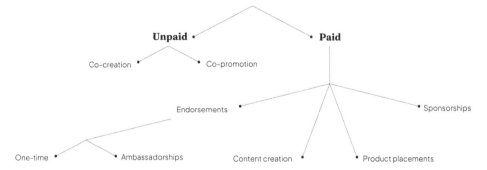

FIGURE 18.2: Brand partnerships

These categories aren't mutually exclusive: brand partnerships can take many forms and often include more than one reward mechanism. Brands might agree to both co-create and co-promote a new line of products. A brand might work with an individual to endorse and receive products, while also being financially rewarded. The above typology is more of a buffet than a prix fixe menu.

In securing these engagements, brands can decide to work with organizations or individuals. Increasingly, influential content creators (**influencers**) are becoming a household strategy for brands around the globe. Emerging from the popularization of social networking platforms like Instagram and TikTok, these creators offer decentralized access to niche audiences in exchange for cash compensation, in-kind payments, or a mix of both.

As content creators surge, we're seeing a shift toward engaging customers as partners. User-generated campaigns elevate everyday customers who genuinely use and recommend one's brand. This strategy can come off as a more authentic way to convey benefits and can be either rewarded or unpaid.

TABLE 18.4: Types of Brand partners

Brand <> Brand	Brand <> Individual

• Brands with complementary products
• Audience colleagues
• Reference brands with broad reach
	• Celebrities
	• Content creators:
	  • Artists (platform size irrelevant)
	  • Nanoinfluencers
	  • Microinfluencers
	  • Macroinfluencers
	• Industry experts
	• Customers

The variety of potential partners will expand as communication channels transform, but you will find a recap of the most common associates brands can engage below:

NOTES

1. Petty, R. E., Cacioppo, J. T., & Schumann, D. (1983). Central and peripheral routes to advertising effectiveness: The moderating role of involvement. *Journal of Consumer Research, 10*(2), 135–146. Cacioppo, J. T., & Petty, R. E. (1984). The Elaboration Likelihood Model of Persuasion. *ACR North American Advances, NA-11.* https://www.acrwebsite.org/volumes/6329/volumes/v11/NA-11/full

2. Cialdini, R. B. (1993). *Influence: The Psychology of Persuasion* (Rev. ed). Quill/William Morrow.

3. Cialdini, R. B. (2016). *Pre-Suasion: A Revolutionary Way to Influence and Persuade.* Simon and Schuster.

4. Krugman, H. E. (1965). The impact of television advertising: Learning without involvement. *The Public Opinion Quarterly, 29*(3), 349–356.
Krugman, H. E. (1966). The measurement of advertising involvement. *The Public Opinion Quarterly, 30*(4), 583–596.

CHAPTER 19

DESIGNING MEMORABLE BRAND EXPERIENCES

DOI: 10.4324/9781003336693-23

The word experience is borrowed from Latin *experientia,* which means *testing of possibilities.* Brands can go to market without a defined experiential journey, and may even succeed at selling products, but only **brand experience mapping** can make that success scalable and sustainable over time.

Upon growing, companies find that the unique touchpoints that secured their initial success hinge on systems to survive. Trusting that one team member to carry the weight of the brand's essence on their shoulders is unrealistic. People change and so do their moods and energy levels. An intentional brand journey map locks the special moments your customers know and love you for through processes that make them truly repeatable.

In Chapter 11, we saw how Brandverses can provide a platform for brands to engage their customers through rich, sensory experiences. We defined this space and selected symbols that could best express its look and feel. Throughout this chapter, we will focus on the activities and processes that turn that setting into a fully-fledged experience for customers.

A **brand experience** is a thoughtfully designed journey through which customers interact with a product or service— the cohesive set of touchpoints in which a brand's story unfolds.

Now that we've shaped that story, brand experience mapping will give us tools to put it into action. To turn settings, characters, and intentions into living encounters and events where we'll connect with customers.

THE CEM FRAMEWORK

One of the most widely applied business tools to define these encounters is Schmitt's Customer Experience Management (CEM) framework[1]. It involves five steps for creating meaningful experiences with customers and improving customer loyalty.

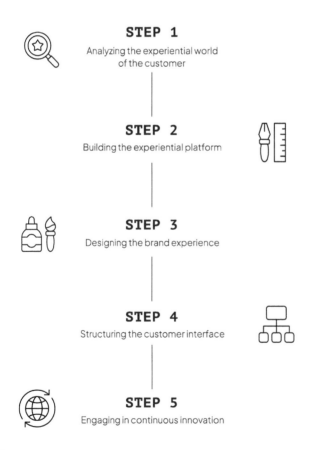

5 STEPS OF THE

CEM Framework

STEP 1
Analyzing the experiential world
of the customer

STEP 2
Building the experiential platform

STEP 3
Designing the brand experience

STEP 4
Structuring the customer interface

STEP 5
Engaging in continuous innovation

FIGURE 19.1: CEM framework

The first step in Schmitt's CEM framework is **analyzing the experiential world of the customer.** This step is about understanding the sociocultural and business context in which customers operate. By understanding these intricate factors, brands can foster a sense of empathy, enabling them to develop persona profiles that drive targeted brand strategies.

Imagine Sunlit Soirees, a company specializing in outdoor furniture. To truly understand their customers, they conduct in-depth research on how people interact with outdoor spaces in various sociocultural contexts, considering factors like climate, regional customs, and lifestyle preferences. By analyzing customer behaviors and preferences, Sunlit Soirees can create furniture that caters to the unique experiential needs of their customers, enhancing comfort and enjoyment in diverse outdoor settings.

In Chapter 6, we learned how to synthesize these customers' traits in **persona profiles** that can drive brand strategy. Once brand managers understand who their target customers are, they can craft a message that resonates with them. For example, if the target market is young entrepreneurs, messages that emphasize independence, ambition, and motivation can be more effective. Knowing who you're marketing to and understanding their needs unlocks empathy.

The second step in the CEM framework is **building the experiential platform**. This involves designing a dynamic, multisensory representation of the desired customer experience. This step in the CEM framework allows brands to weave together unique elements that capture the essence of their offerings, creating a distinct brand identity.

Consider a gourmet popcorn brand: they recognize that customers crave not just delicious popcorn but also a memorable, multisensory experience. The brand decides to create an experiential platform centered around "Adventurous Flavor Journeys". They develop unique, global-inspired popcorn flavors and colorful packaging that transport customers to different countries with each bite. This platform enables the brand to differentiate itself from competitors and create a strong identity.

The third step is **designing the brand experience.** At this stage, brands must incorporate experiential features, aesthetics, and messaging in logos, signage, packaging, retail spaces, and advertising.

Let's take a wearable tech brand as an example. They create sleek, modern devices that seamlessly integrate into daily life, offering an appealing "look and feel" that complements various fashion styles. The brand's advertising and marketing materials highlight the ways their products can enhance everyday experiences, like monitoring fitness levels, organizing schedules, and simplifying communication, all while maintaining a stylish appearance.

In the next section, I'll walk you through the process of mapping out the customer experience from when they become aware of the brand to when they purchase it. We'll consider the various touchpoints such as emails, website visits, and in-person interactions where the brand interacts with its audience. This comprehensive approach helps brands understand how to optimize each interaction for a seamless, memorable experience.

Up next in the CEM framework is **structuring the customer interface**. Once the experiential platform and experience are designed, this step is about implementing them;

ensuring consistency among various touchpoints. A coherent journey reinforces the brand's promise at every turn.

As an example, let's analyze an eco-friendly grocery store chain's implementation of an experiential platform: "Sustainable Living Made Easy". They decide to enact this promise across all brand touchpoints, from the store layout and signage to employee interactions and their online presence. Each customer interaction reinforces their commitment to eco-friendly practices and products, creating a seamless shopping experience that aligns with customers' values.

The last step is an ongoing task: **engaging in continuous innovation.** Innovate based on the experiential platform, ranging from major inventions to small product improvements. This step helps build customer equity.

A boutique travel agency, for example, decides to constantly innovate its experiential platform: "Authentic Cultural Immersion". The brand regularly explores new destinations, develops partnerships with local businesses and artisans, and designs unique, off-the-beaten-path itineraries. By continuously refining their travel packages, they're able to attract new customers and maintain the loyalty of existing ones, ultimately building strong customer equity and fostering growth.

Schmitt's CEM framework is a versatile, adaptable approach that empowers brands to tackle a wide array of challenges, including changing customer perceptions, increasing loyalty and satisfaction, and introducing new products. By combining analytical and creative paradigms and focusing on both internal (employee) and external (customer) experiences, the CEM framework allows brands to achieve unparalleled success in creating unforgettable customer experiences.

MAPPING BRAND EXPERIENCES

Empathy is the key to unlocking brand innovation. Caring about customers' needs and taking the time to uncover them is the rock cult brands stand on.

A **brand experience map** zooms into the essential moments driving customers' interactions with your brand and slices them to design empathetic strategies at every step.

There is no wrong level of zoom or approach to slice these moments, but you will benefit from learning this general framework and adapting it to your brand's specifics.

At a high level, your brand experience map can set a division between pre-purchase, purchase, and post-purchase touch-points. Your next level of detail consists in breaking down each of those phases even further:

- Which moments are taking place **before** customers purchase? Consider research, referrals, consideration, consultative selling, and sales support activities.
- Which specific touchpoints and steps are part of your customer's **purchase** moment? Break down your shopping and checkout moments to better identify opportunities. What interactions do you typically have with customers **after** they've made an initial purchase? Review product support, referral, cross-selling, upselling, and repeat purchasing events.

JOURNEY MAPPING: BOOSTING DELIGHT AND REDUCING FRICTION

This process is about empowering customers to move confidently in the direction of their purchase intention and securing their patronage long term. To help you construct an intentional journey for customers, the journey map below outlines a series of stages and strategy questions to resolve.

Brand Experience Map

	RESEARCHING	ENTERING	SEARCHING	ASKING	PURCHASING	LEAVING	POST-SALE
What is your customer doing?							
What is he/she thinking?							
What is he/she feeling?							
What is your brand saying at this point? How?							

FIGURE 19.2: Brand experience map

From left to right, you'll find a series of **columns** for customer touchpoints and **rows** with experience-related questions. As customers progress through these stages, take a moment to consider:

- ***What they're doing:*** Focus on your customer's job-to-be-done at this stage. What specific actions are they taking as they research, enter, search, ask, purchase, leave, or actually use the product/service?
- ***What they're thinking:*** Consider your customer's thoughts and hesitations. Is there something creating doubt or are there unmet expectations (cognitive dissonance) hurting their experience?
- ***What they're feeling:*** Empathize with their emotions. Is there friction, frustration to address? Excitement or joy to amplify?
- ***What is the brand doing and saying?*** Think proactively about the brand's response and tone. How are we reassuring customers in moments of frustration? How are we delighting them in unexpected ways during each touchpoint? What is best left unsaid (what is the brand *not* doing, by design)?

EVALUATING BRAND EXPERIENCES

Compelling brand experiences create lasting impressions that engage our minds, senses, and emotions. Cognizant of this holistic character, Brakus et al. defined a brand experience as the set of "sensations, feelings, cognitions, and behavioral responses evoked by brand-related stimuli that are part of a brand's design and identity, packaging, communications, and environments"[2].

TABLE 19.1: Brand Experience Scale

Scale name	Brand Experience Scale
Authors	Brakus et al. (2009)
Type of scale	7-point Likert
Anchors	From "Strongly disagree" (1) to "Strongly agree" (7)
Dimensions	*Sensory, Affective, Intellectual, Behavioral*
Items	**Sensory** • This brand makes a strong impression on my visual sense or other senses • I find this brand interesting in a sensory way • This brand does not appeal to my senses* **Affective** • This brand induces feelings and sentiments • I do not have strong emotions for this brand* • This brand is an emotional brand **Intellectual** • I engage in a lot of thinking when I encounter this brand • This brand does not make me think* • This brand stimulates my curiosity and problem solving **Behavioral** • I engage in physical actions and behaviors when I use this brand • This brand results in bodily experiences • This brand is not action-oriented* ** Item should be reverse coded*

They also developed a scale to visualize and fine-tune this brand experience within all kinds of organizations. Dimension and item details are included below for ease of application.

NOTES

1. Schmitt, B. H. (2003). *Customer Experience Management: A Revolutionary Approach to Connecting with Your Customers.* John Wiley & Sons, Incorporated.
2. Brakus, J. J., Schmitt, B. H., & Zarantonello, L. (2009). Brand experience: What is it? How is it measured? Does it affect loyalty? *Journal of Marketing, 73*, 52–68.

CHAPTER 20

BRAND PORTFOLIO MANAGEMENT

EXTENSIONS, ARCHITECTURE, AND REBRANDING

DOI: 10.4324/9781003336693-24

The year is 1946. Josephine Esther Mentzer walks around the streets of Manhattan demonstrating her makeup and creams to women while they are sitting under hair dryers. This entrepreneurial daughter of immigrants decides to go by Estée and marries Joseph Lauder. And the rest is history.

Estée Lauder is the global cosmetics brand a young Josephine could only dream of. Dozens of brand acquisitions, product extensions, market expansions, and one IPO later, The Estée Lauder Companies (NYSE: EL) now own cult brands like Aveda, Clinique, Origins, La Mer, MAC, and Too Faced[1].

Like Estée and Joseph's small business, brands evolve from the minute they're created. The brand we're designing today must not only stand the test of time, but be prepared to accommodate the strategic pivots we will inevitably face. We're building for now and for later, simultaneously.

That's where the concept of a **brand portfolio** comes in: it's a framework to manage the living, expansive entity that is a brand.

As brand managers, we are challenged to build ever-more global, scalable, and ambitious brands. New growth opportunities at our disposal make brand building a more ambitious, unsettled endeavor.

Throughout this chapter, we will explore different kinds of brand portfolios, learning how to organize and reorganize organizational structures as brands families expand.

BASICS OF BRAND ARCHITECTURE

Brand architecture is a blueprint that lays out how a company's various brands, products, or services relate to one another.

Think of it as the master plan that makes it easier for customers to understand what a company has to offer, while helping businesses strengthen their position in the market and create loyal customers[2]. For example, consider how Apple seamlessly organizes its products, like the iPhone, iPad, and MacBook, within its brand ecosystem.

When a company nails its brand architecture, it not only highlights the connections between its brands but also helps customers clarify each product's value added in a differentiated way. For instance, the way Unilever manages its wide range of products, including Dove, Ben & Jerry's, and Lipton, creates a harmonious environment where each brand can grow and support one another. This strategic organization helps guide consumer choices and opens up opportunities for cross-selling.

Jan Noel Kapferer summarized the brand architecture challenge well in five essential questions[3]:

1. What should we call new products in the portfolio?
2. How many brand levels should we adopt?
3. How much visibility should the parent brand have, if any?
4. Should the corporate and commercial brand names be different?
5. Should the architecture change based on the market?

BRAND PORTFOLIO

While brand architecture describes the strategy, structure, and relationships among a company's various brands, the term **brand portfolio** is a way to refer to the set of brands managed by this company.

By diversifying its portfolio, a company can target different market segments and reduce risks associated with a single brand. Managing a brand portfolio requires balancing the resources allocated to each brand and ensuring that they complement and support each other.

Think of a brand portfolio as a diverse array of offerings, like the many branches of a tree, each with its own unique qualities and purpose. This collection of brands caters to different customer segments, markets, and needs, providing businesses with a competitive edge. For instance, Toyota's brand portfolio includes Toyota, Lexus, and Scion, each targeting different customer groups with distinct offerings. Meanwhile, brand architecture is like the tree's trunk and roots, providing a stable, structured foundation that supports and connects all those branches, ensuring the tree thrives and prospers.

Managing a brand portfolio involves making strategic decisions about the creation, nurturing, and growth of individual brands within the portfolio. It requires a keen understanding of market dynamics, customer preferences, and competitive landscapes. A strong brand portfolio can help businesses expand their market reach, optimize resource allocation, and mitigate risks associated with market fluctuations.

For example, Marriott International's brand architecture clearly communicates the different experiences offered by its range of hotel brands, such as the Ritz-Carlton, Courtyard by Marriott, and Aloft Hotels.

BRAND ARCHITECTURE STRATEGIES

To create the perfect brand architecture, companies need to think about all the factors that shape how their audience sees and understands their offerings[4]. By diving deep into research and analysis, businesses can establish a brand framework that effectively communicates their core values, guides customers, and boosts brand equity. Just look at how Coca-Cola successfully differentiates its brands, like Diet Coke, Sprite, and Fanta, within the same portfolio.

Nestlé has built a strong brand architecture with its numerous products, such as Nespresso, KitKat, and Purina. Procter & Gamble manages its extensive range of brands, from Pampers to Gillette, with a clear and efficient structure.

In the end, a well-thought-out brand architecture strategy can make a huge difference to a company's success. It drives brand recognition, sets brands apart, and fuels growth in an ever-competitive market[5]. Whether you're managing a small business or a global powerhouse, a solid brand architecture can work wonders.

Aaker and Joachimsthaler proposed four main types of brand architecture, each with different sub-strategies. These types are the branded house, sub-brands, endorsed brands, and house of brands[6].

BRANDED HOUSE

A branded house strategy places the corporate brand at the forefront, with all products or services promoted under the corporate brand name. This strategy comprises two sub-strategies:

- **Different identity:** Unleash the power of unique brand identities while retaining the essence of the master brand. This approach presents an opportunity to diversify and expand into new markets.

Brand Relationship Spectrum

DAVID AAKER AND ERICH JOACHIMSTHALER

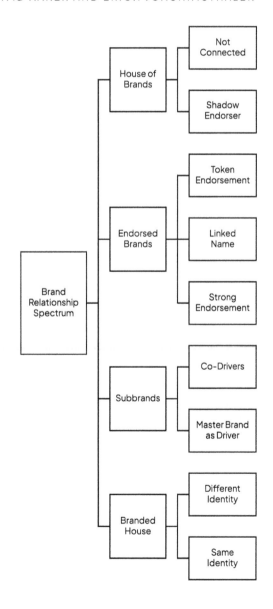

- Samsung Galaxy, Samsung Smart TV, Samsung Gear, and Samsung Home Appliances all go under the Samsung brand, while each product line maintains a distinct identity.
- **Same identity:** Embrace a unified brand identity across products and services, creating a cohesive brand experience that resonates with consumers and amplifies brand equity.
  - Virgin's Virgin Atlantic, Virgin Mobile, and Virgin Galactic.

SUB-BRANDS

Sub-brands fuse the parent brand with an independent brand identity, enabling the subsidiaries to establish their unique positions while still benefiting from the parent brand's equity. This model contains two sub-strategies:

- **Co-drivers:** Master and sub-brands work hand-in-hand, strengthening each other's positioning and leveraging the parent brand's reputation.
  - *Nestlé's KitKat, Nespresso, Nesquik, and Purina*
- **Master brand as a driver:** The magnetic pull of the master brand drives the sub-brand forward and serves customers with a consistent brand promise.
  - *Ford's Ford Mustang, Ford Focus, Ford Explorer, and Ford F-150*

ENDORSED BRANDS

Endorsed brands maintain their unique identities but are associated with a parent brand for endorsement or support. This model features three sub-strategies:

- **Token endorsement:** A subtle endorsement from the master brand, providing credibility and support while allowing endorsed brands to shine independently.
  - Xoom, a PayPal Service: PayPal connects its Xoom sub-brand, an international money transfer service, using the "a PayPal Service" structure in the logo to link it with the parent company.
- **Linked name:** There's an artful, linguistically creative linkage between the master brand and endorsed brand, creating a connection through visual and verbal cues that inspire brand recognition.
  - Amazon employs the "Amazon" prefix to link its sub-brands, such as Amazon Prime, Amazon Web Services (AWS), and Amazon Echo.
- **Strong endorsement:** Provided by the master brand, this endorsement forges a powerful connection and infuses the endorsed brand with credibility and trust. Endorsed brands are typically prefixed with "by" to clearly indicate ownership.
  - InfinitiPRO by Conair: Conair, a manufacturer of personal care and small appliances, connects its InfinitiPRO sub-brand, which offers a range of beauty tools and accessories, using "by" in the logo to link it with the main brand, creating a cohesive brand identity.

HOUSE OF BRANDS

A **house of brands** comprises a collection of unrelated, distinctive brands, each with its unique identity. The corporate brand typically assumes a limited role in this strategy. There are two sub-strategies:

- **Not connected:** A sense of independence where unique brands operate autonomously and cater to distinct markets without interference from the parent brand.

- Luxottica owns various eyewear brands like Ray-Ban, Oakley, and Persol, without connecting them to the parent brand, allowing each sub-brand to maintain its own identity.
- **Shadow endorser:** A subtle connection between the parent brand and its subsidiaries, offering a gentle nod of endorsement while allowing the individual brands to flourish in their respective niches. The endorsement is often only visible when one actively looks for it in non-prominent marketing spaces or small print.
  - Unilever employs a shadow endorser sub-strategy for sub-brands such as Dove, Lipton, and Ben & Jerry's. The Unilever name is not prominently displayed on the products but can be found in small print on packaging, subtly connecting the sub-brands to the parent company.

BRAND EXTENSIONS

Brand extensions harness the power of an existing brand's equity to introduce offerings in new categories. This strategy can capitalize on the brand's reputation, reduce marketing costs, and increase the likelihood of consumer acceptance. However, brand extensions can also dilute brand equity if not managed carefully.

Strategic brand extensions enable companies to benefit from the positive associations and trust that consumers have with their established brand. By extending the brand into new categories, organizations can reduce the need for substantial marketing investments and lean on the original brand's familiarity to increase the likelihood of the new product's success. In order to preserve the value of a brand, companies must ensure that their new offerings are compatible with their core brand values. Failing to do so could mean a loss of brand equity.

To maximize the effectiveness of brand extensions, organizations must ensure that their new products or services align with the brand's core values and image, and that the extension does not overstretch the brand's positioning. Failure to maintain this alignment can lead to potential confusion among consumers, dilution of the brand's distinct identity, and ultimately, weakened brand equity.

In one of the first studies on **brand extension fit**, Aaker and Keller found three key influential factors: substitutability, complementarity, and transferability[7]. Put simply, the affinity between original and new product/s must be such that they can be used interchangeably, in a complementary way, or produced efficiently as part of a single operation.

A remarkable illustration of complementary offerings can be found in Adobe's Creative Cloud suite, where various applications seamlessly integrate, empowering users to unleash their full creative potential.

Transferability is another essential component of solid brand extension fit. Tesla's foray into solar power and energy storage, for example, exemplifies the strategic transfer of core competencies into new domains and products like the Powerwall and Solar Roof.

Professors Franziska Völckner and Henrik Sattler also identified five factors that significantly influence brand extension success[8]:

- Fit between the parent brand and the extension product
- Marketing support for the extension's release

- Parent brand conviction
- Parent brand experience
- Retailer acceptance

All in all, parent and extension brand fit surfaces as a determining factor for a given extension's success.

MEASURING BRAND EXTENSION FIT

Brand managers must ensure brand extensions make marketing and operational sense. As we just saw, this notion is known as **Brand Extension Fit.**

Most recently, Deng and Messinger expanded on previous brand extension studies and looked at measurable factors to determine a given brand extension's strength. Six dimensions emerged as a result of their analysis[9]:

- **Feature-based fit:** Is there alignment between facets of the original and extension brands (aesthetic style, quality, price)?
- **Function-based fit:** How well do the original and extension brands' perceived functions integrate?
- **Resource-based fit:** Can the original brand be expected to deliver on the extension, considering its current production capabilities and expertise?
- **Usage-occasion-based fit:** Are these two brands used in a similar context?
- **Target market-based fit:** Does the parent brand have the authority and recognition among the new brand's intended target or can it predictably build it leveraging its current market position?
- **Image-based fit:** Are both brands' deeper meanings, values, and mental associations compatible?

You might be wondering how these common-sense principles can be put to the test. As a result of their analysis, Deng and Messinger built a robust scale to evaluate brand extension fit. Item, scoring, and dimension details are all available below for ease of use.

DESIGNING BRAND EXTENSION STRATEGIES

As you contemplate a brand extension, keep in mind the following strategic decisions:

- **Associations:** Which parent brand associations benefit the extension brand?
- **Naming:** Will the parent brand's name make any kind of appearance in the extension brand's? (Explicit as in logo merger, logo subtext, or implicit/subtle as in marketing subtext for an independent sub-brand)
- **Visual identity:** Will the parent brand's visual identity influence the extension brand's to create portfolio cohesion, or will it diverge? Of cohesive, which design elements will they share?
- **Co-branding:** Does it ever make sense for these brands to market themselves together? In what contexts?
- **Positioning:** Does the extension represent an upward or downward stretch for the parent brand in terms of pricing?
- **Market:** How are the target audiences similar? Different?
- **Channels:** How should the communication channels be similar? Different?
- **Production synergies:** What production processes are shared, hence would benefit/gain efficiencies from scale?
- **Marketing synergies:** Which parent brand partnerships, know-how, and efficiencies benefit the extension *brand?*

TABLE 20.1: Brand Extension Fit Scale

Scale name	Brand Extension Fit Scale
Authors	Deng & Messinger (2022)
Type of scale	7-point Likert
Anchors	From "Extremely dissimilar" (1) to "Extremely similar" (7)
Dimensions	Feature-based Fit, Function-based Fit, Resource-based Fit, Image-based Fit, Usage-occasion-based Fit, Target-market-based Fit
Items	**Feature-based Fit** • How similar are [parent brand (product)] and [extension product], in terms of their specific features and attributes (e.g. size, color, smell, taste, price, etc.)? **Function-based Fit** • How similar are [parent brand (product)] and [extension product], in terms of their basic functions, benefits, and functionality? **Resource-based Fit** • How similar are [parent brand (product)] and [extension product], in terms of the resources required to develop the products (e.g., people, facilities, skills, strategy, knowledge, expertise)? **Image-based Fit** • How similar are [parent brand (product)] and [extension product], in terms of their abstract images and concepts (i.e., associations, concepts, or images that come to your mind when you think about the brand/product)? **Usage-occasion-based Fit** • How similar are [parent brand (product)] and [extension product], in terms of their usage occasions (i.e., where or when to use them)? **Target-market-based Fit** • How similar are [parent brand (product)] and [extension product], in terms of their target markets (i.e., consumers at which a product is aimed)?

Successful brand extensions create synergistic ecosystems that elevate the user experience. They lean on the foundation of past success to expand their horizons by capitalizing on the expertise, infrastructure, and human talent that propelled their original offerings to prominence.

GOING GLOBAL

As brand architectures get more complex, so do the opportunities for geographical expansion. When a brand has built a strong foundation in a given market, there's a temptation to merely export that essence and conquer new regions the "x brand" way. By all means, *resist that temptation.*

While there are distinctive identity elements that could potentially set this brand apart in any market, it is crucial to analyze how local cultures interpret these ideas. Out of respect for these future customers and due diligence for the brand's success, organizations must explore new markets with the fresh, unbiased eyes of curiosity.

Getting out of one's own "normal" is essential. Markets vary in their value priorities, communication styles, and predominant cultural dimensions. Let's look at how these three factors can make a real difference for brand marketing.

On one hand, cultures differ in their preferred communication styles. First introduced by anthropologist Edward T. Hall, the concepts of **high and low-context communication** help explain the cultural variations in how we speak to each other:

A high context communication or message is one in which most of the information is already in the person, while very little is in the coded, explicit, transmitted part of the message. While a low context communication is just the opposite; the mass of the information is vested in the explicit code. (Hall 1976)[10]

A high-context culture relies heavily on non-verbal cues, such as facial expressions, gestures, and tones of voice, for communication. Many Asian countries, such as Japan and China, have high-context cultures. As opposed to high-context communication, low-context communication involves explicit, direct, and precise verbal communication. People in low-context cultures tend to rely on words instead of non-verbal cues to convey meaning. The United States, Germany, and Scandinavian countries are examples of low-context cultures.

How we say certain things varies across cultures, and so do the things we choose to say and do. Depending on our upbringing and context, we come to hold certain values in high regard. These values, in turn, become strong predictors and drivers of our behavior. Schwartz found that there's a relatively universal set of values whose valence changes depending on the culture you're looking at[11].

Schwartz identifies ten motivationally distinct, broad, and basic values that stem from the three universal human needs: the biological needs of an individual, the need for coordinated social interaction, and the need for communal well-being[12].

Universal
Values

SCHWARTZ

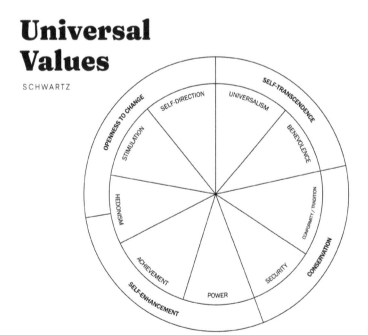

FIGURE 20.2: Schwartz value system

Across cultures, these ten basic values tend to be recognized as core values:

1. **Self-direction:** Self-direction is all about independent thinking, taking action, and cherishing personal freedom.
2. **Stimulation:** This dimension is all about seeking excitement, novelty, and embracing change.
3. **Hedonism:** Think of hedonism as the pursuit of life's pleasures and personal indulgence.
4. **Achievement:** Achievement is all about the importance a culture places on personal success, ambition, and competence.
5. **Power:** Countries with high power value respect authority and social status, while those with low power value treasure equality and autonomy.
6. **Security:** Security is all about the importance of safety, harmony, and stability in society, relationships, and oneself.
7. **Conformity:** Conformity involves refraining from actions or inclinations that could harm others or violate social norms.
8. **Tradition:** Tradition represents the respect for customs and ideas passed down from previous generations.
9. **Benevolence:** Benevolence focuses on preserving and enhancing the well-being of those we interact with regularly.
10. **Universalism:** Universalism is all about understanding, tolerance, and protecting the welfare of all people and nature.

Another way to look at these underlying differences is through the lens of **cultural dimensions.** Dutch social psychologist Geert Hofstede created a framework to pinpoint specific traits with high variance across cultures[13]. Following are his six cultural dimensions, which have deeply influenced the field of cross-cultural communications[14]:

1. **Power distance index (PDI):** In every society, power is either concentrated, shared equally among its members, or a mix of both. High power distance cultures welcome hierarchy, while low power distance cultures champion equal power distribution and collaborative decision-making.
2. **Individualism vs. collectivism (IDV):** Some societies prioritize personal goals, while others value group harmony. Individualist cultures cherish autonomy and self-expression, whereas collectivist cultures treasure unity and social cohesion.
3. **Masculinity vs. femininity (MAS):** Imagine a society valuing traits like ambition and assertiveness versus one that prizes empathy and cooperation. That's what this dimension explores.
4. **Uncertainty avoidance index (UAI):** This dimension uncovers how societies react to uncertainty. High uncertainty avoidance cultures create rules to minimize risks, while low uncertainty avoidance cultures embrace change and ambiguity.
5. **Long-term orientation vs. short-term orientation (LTO):** This dimension explores whether a society values long-term planning and future investment over instant gratification and short-term gains.
6. **Indulgence vs. restraint (IVR):** Imagine a world where fun and personal enjoyment are either encouraged or restricted by social norms. Indulgent cultures prioritize leisure, while restrained cultures emphasize self-discipline.

Understanding Hofstede's six cultural dimensions can unlock our potential to connect with people across cultures, craft winning brand strategies, and adapt to the kaleidoscope of cultural environments.

WHERE TO FROM HERE?

What are all the possible ways a brand can extend itself into a new market? The two obvious extremes of this answer are exporting its exact identity or adapting to the new context entirely.

Bartlett and Ghoshal developed a typology of multinational companies that surfaces four potential strategies[15]:

- **Internationalization:** a quite literal rinse and repeat from one market to the next, without meaningful changes to pricing structures or feature sets. Focusing on centralized decision-making and a strong connection to their roots, these firms offer standardized products with minimal tweaks for local markets.
- **Global strategy:** variance in local preferences is not very important, but pricing is. Companies adopting this strategy are masters of standardization and integration, striving for cost efficiencies and economies of scale through centralized decision-making and minimal localization. They offer a consistent brand image and product line across the globe.
- **Transnational strategy:** tries to balance the desire for lower costs and efficiency with the need to adjust to local preferences within various countries. A middle ground between the global and multi-domestic strategies. Companies that embrace this strategy expertly balance a consistent global brand image with local market adaptations.
- **Multidomestic:** Emphasizes responsiveness to local requirements within each of its markets, regardless of

cost or efficiency implications. This approach is all about embracing local flavors. By customizing products and services for individual markets, subsidiaries enjoy more autonomy and decision-making power, adapting their offerings to the local environment like a chameleon.

NOTES

1. Estée Lauder. *A Family in Business*. Retrieved from https://www.elcompanies.com/en/who-we-are/the-lauder-family/a-family-in-business
Estée Lauder. *The Estée Story*. Retrieved from https://www.elcompanies.com/en/who-we-are/the-lauder-family/the-estee-story
2. Aaker, D. A., & Joachimsthaler, E. (2000). The brand relationship spectrum: The key to the brand architecture challenge. *California Management Review, 42*(4), 8–23.
3. Kapferer, J.-N. (2008). *The New Strategic Brand Management: Creating and Sustaining Brand Equity Long Term*. Kogan Page Publishers.
4. Bengtsson, A., & Servais, P. (2005). Co-branding on industrial markets. *Industrial Marketing Management, 34*(7), 706–713. https://doi.org/10.1016/j.indmarman.2005.06.004
5. Hankinson, G., & Cowking, P. (1993). *Branding in Action: Cases and Strategies for Profitable Brand Management*. McGraw-Hill.
6. Aaker, D. A., & Joachimsthaler, E. (2000). The Brand Relationship Spectrum: The key to the brand architecture challenge. *California Management Review, 42*(4), 8–23.
7. Aaker, D. A., & Keller, K. L. (1990). Consumer evaluations of brand extensions. *Journal of Marketing, 54*(1), 27.
8. Völckner, F., & Sattler, H. (2006). Drivers of brand extension success. *Journal of Marketing, 70*(2), 18–34. https://doi.org/10.1509/jmkg.70.2.018
9. Deng, Q. (Claire), & Messinger, P. R. (2022). Dimensions of brand-extension fit. *International Journal of Research in Marketing, 39*(3), 764–787. https://doi.org/10.1016/j.ijresmar.2021.09.013
10. Hall, E. T. (1976). *Beyond Culture*. Knopf Doubleday Publishing Group.
11. Schwartz, S. H. (1992). Universals in the content and structure of values: Theoretical advances and empirical tests in 20 countries. In *Advances in Experimental Social Psychology* (Vol. 25, pp. 1–65). Academic Press.

12. Schwartz, S. H. (2012). An overview of the Schwartz theory of basic values. *Online readings in Psychology and Culture, 2*(1), 11.

13. Hofstede, G. H. (2001). *Culture's Consequences: Comparing Values, Behaviors, Institutions, and Organizations Across Nations* (Second edition). Sage.

14. Hofstede, G., Hofstede, G. J., & Minkov, M. (2010). *Cultures and Organizations: Software of the Mind* (Third Edition). McGraw Hill Professional.

15. Bartlett, C. A., & Ghoshal, S. (2002). *Managing Across Borders: The Transnational Solution.* Harvard Business Press.

CHAPTER 21

BRAND INTELLIGENCE

DOI: 10.4324/9781003336693-25

A brand's strategy can be meticulously designed on paper and fail spectacularly when put to the test. Only through diligent measurement and analysis can a team unlock sustainable brand growth. In my experience, these brand intelligence habits must become formal processes within organizations to maintain their periodicity and importance.

There's a misconception in the business world that the return on brand-building investments and activities cannot be measured. In fact, there's a wide range of objective scales and tools to quantify the impact of our actions.

Knowing your brand's inner trends is essential, but so is taking a pulse on the wider industry. Are there meaningful shifts taking place that have implications for what you're building? Have consumer preferences evolved since you last studied the market? What are direct and indirect competitors trying that sets new expectations from your target customer?

This simultaneously present and prospective mindset drives all sustainable brand strategy. Throughout this chapter, we will review options available to brand managers as we assess key health indicators like affect, loyalty, demand, perception, and awareness. Then, we will look at trendspotting and forecasting techniques to stay ahead of external changes and seize opportunities.

TRENDS: KEEPING YOUR FINGER ON THE PULSE

In Chapter 6, we discussed the most popular types of research questions in marketing, focusing on segmentation research.

We saw how primary and secondary sources can provide insights to build a brand's audience personas.

Now, let's turn our attention to trend research, an essential tool to keep up with market changes.

Identifying trends as they emerge keeps brands fresh and relevant. Even if you've consciously gone through every exercise in this book, changing conditions will challenge your assumptions. Keeping your finger on the pulse of change is crucial for brand survival.

However, analyzing the vast amount of available information to distill actionable insights can be a daunting task. What to monitor, what to look out for, and how to use this data are all important questions.

ENTER THE BRAND RADAR

A **brand radar** is a trend data collection system that allows you to identify meaningful shifts and act on them through informed brand innovations.

Seizing opportunities requires being aware of them in a timely fashion. If you intend to do this sustainably, your trendspotting should also be process-driven and deliberate.

Hearsay can lead to random moments of serendipity, but a solid trend research practice will keep your execution predictably sharp long term.

BUILDING A BRAND RADAR

At its most basic, a brand radar contains:

1. Source name
2. Relationship of the source to one's brand
   - Direct competitor
   - Indirect competitor
   - Industry reference
   - General reference
3. Direct link to access emerging updates
4. Core strength or channel to look out for

Maintaining a brand radar involves two stages: **monitoring sources** and **storing insights**.

For monitoring, you can access a set of links manually or lean on an RSS reader.

Insights storage can be as simple as populating a database/spreadsheet or using a more elaborate bookmarking tool like Pinterest or Evernote. Store these notes in a place that's accessible to your team.

With the amount of sources you'll monitor, the ability to synthesize what matters most is key. For every source with noteworthy updates, consider recording the following ideas:

- What can we take away from this?
- If not immediately actionable, how can we translate this tactic to our audience?
- Why did this work?

Brand radar

WRITING TOOL BRAND FOR MILLENNIAL WOMEN

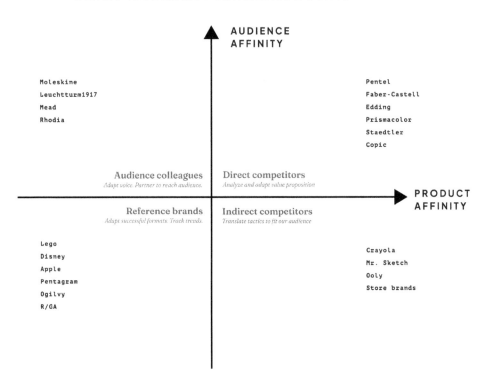

FIGURE 21.1: Brand radar for a new writing tool brand

HOW TO SELECT SOURCES

As the amount and accessibility of information become virtually endless, being strategic about the brands on our radar
is essential to making trend research sustainable. Read on
to learn how to inform your brand radar with four kinds of
sources, mapping them based on how close they are to your
brand's product or service (product affinity) and target customer (audience affinity).

Whose developments should you follow and why? On one hand, you have **direct competitors**: brands with a similar product that are also aiming for the same audience segment/s. Include brands with different price points, being mindful of which of these are most closely related to yours. As you plot them on our brand radar, put an intentional amount of distance to reflect the pricing difference along the X-axis (product affinity).

If you're a new brand of writing tools (pens, pencils, and markers) catering to design-minded women born between 1980–2000 (roughly the Millennial Generation), your direct competitors might include Pentel, Faber-Castell, Edding, Prismacolor, Staedtler, and Copic.

You should also watch brands with a similar product that are speaking to a different segment. Following these **indirect competitors** can provide actionable insights, pending an audience translation. Because they're not directly addressing your core audience, the chance of learning something that will come across as innovative is even higher.

For our earlier example of a writing tool company, you could consider following brands like Crayola, Mr. Sketch, Ooly, or store-branded alternatives (Amazon, Target, etc) targeting *children* instead of Millennial women. While not directed at your core audience, these brands' moves can provide actionable inspiration for your own tactics.

There's also value in learning from **audience colleagues**, brands selling a different product to your same audience. In these cases, look for style and strategy choices aimed at connecting with this group. Your brand can adapt these insights to communicate its product's unique features and benefits. Because they reach an audience you're also targeting, with a noncompetitive offering, brands in this group might be valuable promotion partners.

Continuing with our writing tool example, one might look at brands selling notebooks to the same audience segment: Moleskine, Leuchtturm1917, Mead, and Rhodia. As you can tell, these brands make strong partner candidates due to their complementary nature with the product we sell.

Finally, look out for innovations from **referential brands** that are generally effective communicators without there being a product or audience affinity with yours. Following these general references can provide impactful ideas to navigate larger industry shifts and leverage emerging channels.

To take a temperature check on the larger creative industry, we might decide to include household brands like Lego, Disney, and Apple or award-winning agencies like Pentagram, Ogilvy, and R/GA. Their leadership position in our brand's larger space gives them a unique perspective on what's next—and that's exactly the temperature we want to be able to check.

HOW TO LEVERAGE TRENDS

Here are some next steps to power brand innovation with these findings:

- Gathering inspiration for brand campaign ideas
- Adapting copy formulas
- Creating trend reports for customers
- Informing new product development directions
- Brand design tactics

CONCLUSION AND EMERGING DIRECTIONS

DOI: 10.4324/9781003336693-26

We're permanently navigating this transitional spot where you can see the calm river you've been mapping and the wild ocean ahead. Open waters that could take you, quite literally, anywhere on earth. We see this and wonder: where to?

In the midst of these short and long-term perspectives, we find ourselves constantly stepping out from the comfort of our knowns into the often uncharted, untested territories of brand innovation.

In this final chapter, we'll review the emerging concepts of nostalgic, place, and personal branding, as well as some final thoughts on brand innovation and the shifts that will transform our field next.

NOSTALGIC BRANDING

As we've seen, internal influences dictate our ability to perceive the stimuli around us and tint the lens with which we see them. One such internal influence is our proneness to experience nostalgia. The more turbulent and disruptive the times, the more we find ourselves returning to the tried-and-true for comfort, no matter how mundane. While originally linked to a disease or state of melancholy, nostalgia is now emerging as a largely positive avenue for brands.

Holbrook and Schindler defined **nostalgia proneness** as "a preference toward objects that were more common when one was younger," clarifying that youth here refers to "early adulthood, adolescence, childhood, or even before birth[1]". This last point is essential in understanding nostalgia's impact for brand development: human beings don't just experience a sense of **personal nostalgia** around events within their own lifetime, but can also be powerfully drawn by **historical nostalgia** toward events that happened before they were born[2]. These symbols go beyond our individual memories, but compel us insofar as they allow us to affirm and express our identity associating it with ideas from a distant past.

The relationship between nostalgia and brand perception has been studied by various psychologists, sociologists, and researchers. Some have explored the impact of nostalgia on purchase intention and attitudes towards the brand in different scenarios: when the "need to belong" is active[3], within online brand communities[4], when the attitude towards the past is favorable and/or consumers long to relive it[5], when advertisements include nostalgic themes[6], when products are not primarily aesthetic[7], when consumed privately[8], and when the value of "materialism" is low[9].

To understand the relationship between nostalgia and brand preference effects, we turn once again to the concept of self, or self-concept, as defined by Hazel Rose Markus from social psychology (see Chapter 5). In her article "Possible Selves," Markus clearly establishes that past selves (self-concepts) "can become possible selves insofar as they can define an individual anew in the future"[10]. Under certain circumstances, Markus argues, this past self (self-concept) can be activated and influence an individual's behavior.

Far from being conditioned like machines, human beings make decisions to reduce the tension (distance) between the current self and the desired self; a process in which possessions play the fundamental role of being symbolic (cognitive) bridges between who we have been (past self), who we are (current self), and who we can become (possible self)[11].

Nostalgia's power to connect with our emotions is well-deserved, as it has been shown to influence self-management functions positively in a number of ways. It elevates our perceived sense of purpose, social connectivity, self-continuity, and self-esteem[12].

When brands evoke a feeling of the past, these elements serve as materializations of an individual's memory and build positive associations with the brand.

BUILDING NOSTALGIC BRAND STORIES

We explored storytelling in depth in Chapter 4, but nostalgic branding calls for a different twist on our storyboard approach. Nostalgic brand narratives feature a vivid historical setting, well-developed characters, and often incorporate a touch of fantasy. Some are comparable to legends.

To begin, decide whether the central focus of the nostalgic brand's story will be the product or its creator. When the focus is on the product or service offered, the narrative revolves around explaining the origins of its unique features and why. When the focus is on the creator, it becomes more important to tell the circumstances that led to the brand's launch, as well as the personal characteristics of the individuals behind it.

It's also crucial to define whether the story will be told from a fiction or non-fiction perspective. By definition, a legend incorporates fantastic elements, so only the fiction angle will allow you to develop this type of narration. Based on this criterion, your nostalgic brand story will be framed as a legend or a historical recount.

Thus, four types of nostalgic brand stories emerge:

TABLE 22.1: Nostalgic brand storytelling modes

	Creator focus	Product focus
Fiction	**Creator Legend** Elements of fantasy are incorporated when telling the personal story of the brand's founder or, alternatively, the founding team.	**Product Legend** A legendary origin of the product, service, or brand is invented, incorporating elements of fantasy. The real creators are not necessarily mentioned. On the contrary, the entire story is a product of the imagination.
Non-fiction	**Creator History** The history of the brand's founder or founding team is told as it happened. Being a narration of real events, it is recommended to use this angle as long as the brand has a proven track record in the market.	**Product History** The history of the birth of the product, service, or brand is told as it happened. Being a narration of real events, it is recommended to use this angle as long as the brand has a proven track record in the market.

PLACE BRANDING

Place branding is understood as the intentional development of a brand system around a location to convey its unique values and benefits. Target audiences range from investors to tourists, to local citizens, who find themselves betting on the place's future permanently through their taxes. Believing in this place's potential to suit one's needs can feel like an act of faith. It is the place brand strategist's role to make it less so: to position this geographical location as the catalyst for whatever is in the prospect's mind.

Over time, a number of researchers and practitioners have tried to create a common language and understanding of what place branding entails. They've built models to examine the relationships between a location's economy, resources, stakeholders, idiosyncracies and the role they play in shaping its place brand.

In 2004, Hankinson developed the idea of a "relational network brand", where the personality and reality of the place define its core identity[13]. Think of New York with its fast-paced, vibrant energy—these unique traits define the city's brand. In another influential development in this field, Hanna and Rowley created the Strategic Place Brand Management model, which sees a place's brand as the interplay between what it offers (functional and experiential attributes), its ongoing development, and how stakeholders are engaged[14]. Place brands must articulate the location's unique infrastructure, stakeholder relationships, and identity to shape a strong communications plan. These elements come to life as the place brand's experience, which must then be evaluated in light of what customers actually perceive to keep the feedback loop active and the brand evolving over time.

Perhaps no other branding application makes stronger use of the Brandverse framework (Chapter 11) than **place branding.** To build desire around a location, it's essential to define what it is that differentiates it as vividly as possible. *What are the sounds, sensations, sights, and scents that you find here and nowhere else?*

In 2018, inspired by these and other insights, I took on the project of designing a city brand for Santa Marta, Colombia. Our raw creative materials were all of the existing associations triggered by the city. To discover them, we applied a unique combination of qualitative and quantitative research techniques:

- We placed whiteboards strategically across the city, asking bypassers to draw or write the first idea that came to mind when thinking about the city's name. This projective technique allowed us to access rich associations that a questionnaire couldn't have unveiled.
- We organized focus groups with relevant citizen organizations like business owners, tourist guides, and political leaders. Their perceptions and ideas were collected through in-depth discussions over the course of 10 weeks.

- Once we identified the most outstanding brand associations, we reached over 10,000 citizens with a structured questionnaire that gave us an idea of salience:
  which were first, second, and third-order associations?
  Which first-order associations should be reinforced in
  the new brand system? Which second and third-order
  links should be brought into messaging to strengthen
  the city/brand's overall associative network?

The outcome of this process was a city Brand System defined
by the promise "Santa Marta: Naturally Magical". As a result
of its co-design with key stakeholders, the Brand System has
become widely accepted as a useful tool for communicating
the city's unique features at home and abroad.

FIGURE 22.1: City brand
development process

PERSONAL BRANDING

We live in an era where the individual has access to the large-scale communication platforms corporate brands in the 70s could only dream of. This environment has led to the popularization of **personal branding**, an attempt to build a brand platform around a single person's character, values, or lifestyle. Ultimately, all successful personal branding is based on the idea of **influence**: building it, exerting it, and strengthening it over time. Personal branding is especially essential for political candidates, who must build robust communication platforms around a set of key messages.

Contrary to popular belief, personal branding should start with therapy, not strategy. In order to communicate meaning, one must find it. Dr. Viktor Frankl, father of logotherapy, phrased it well:

> Life is not primarily a quest for pleasure, as Freud believed, or a quest for power, as Alfred Adler taught, but a quest for meaning. The greatest task for any person is to find meaning in his or her own life.[15]

The process of building a strong personal brand starts with the desire to explore one's deeper intentions in life (**self-discovery**), which leads to a more acute awareness of who we are (**self-knowledge**), an elevated perception of self (**self-esteem**), and, ultimately, yes, confident communication (**self-promotion**). The reason personal branding is often stigmatized as self-aggrandizing is *many human beings are too loud about meanings they've explored too little.* You can't microwave personal purpose.

Personal Branding Process

BUSCHE

FIGURE 22.2: Personal branding process

Like other forms of brand development, building a personal brand comes with a set of **benefits** that can propel an individual's life project:

1. **Thought leadership:** A strong personal brand positions you as a thought leader in your industry. When potential customers think about their problem, you will be a top-of-mind solver.

2. **Direction:** In figuring out your personal brand's values, mission, and vision, you will find a strong sense of direction. Knowing which investments and partnerships get you where you want to go will save you time, money, and effort.

3. **Captive audience:** Building your personal brand implies defining and attracting an audience that will be willing to pay for what you offer.

4. **Collaborations:** Because you offer clarity of scope and vision, other (corporate or personal) brands will want to collaborate with you. This brings added exposure and new potential customers.

5. **Premium pricing:** Personal branding adds to the value that you already offer for your products/services, and may help develop a premium pricing

strategy. Therefore, you might charge more than your competitor for a similar item based on the fact that customers know and trust the personal brand that you've built.

6. **Motivation:** Entrepreneurship and all kinds of creative work are not without their hassles. Some days are bright, some are messy. Some days revenue is flowing in, and some days the well is dry. A strong sense of your personal brand helps you stay strong even when everything else is falling apart. You know who you are, what you offer, what you're capable of, and "this is just a small bump on the road".

7. **Creative license:** When you've positioned your personal brand among an audience, there is a certain "creative license" that allows you to come up with new products and services that are instantly well-received. Because you have taken the time to communicate a clear message and promote your brand's values, it becomes easier to launch innovative products with your audience's support.

CONCLUSION

Brands speak to the *homo significans* within us. The human being in search of meaning, prone to symbolism, intrigued by transcendence. They provide a reason to try something beyond its utilitarian value, satisfying our self-identification, affirmation, and expression needs.

Strong brands immunize products and ideas against oblivion. They encapsulate layers of value, memories, and affect that remind us to keep this relationship. At their most basic level, brand relationships can drive affinity. At their best, they foster affect, loyalty, and recommendation.

Intentionally built brand experiences create lasting impressions. Our senses and minds are engaged. Our needs and aspirations are satisfied. Our imaginations are fed.

Branding is an exercise that demands mindful communication, but it can also happen spontaneously in the background. Rest assured: left to their own devices, customers will also give shape to your brand's story informed by their own interactions, perceptions, and emotions. If your brand's story isn't a dialogue, it will be a monologue.

Actively shaping brand associations is one of the most strategic functions of a brand manager. It's also a North Star for every other person impacting brand experience touchpoints. From a support representative to a CEO, sound brand management involves a conscious responsibility to signify at every step.

NOTES

1. Holbrook, M. B., & Schindler, R. M. (1991). Echoes of the dear departed past: Some work in progress on nostalgia. *ACR North American Advances, NA-18*. http://acrwebsite.org/volumes/7181/volumes/v18/NA-18
2. Stern, B. B. (1992). Historical and personal nostalgia in advertising text: The fin de siecle effect. *Journal of Advertising, 21*(4), 11–22.
3. Loveland, K. E., Smeesters, D., & Mandel, N. (2010). Still preoccupied with 1995: The need to belong and preference for nostalgic products. *Journal of Consumer Research, 37*(3), 393–408. https://doi.org/10.1086/653043
4. Brown, S., Kozinets, R. V., & Sherry Jr, J. F. (2003). Teaching old brands new tricks: Retro branding and the revival of brand meaning. *Journal of Marketing, 67*(3), 19–33.
5. Sierra, J. J., & McQuitty, S. (2007). Attitudes and emotions as determinants of nostalgia purchases: An application of Social

Identity Theory. *The Journal of Marketing Theory and Practice, 15*(2), 99–112.

6. Pascal, V. J., Sprott, D. E., & Muehling, D. D. (2002). The influence of evoked nostalgia on consumers' responses to advertising: An exploratory study. *Journal of Current Issues & Research in Advertising, 24*(1), 39.

   Muehling, D. D., & Pascal, V. J. (2012). An involvement explanation for nostalgia advertising effects. *Journal of Promotion Management, 18*(1), 100–118. https://doi.org/10.1080/10496491.2012.646222

7. Schindler, R. M., & Holbrook, M. B. (2003). Nostalgia for early experience as a determinant of consumer preferences. *Psychology and Marketing, 20*(4), 275–302. https://doi.org/10.1002/mar.10074

8. Stern, B. B. (1992). Historical and personal nostalgia in advertising text: The fin de siecle effect. *Journal of Advertising, 21*(4), 11–22.

9. Rindfleisch, A., Freeman, D., & Burroughs, J. E. (2000). Nostalgia, materialism, and product preferences: An initial inquiry. *Advances in Consumer Research, 27*(1), 36–41.

10. Markus, H., & Nurius, P. (1986). Possible selves. *American Psychologist, 41*(9), 954–969. https://doi.org/10.1037/0003-066X.41.9.954

11. Belk, R. W. (1990). The role of possessions in constructing and maintaining a sense of past. *ACR North American Advances, NA-17.* http://acrwebsite.org/volumes/7083/volumes/v17/NA-17

12. Sedikides, C., Wildschut, T., Arndt, J., & Routledge, C. (2008). Nostalgia: Past, present, and future. *Current Directions in Psychological Science, 17*(5), 304–307.

13. Hankinson, G. (2004). Relational network brands: Towards a conceptual model of place brands. *Journal of Vacation Marketing, 10*(2), 109–121.

   Hankinson, G. (2010). Place branding research: A cross-disciplinary agenda and the views of practitioners. *Place Branding and Public Diplomacy, 6*(4), 300–315. https://doi.org/10.1057/pb.2010.29

14. Hanna, S., & Rowley, J. (2011). Towards a strategic place brand-management model. *Journal of Marketing Management, 27*(5–6), 458–476. https://doi.org/10.1080/02672571003683797

15. Frankl, V. E. (1985). *Man's Search for Meaning.* Simon and Schuster.

INDEX

Page numbers in *italics* refer to figures, those in **bold** indicate tables.

Aaker, D. A. 24; and Joachimsthaler, E. 340–2; and Keller, K. L. 345
Aaker, J. L. 25, 173
Aaronson, B. S. 250
abstract marks 221
access control of channels 313
advertising, history of 23, 24, 27
aesthetic pleasure of logos 219
ambiance: brandverse framework 194
"ambient scent" 267–8
analogical learning 86
analogous color scheme 256
anchor pricing 167–8
anchoring bias 124
angular and circular logos 223, *225*
archetypes 175–83
Ares, G. and Deliza, R. 271
Arora, S. et al. 152
associations 131; acting on 147–8; brand concept mapping (BCM) 142–4; color 249–51, *252*; importance of 144–7; looking inside the mind 138–42; and relationship-building 294, *see also* positioning
asymmetrical and symmetrical logos 223–5
attention 82; AIDA response model 288–9
attitude 139; -based segmentation 112
attributes and benefits of products 139
audience colleagues 361–2
audiobranding 265–6
authenticity of brand story 87, 88
authority principle of persuasion 317–18
availability bias 124
awareness 289, 293

B2B service brand equity scale 304–6
baby boomers *115*, 116
Bandura, A. 17–18
Bartlett, C. A. and Ghoshal, S. 353–4
behavioral economics 30
behavioral segmentation 112

behaviorism 12–13, 20; and cognitive perspective 15
Belk, R. 19, 98–9, 102
benefit-based segmentation 112
benefits and attributes of products 139
biases: anchoring effect 168; in research 123–4
black associations 250
blue associations 249–51
Blumer, H. 18
Bonde, A. and Hansen, A. G. 266
Bone, P. F. and Ellen, P. S. 268
books and style guides 271–4
Bradford, K. D. and Desrochers, D. M. 267–8
Brakus, J. J. et al. 334–5
brand: etymology of term 22; and psychological paradigms 20
brand advocacy 299
brand applications 268–70
brand architecture 337–8; strategies 339–44
brand asset management model 64–6
brand associations *see* associations
brand attachment 294–5
brand awareness *see* awareness
brand clarity 4
brand concept management (BCM) model 67–8
brand concept mapping (BCM) 142–4
brand design management model 70–1
brand differentiation 295
brand equity 24, 61; as path forward 61–3; *see also* brand relationships
brand experiences 327; customer experience management (CEM) framework 328–31; evaluating 334–5; mapping 332–4
brand extensions 344–6; designing strategies 347–8; fit measurement 346–7; fit scale **348**
brand familiarity 293

brand image 23–4, 293–4; scale **141**
brand imagery 261–2; defining guidelines 263–4; importance of 262–3
brand intelligence 357–62
brand loyalty 297–8
brand management 25, 64; models 64–75; promise fulfilment 93
brand messaging mix: building blocks and use 319–22
brand packaging 270–1
brand partner quality 301
brand personality *see* personality
brand portfolio management *see* brand architecture; brand extensions; global/cultural issues
brand preference 296
brand promise 92–4
brand radar: building 359, *360*; leveraging trends 362; selecting sources 360–2
brand relationships 287; hierarchy of effects model and dimensions 288–91, 292–9; lasting 300–2; response models 288–91; *see also* internal branding
brand sentiment 294
brand story 79–80, 140; in brand system *275*, *276*; co-constructed 89; consumer shape and recall of 81–4; defining value 80–1; four elements of 87–8; nostalgic 367, **368**; role of individual perception 84–7; storyboard building 89–92; strong 88
brand theme/score 266
brand trust 296–7
branded house 340–2
branding, definition of 25
brandverse 191–2, 263, 327; building 197–8; embodied cognition 196–7; framework 194; sensory engagement 192–3, 195–6
brown associations 251
bundling: pricing strategy 167
business impact of logos 220
business vocabulary, historical evolution of 22–5

caregiver archetype 182
central and peripheral routes of persuasion 316–17, 319

channels: brand building and 311–12; brand communication and art of persuasion 316–17; brand messaging mix: building blocks and use 319–22; brand partnerships 323–5; and brand story 88; dimension of strategy 278–9; earned, paid, and owned 312–16; principles of persuasion 317–18; putting to work 319
Christodoulides, G. et al. 83
Cialdini, R. 317–18
circular and angular logos 223, *225*
city branding 369–70
classical conditioning 12–13
closure: Gestalt principle 210–11
co-branding and partnership 140
co-constructed brand stories 89
cognition, embodied 196–7
cognitive bias *see* biases
cognitive perspective 15, 20, 81–3
Coleman, D. et al. 304–6
color 247–8, 261; art and science of 248–9; associations 249–51, *252*; combinations 255–7; many facets of 251, 253–5; packaging 270, *271*; surface in visual perception 204–5
commitment in brand relationship 301
common fate: Gestalt principle 213
communication: high and low-context 349–50; strategic 88; *see also* channels; culture
competence: brand personality 172, 240, 250–1
competition-based pricing 162, 164
competitor analysis 113
competitors, direct and indirect 361
complementarity: brand extension fit 345
complementary color scheme 256
comprehension 82
conceptual fluency of logos 222
conciseness of brand story 87–8
confirmation bias 123
consensus principle of persuasion 318
consistency: coherence and fulfilment of brand promise 93; and congruence of logos 227–8; principle of persuasion 318

consumer behavior 9–10, *11*; overall model of 83–4; psychological paradigms 11–19, 20; research 23
consumer culture (1900-1930s), rise of 27, **28**
consumer psychology research, historical evolution of 27–31
consumers: and customers: terminology 125, 126; shaping and recalling brand story 81–4; *see also entries beginning* customer
content control of channels 313
content creators (influencers) 324
content marketing 140
continuity: Gestalt principle 211
continuous innovation 331
continuous measurement, importance of 124–5
control of channels, third party 313
conviction 290, 296–7
cost-based pricing 162, 163
creator archetype 182
culture: authenticity of logos 226; brand asset management 66; and color 248–9; cross-cultural analysis 114; dimensions and cross-cultural communication 351–3; going global 348–53
customer acquisition cost (CAC) 277
customer experience management (CEM) framework 328–31
customer interface, structuring 330–1
customer-based brand equity 61
customer-based pricing 162, 165–6
customer-centric brand story 88, 92–3
customers: and consumers: terminology 125, 126; dimension of strategy 277–8; *see also entries beginning* consumer

Davis, S. 64–6
decoy pricing 168–9
demographic segmentation 113
Deng, Q. and Messinger, P. R. 346–7
desire 98; AIDA response model 288–9
desired self and actual self 102–3
desired social identities, enacting 104
diagonals in logo design 225, *226*
Dichter, E. and Krugman, H. 27–8
digital and physical brand applications **269**

Doyle, J. R. and Bottomley, P. A. 228
dual coding theory 195–6
dynamic pricing 163

economic man 11–12
economic value to customer (EVC) 165
Egyptian/slab serif typefaces 239
elaborate and natural logos 223, *224*
elaboration likelihood model (ELM) 316–17, 319, 321
Elliott, R. and Wattanasuwan, K. 100–1
emblem logos 221
embodied cognition 196–7
emotions: and color associations 249–51, *252*; and memories 268
empathy maps 118–19
employee brand equity (EBE) scale 304
endorsed brands 342–3
Escalas, J. 102
excitement: brand personality 172, 240, 250
experience control of channels 313
experiential marketing 140
experimenter bias 124
experiments 119
explorer archetype 177
exposure 81–2
extended self 19, 99

Fench, A. and Smith, G. 139
figure-ground: Gestalt principle 212
firm-based brand equity 61
first-order/core brand associations 138–9, 140–1, 144; reinforcing 148
focus groups 118
fonts *see* typography
Fournier, S. 300–2
frames in logo design 226
Frankl, V. 371
freemium pricing 165–6
Freud, S. 14

Gardner, B. B. and Levy, S. 23–4
Generation X *115*, 116
Generation Y/Millennials 114, *115*, 116
Generation Z 114, *115*, 116
generational cohorts 114–17

Gentner, D. 86
geographic segmentation 112
geometric sans-serif typefaces 239
Gestalt principles 206–7, 206–13; commonly
    applied 208–13; design 213; history 207–8
global strategy 353
global/cultural issues 348–53
"Golden Age of Capitalism" 23
Gorn, G. J. et al. 249–50
green associations 250–1
Grohmann, B. et al. 240
gross margin pricing 163
group affiliation, signalling 104

Hagtvedt, H. 243
Hall, E. T. 349
halo effect 123
Hawkins, D. et al. 83
Hawthorne effect 124
Henderson, P. W.: and Cote, J. A. 223; et al.
    241–2
hero archetype 178–9
hierarchy of effects model and dimensions
    289–91, 292–9
hierarchy of needs 16, 145–7
historical evolution of branding 20–2;
    business vocabulary 22–5; timeline 25–31
Hofstede, G. 351–3
Holbrook, M. B. and Schindler, R. M. 365–6
house of brands 343–4
hue 253, 254, 255
human-centered brand management 71–5
humanist typefaces: old-style 238; sans-serif
    239
humanistic perspective 16–17, 20
humor of brand story 87, 88

ideas 4–5; brand naming process 154, **155–6**
identity/ies: branded house strategy 340–2;
    enacting desired 104; narrative 16–17;
    see also self-brand identification; personal
    branding
illuminance in visual perception 204
impulse purchase/impulse buying theory 290–1
incomplete typefaces 243

individual perception, role of 84–7
industrial analysis 114
Industrial Revolution 26, **27**
information processing 15, 20, 81–3
innocent archetype 176, *177*
innovation, continuous 331
intentional/mindful branding 5
interdependence 300
internal branding 303–6; resource/Brand
    System 274–9
internationalization 353
internet, growth of 30
interval scales 121
interviews 118
intimacy in brand relationship 301

Jacoby, J. and Kyner, D. B. 298
James, W. 18, 19, 97, 102
jester archetype 181
jingles 265
Jung, C. 14, 175

Keller, K. L. 139; Aaker, D. A. and 345; Kotler,
    P. and 25
Killian, K. 265–6
King, C. et al. 304
Kleine, R. E. 100
knowledge 289, 293–4
Kotler, P. 109, 306; and Keller, K. L. 25

Lavridge, R. J. and Steiner, G. A. 288–9
letterform logos 221
lifetime value (LTV) 278
liking 289–90, 294–5; principle of persuasion
    318
linked name 343
location: in visual perception 205–6; see also
    place branding
logical brand management model 68, *69*
Logman, M. 68, *69*
logos 217–18, 261; art and science of design
    223–7; audio/sound 265, 266; consistency
    and congruence 227–8; dual coding 196;
    importance of 218–20; psychological
    impact of 222; types of 220–1

love: and belongingness needs 146; brand relationship 300
lover archetype 181
Low, G. S. and Lamb Jr, C. W. 141
lower and uppercase characters 242
Lupton, E. 237–8

magician archetype 179, *180*
manifesto 6–7; brandverse framework 194, *195*
maps/mapping: brand concept (BCM) 142–4; brand experiences 332–4; empathy 118–19; perceptual brand positioning 134–7
Mark, M. and Pearson, C. S. 175, 176
market trend analysis 113
"marketer scent" 267
markup pricing 163
Markus, H. and Nurius, P. 16, 20, 97, 366
Marshall, A. 11
Maslow, A. 16, 145–7
material self 18, 97, 102
materiality in visual perception 205
maximum likelihood (ML) analysis 137
Mead, G. H. 18, 103
means–ends theory 144–5
memory 20; associative network model 138–9; and scent 268
metaphors: brand name ideation **156**; visual 225–6, 263
Millennials/Generation Y 114, *115*, 116
Miller, H. 227, *228*
modern typefaces 239
monitoring: competing brands 148; sources and storing insights 359
monochromatic color scheme 256
Montaña, J. et al. 70–1
Moore, G. 132
Moore, K. and Reid, S. 21, 26
morphological devices *158*, 159
motion principles 264
multidimensional customer-based brand equity scale 82–3, 296
multidisciplinary approach to consumption 98

multidomestic strategy 353–4
multinational companies: typology of strategies 353–4
multisensory experiences 192–3
Munuera-Alemán, J. L. et al. 297
music/songs 265, 266

naming 151–2; creative transformation 157–9; process 153–7; types of 152, *153*
narrative identity 16–17
natural and elaborate logos 223, *224*
'neighbor': brandverse framework 194
net promoter score (NPS) 299
Neumeier, M. 132
nominal scales 120
nostalgic branding 365–7; stories 367, **368**
not connected: house of brands 343–4

objects: brandverse framework 194
observation 118
odd-even/psychological pricing 166
Odin, Y. et al. 298
Ogilvy, D. 24
olfactive branding 267–8
online retail/service (ORS) brand equity scale 63
opacity, color 254
operant conditioning 13
ordinal scales 120–1
orthographic devices *158*, 159
outlaw archetype 179
overall model of consumer behavior 83–4

parity pricing/price match 164
Park, C. et al. 67–8, 295
partnerships 323–5; and co-branding 140; non-competing brands 148
past selves 366
patterns *see* Gestalt principles
Pavlov, I. 12–13
pay-what-you-want pricing 166
penetration pricing 164
perceived quality 296

perceptual brand positioning maps
134–7
perceptual fluency of logos 222
peripheral and central routes of persuasion
316–17, 319
personal branding 371–3
personality 171; archetypes 175–83; color
associations, emotions and 249–51, *252*;
definition of 25; dimensions, framework
and scale 171–5; font selection 240; impact
of logos 226–7; and voice/tone 183–6
personas/persona profiles 125–7, 329
persuasion, art and principles of 316–18
Petty, R. E. et al. 316–17
phonetic devices *158*, 159
pictorial marks/brand symbols 221
place branding 368–70; brandverse
framework 194, 369
positioning 131–4; perceptual brand
positioning maps 134–7; segmentation,
targeting, and (STP) 109–10; top-of-mind:
achieving dominant position 137–8
possible selves 16, 20; activation of 102; and
actual selves 97–8; and past selves 366
post-Second World War era (1940-1950s)
23–4, 27
preference 290, 295–6
premium pricing 165, 372–3
price discrimination 164
price match/parity pricing 164
pricing 161; popular techniques 162–6;
strategic presentation, recurrence, and
discounting 167–9
processing fluency of logos 222
"product scent" 267, 268
product sounds 266
products, dimension of strategy 279
proto-brands 21–2, 26
proximity: Gestalt principle 209
psychodynamic perspective 14–15
psychographic segmentation 112
psychological paradigms 11–19, 20
psychological/odd-even pricing 166
purchase 290–1, 297–9
purple associations 250, 251

qualitative and quantitative research
techniques 117–22, 126–7
questionnaires 119; common scales **122**;
design 120–1

ratio scales 121
rebranding 279
recall device, logo as 219
reciprocity principle of persuasion 317
red associations 249–50, 251
referential brands 362
regular guy/gal archetype 180–1
Reichheld, F. F. 299
reinforcement 13; first-order/core brand
associations 148
repositioning 132
research 108; avoiding common biases 123–4;
generational cohorts 114–17; importance
of continuous measurement 124–5;
primary and secondary research 111–14;
qualitative and quantitative techniques
117–22; segmentation research 108–11;
targeting: building personas 125–7, 329
response bias 123
response models 288–91
reversal of brand story 87, 88
Ricoeur, P. 16–17
Ries, A. et al. 138
roundness of typeface 243
ruggedness: brand personality 173, 240,
250–1
ruler archetype 182, *183*

sage archetype 177–8
Sample, K. et al. 202
sampling/selection bias 123
saturation, color 253–4
Saussure, F. de 217
scarcity principle of persuasion 317
scent/olfactive branding 267–8
Schmitt, R. H. 328–31
Schwartz, S. H. 350–1
seals, historical 21–2
second and third-order associations 140, 144;
connecting 148

secondary research 112–14
segmentation, targeting, and positioning (STP) 109–10
segmentation research 108–11
selection: bias 123; brand naming process 154, **157**
selective and voluntary exposure 82
self-actualization 20; needs 16, 146–7
self-affirmation 101–2
self-brand connection scale **102**
self-brand identification 97–8; brands as social and self-symbolism 100–5; symbolic consumption 98–100; *see also* personal branding
self-concept: and extended self 19, 99; and symbolic interactionism 18; *see also* possible selves
self-connection 300
self-enhancement 102–3
self-esteem needs 146
self-expression 103–5
semantic devices *158*, 159
semiology and semiotics 217–18
semiotic significance of logos 219
sensory engagement and branding 192–3, 195–6
serif and sans-serif typefaces 237–9, 242
shades, color 254
shadow endorser: house of brands 344
shape in visual perception 204
signifiers 217
silent generation *115*, 116
similarity: Gestalt principle 209–10
sincerity: brand personality 171–2, 240
skimming pricing 165
Skinner, B. F. 13
slab/Egyptian serif typefaces 239
Smith, A. 11
social desirability bias 123
social expectations 103–4
social learning theory 17–18, 85
social media, rise of 30
social performance, guiding 104
social proof and user-generated content 140
social and self-symbolism 100–5

sociocultural perspective 17–19, 20
solid typefaces 243
Solomon, M. R. 99–100
songs/music 265, 266
sophistication: brand personality 172, 240
sound/sonic branding 265–6
soundscape 266
split complementary color scheme 256
statistical analysis 119; maximum likelihood (ML) 137
Stern, H. 291
storytelling *see* brand story
strategies: brand system *275*, 277–9; multinational companies 353–4; pricing 167–9
strong endorsement 343
style guides and books 271–4
sub-brands 342
subscription pricing 169
success, dimension of strategy 277
suitability: brand extension fit 345
surface color in visual perception 204–5
symbolic consumption 19, 98–100
symbolic interactionism 18–19, 20
symbolic meaning 24
symbols in brand system *275*, 277
symmetrical and asymmetrical logos 223–5
symmetry: Gestalt principle 212

targeting: building personas/persona profiles 125–7, 329; segmentation, targeting, and positioning (STP) 109–10
team members *see* internal branding
Thaler, R. 30
third party control of channels 313
tints, color 254
token endorsement 343
tones: color 254; voice and 183–6
top-of-mind: achieving dominant position 137–8
touch and packaging 271
Townsend, C.: and Kahn, B. E. 262–3; and Sood, S. 100
transferability: brand extension fit 345

transformation: brand naming process 154, **156**; creative 157–9
transitional typefaces 238–9; sans-serif 239
transnational strategy 353
triadic color scheme 256–7
typesetting 242
typography 233–4, 261; anatomy 234–7; classification 237–9; congruence of fonts 228; psychological impact of 240–3

unconscious mind 14
unity principle of persuasion 318
upper and lowercase characters 242
user-generated content and social proof 140
utility maximization 11

value-based pricing 165; color 254; defining 80–1
values, basic and universal 350–1

visual perception 201–2; defining 202–6; recognizing patterns *see* Gestalt principles
voice and tone 183–6
Völckner, F. and Sattler, H. 345–6
voluntary and selective exposure 82

Watson, J. 14
Wengrow, D. 21
Wertheimer, M. 207–8
Wheeler, A. 220
wordmarks/logotypes 221
Wundt, W. 12, 23

yellow associations 249, 250, 251; green- 250, 251
Yoo, B. and Donuth, N. 82, 296

zone pricing 164